A COMPLETE GUIDE TO BIRD FEEDING

A COMPLETE GUIDE TO BIRD FEEDING

John V. Dennis

Drawings by Matthew Kalmenoff

Alfred · A · Knopf
New York
1994

THIS IS A BORZOI BOOK
PUBLISHED BY ALFRED A. KNOPF, INC.

Copyright © 1975, 1994 by John V. Dennis
Illustrations copyright © 1975 by Alfred A. Knopf, Inc.

All rights reserved under International and Pan-
American Copyright Conventions. Published in the
United States by Alfred A. Knopf, Inc., New York,
and simultaneously in Canada by Random House of
Canada Limited, Toronto. Distributed by Random
House, Inc., New York. Originally published in
different form in 1975 in hard cover.

Library of Congress Cataloging-in-Publication Data
Dennis, John V   A complete guide to bird feeding.
Includes bibliographical references.
1. Birds—Foods. 2. Bird feeders. I. Title.
QL676.5.D44   1975   639'.97'82   74-21277
ISBN 0-679-75052-5 (pbk)

Published August 29, 1975
Revised, First Paperback Edition Published March 27, 1994
Second Printing, April 1994
MANUFACTURED IN THE UNITED STATES OF AMERICA

To all those who watch and enjoy birds
and especially Mary Alice,
who has shared this hobby with me

CONTENTS

ILLUSTRATIONS

PREFACE

When, some forty-five years ago, I was managing a bird sanctuary for the Massachusetts Audubon Society, I conceived the idea of a book exclusively on bird feeding. Inspiration for such a book came from the many questions people asked me about bird feeding and the birds that come to feeding stations. Now, after a long interval and experience in feeding birds in Florida, Virginia, and other eastern states, a book has emerged. Much of the information in this book has been supplied by numerous correspondents and friends who, like myself, have delved deeply into this intriguing hobby. I owe a debt of gratitude to all of them and to my editors at Alfred A. Knopf: Angus Cameron and Barbara Bristol.

Although this book is primarily for use in states that lie east of the Great Plains, the techniques described can be used anywhere. Also many of the species that come to feeders in the East have wide ranges and, in many cases, will be found at feeding stations throughout much of North America. In addition, many species regarded as exclusively western have close counterparts in the East. These western cousins behave in much the same way as their eastern counterparts. So wherever the reader may happen to live, this book should prove helpful.

LEARNING HOW

part one

To many, the joy of feeding birds is that it takes so little skill and equipment. Without much more than daily offerings of food and a feeder or two we can set up a contact with birds that is rewarding both to them and to us. But establishing a really satisfactory bird feeding program does take a certain amount of skill and some work too. I say this at the risk of dampening the enthusiasm of those who would rather not become deeply involved. There is still a place for casual or part-time bird feeding. Some good, and perhaps no harm, will come of it so long as the birds' habits are not molded to the degree that they become overly dependent upon their human friends for food. This book, however, is primarily for those who would improve their skills and make bird feeding into something that is of real assistance to birds. Doing this will in turn result in a deep sense of satisfaction. The first few chapters of this book will see the reader through the troublesome features of this hobby. Thereafter it is clear sailing with most emphasis upon enjoying the varied clientele that will respond to our efforts.

Taming birds, finding out what they eat and how they pass their time are parts of this hobby that can become very absorbing. If we are to get the most out of this side of bird feeding, it is important that we become proficient at bird identification. Once this art has been learned, a whole new field of activity is opened to us. Whether we will go on to listing, reporting, and conducting field studies is a matter of time and individual taste. It is enough to say that a feeding station brings birds ever so much closer to us, where we can study them under favorable circumstances. You learn about birds by seeing them and seeing them often and well.

Is there a harmful side to feeding birds? Many wonder if through feeding we make birds too dependent and perhaps weaken their urge to seek out natural foods. The only answer I can give to this is that it takes skill and ingenuity to hold most birds to an artificial source of food. Some, to be sure, are overly attentive to the feeding station and we could not budge them if we wished. But most species that visit us are inquisitive and restless. These visitors are constantly looking for new sources of food. Over much of the year, natural foods take priority over anything that we may offer them. Many species desert us completely when insect food becomes plentiful enough to meet their needs. Even during northern winters chickadees, nuthatches, and woodpeckers spend a large share of their time away from feeders looking for natural foods. I have never been worried about birds becoming overly dependent; my biggest problem is usually in holding the birds I most want to see at my feeders.

If there is any harm in this hobby, it is in commencing a sizable bird feeding program and then not continuing it during food-scarce periods of the year. Once we begin, we have an obligation to continue until birds can safely be on their own.

Any other harm in feeding birds comes under the heading of unsanitary or unsafe conditions at bird baths and feeders. No one intentionally creates bad conditions. However, unsafe foods, unsanitary bird baths and feeders, and inadequate cover near feeders impose hazards that may offset the help we hope to provide. Readers who would take extra precautions should pay special attention to the sections that follow on food, special needs, and things that go wrong. Also check the list in Appendix A for unsafe foods and other hazards at feeders and bird baths. We cannot expect to make our grounds completely safe for birds; in fact, interference with the natural processes that take place near us is in itself an unwise undertaking. But we should try to make sure that we have not unintentionally subjected birds to new and unnecessary hazards. At the same time we should not go beyond the immediate goals of our bird feeding program and try to remold the birdlife we see about us.

BIRD FEEDING AS A HOBBY

It is safe to say that little or no thought was given to feeding birds during the early days of the United States. By the early nineteenth century there are indications that birds had found at least a few friends. Audubon told of the companionable snowbirds that appeared at the approach of hard weather and that were sometimes fed by persons from the old country. The snowbird, or junco, is still the bird that elicits the sympathy of nearly everyone when cold weather sets in. In 1845, Henry David Thoreau at his Walden Pond cabin made a habit of scattering corn and bread crumbs outside his door. Among the guests that enjoyed this fare were rabbits, red squirrels, blue jays, and chickadees.

Fifty years later another naturalist, John Burroughs, invited guests to his door with equally simple fare. Burroughs was struck by the wildness of the birds that appeared in the woodlands and fields near his cabin retreat. "They sweep by me and around me in flocks," he wrote, "the Canada sparrow, the pine grosbeak, the redpoll, the cedar-bird—feeding upon frozen apples in the orchard, upon cedar-berries, upon maple buds and the berries of mountain ash, and upon the seeds of the weeds that rise upon the snow in the fields, or upon the hay-seed dropped where the cattle have been foddered in the barn-yard or about the distant stock; but yet taking no heed of man, in no way changing their habits so as to take advantage of his presence in nature."

When Burroughs wrote these lines, birds were regarded largely as objects for food or sport; the feathers of many were used to decorate women's hats. So ruthless had the plume trade become that by the end of the century many of the birds that furnished them had been slaughtered to the point of extinction. Unless something were done soon, egrets, herons, and terns would be joining the lengthening list of vanished species. Persecution was the reason for the wariness and lack of response that Burroughs had noted.

As has happened so many times in this country, there was a sudden awakening when conditions began to get too much out of hand. Toward the end of the century, a strong conservation movement made its appearance. No goal seemed to be more pressing than that of saving birdlife. Under the leadership of the National Association of Audubon Societies,* people banded together to do what they could. It wasn't long before the plume trade was outlawed and bird protection had become a byword. Laws were passed, sanctuaries established, and scientific studies initiated that would show the true economic value of birds.

Still another approach to bird protection was all but unnoticed at first. Later it was found that through feeding, bird baths, birdhouses, and special plantings, even the smallest yards could be made into havens for songbirds. The concept of a home sanctuary goes back many hundreds of years in European countries. It was considered good luck to have storks nesting on the chimney and swallows building nests under the eaves. In northern countries it had long been a tradition to feed birds at Christmas time. It was a Scandinavian custom to tie a sheaf of wheat or oats to a pole. The pole was raised on Christmas Eve, with families competing to see how high they could raise their sheaf. The custom has continued down to the present time but with the sheaf being placed outside the window. Such sheaves may sometimes be seen in northern states in this country, such as Wisconsin and Minnesota, that were largely settled by Scandinavians.

But to provide food the whole year, or even all winter, is something that seems to have been overlooked until quite recently. The first person in this country to establish a feeding program along the lines we know today seems to have been a housewife who lived in Brattleboro, Vermont. We know of the activities of this lady, Mrs. E. B. Davenport, through an equally devoted student of birdlife who was to make a name for herself as a writer. This was Florence A. Merriam, who in her book *Birds of Village and Field*[†] tells of the Davenport feeders and the birds that came to them. No less than twenty species were recorded during the winter and early summer

*Established in 1905 and the present National Audubon Society.
[†]Boston, Houghton and Mifflin, 1898.

of 1896. Part of Mrs. Davenport's success was a result of the design and location of her feeders. Those intended for shy birds like the ruffed grouse were well away from the house. The ruffed grouse feeder was a barrel lying on its side and supplied with buckwheat. Bolder birds, like chickadees and blue jays, were enticed to suet or pork fixed to tree trunks or food on a window shelf. By using a fairly wide variety of foods, Mrs. Davenport was able to attract birds that were essentially seed-eaters and others that were largely insect-eating. Her menu sounds much like the offerings we provide today. Besides items already mentioned, she used sunflower, hemp, finely cracked corn, nutmeats, and a cornbread that wouldn't freeze in very cold weather. Florence Merriam tells us that when the Davenport family sat down to their meals, they nearly always had birds in view at nearby feeders. Food and water were supplied to birds all summer, and Mrs. Davenport used to conduct a bird census in a nearby orchard.

By 1900 hummingbird feeders had made their appearance. The first crude attempts to attract hummingbirds go back to around 1890, when a young girl, convalescing from an illness in the sunshine of a California garden, tried holding out tubular flowers that she filled with sweetened solutions. First using sugar and then honey, she succeeded in making daily patrons out of two male hummingbirds.[*]

Around 1899, Caroline G. Soule[†] of Brookline, Massachusetts, hung up a bottle of sugar-water with an imitation trumpet creeper flower inserted in the opening. Soon she had so many hummingbirds coming for a drink that she had to fill the bottle twice a day. Since this early experiment, little new has been added to the art of hummingbird feeding.

Having written about the eastern birds, the enthusiastic Florence Merriam, now the wife of a naturalist, was off to the West before 1900 and writing about the birds she found there. Always keenly interested in bird feeding and habits of birds at feeders, she portrayed the western birds with a skill and humor that has rarely been duplicated. If anything, the western birds were tamer and took more readily to artificial fare than their eastern cousins.

We must admire these early enthusiasts. With almost no published material to help them, they were able to devise methods which were highly successful and which we could profitably employ today. We have improved the appearance of feeders, made them more sturdy, and found ways to keep out certain uninvited guests. But we do

[*] Robert Ridgeway, *The Hummingbirds*, 1892.
[†] "A Hummingbird Experiment," *Bird-lore*, II, No. 5:158, 1900.

not have any magic formulas that work better than the foods and methods used around 1900. If we are relying too heavily upon small feeders of modern design, chances are we are excluding as many kinds of birds as we are attracting. In design and placement of feeders and types of foods to use, we can still profit by the example of the New Englanders who had made so many advances by 1900.

How they managed so well without adequate bird guides or field glasses is another matter. Not until 1895 was there anything approaching a field guide. In that year there appeared a *Handbook of Birds of Eastern North America* by Frank M. Chapman. This book, as useful as it was, can hardly be mentioned in the same breath as our excellent present-day bird guides. The situation in regard to field glasses or telescopes was equally poor. The bird watcher in those days was lucky if he had a pair of opera glasses with a standard 3.5 magnification.

Books about birds during this period were largely devoted to conservation themes and to proving the value of birds as destroyers of insects and other pests. Not until the appearance of Gilbert H. Trafton's *Methods of Attracting Birds* in 1910 was there anything available that approached the modern guide to bird attracting. This work was followed in 1915 by *Wild Bird Guests* by Ernest Harold Baynes. Though adding very little more in the way of information on how to attract birds, Baynes did capture as never before the thrill and excitement of feeding birds in winter in a small New England town. He tells how some winters the northern finches, completely fearless of man, swarmed through the village of Meriden, New Hampshire. Sometimes he would sit on the snow-covered ground and let the birds take food from his hands or whatever part of his body they could cling to. Crossbills and redpolls were so tame that he could pick one up in each hand and they would go right on eating!

Thanks to the writers of that period, and especially the New England ornithologist Edward Howe Forbush,* we know a great deal about the birdlife of the northeastern states around the beginning of this century. Forbush was one of the pioneers in establishing ways to attract birds. He tells of his experiments and those of others in *Useful Birds and Their Protection*.

Apparently many birds had begun to lose the wildness that John Burroughs had spoken of and were beginning to take advantage of food and other inducements

---

* *Useful Birds and Their Protection*, Boston, Massachusetts State Board of Agriculture, 1907; *Birds of Massachusetts and Other New England States*, Boston, Massachusetts Department of Agriculture, 1925.

offered by man. Many birds that we know at feeders today had already put in an appearance. Others hadn't shown themselves and were still "essentially wild."

In the early 1900s the starling and evening grosbeak had barely begun the spectacular expansion in range and numbers that has since made them so abundant and widespread. The red-bellied woodpecker, tufted titmouse, mockingbird, and cardinal were dominantly southern in distribution and rarely seen at northern feeders. The red-winged blackbird had not yet taken up feeding station habits. The same was true of a long list of other birds. Our familiar downy and hairy woodpeckers, chickadee, blue jay, nuthatch, and junco were as much in evidence then as now and, except for the blue jay, just as companionable. The house sparrow, at an all-time peak in numbers, was such a nuisance and caused such havoc among native birds that there was scarcely a hand that wasn't turned against it. Not until the years 1915 through 1920, which saw the automobile replacing the horse, did this prolific import from the Old World begin to show a marked decline in population. Today we scarcely realize what a pest this little bird once was.

Many of the changes in bird population that have occurred during this century are directly attributable to feeding stations. The extra food in winter has made it possible for many more birds to stay in the North. Some species have benefited to such an extent that they are far more numerous than they were during the early days of bird feeding. This has occurred in spite of the destruction of habitats and the contaminating effect of pesticides.

There is something in bird feeding for everyone. For some, the joy lies in better opportunities to watch birds. Keeping tabs on arrival and departure dates, changes in population, and unexpected visitors is facilitated by the ease with which birds can be viewed through the window. The same is true when it comes to watching feeding habits and the relationships that birds establish among themselves. Roy Ivor, Alfred G. Martin, Margaret Millar, and Louise de Kiriline Lawrence, on this side of the Atlantic, and Len Howard in England are among those who have written books based largely upon observations of birds at and near feeders.

To many bird feeding enthusiasts the scientific side takes second place or is not a factor at all. The companionship of birds, their song, movement, and beauty are reasons given for a hobby that, in the words of Edwin Way Teale,* fills an ever-

*In introduction to John K. Terres, *Songbirds in Your Garden*, New York, Thomas Y. Crowell, 1968.

growing need in our lives. He points out that as the pressure of population increasingly regiments us and crowds us closer together, we need an association with the wild, winged freedom of birds. Or as Irene Schultz of Lake Bluff, Illinois, put it in a letter published in the April 7, 1972 issue of *Life* magazine: "I can't understand why I get so much pleasure from the collection of birds that dine at our place, but I do. Maybe they're the story of life, told on a diminutive scale, and with beauty."

GETTING STARTED

One of the reasons that bird feeding has such appeal is that it is so easy. You simply toss some food on the ground, put up a feeder or two, and you are in business. You can have a very simple program and feed birds in much the same way that John Burroughs did some one hundred years ago, or you can have a large operation conducted along scientific lines. Whatever your preference, you can be sure that birds will take note of your offerings and reward you well for the trouble you have taken.

WHEN TO START

Psychologically you will be in the right mood when the first cold spell of the fall comes your way. This is the right time, too, to let birds know your intentions. Birds begin to establish feeding territories in early fall. If your yard is going to be included within the rounds of chickadees, nuthatches, and the other birds that join them, you need to start feeding before real winter weather sets in. Very few birds may come at first. But do not let this discourage you. It usually takes something close to a snowstorm to wean sizable numbers of birds away from natural food supplies. In more northern states feeding should be initiated sometime in September; from Virginia and Missouri southward sometime in October.

Do not worry too much about feeders when you are first starting out. Normally people begin with one or two and gradually increase the number as they attract more birds and discover which foods and feeders are best suited to the needs of their birds.

Place feeders where they can be easily viewed from windows. Also find locations that are sheltered from the wind. The most sheltered places are usually on the south side of the house. You may have to try several locations before you find ones that are well suited to your needs and those of your birds. But remember that birds are creatures of habit and do not adjust easily to sudden shifts in feeding locations.

WHAT TO FEED

When you first begin, most of the common bird foods will be ignored. Partly this is because it takes time for birds to recognize artificial foods and partly there is the distraction of natural foods that are usually abundant in the fall. The one food that sometimes gets attention under these circumstances is white bread. Even nutritionally poor white bread is so alluring to birds that they will leave better sources of food for it. Fresh or stale, it holds a strange fascination and brings more variety to a yard than almost any other food. Break the bread into small pieces and scatter where birds can see it. If this does not bring a few customers, nothing will. Your bread will also bring four-footed guests. Because of this and other shortcomings, white bread is not an especially good food to use. Try it only as a lure and then go on to the other foods that are discussed in the next chapter and in Appendixes A and B (pages 249–75).

A number of kitchen leftovers are indispensable for use in recipes for birds, and others are substitutes for food that would otherwise have to be purchased. Both to economize and to please our customers, we should start saving leftovers well ahead of the fall feeding program. First on the list are pan drippings. Whether from bacon or meat roasts, any drippings that do not contain too much seasoning should be saved. Simply pour into cans and store in the refrigerator until needed. Much the same policy should apply to suet. Wrap in pieces of paper and keep under refrigeration. All too often overlooked are eggshells. Properly used, they can be a valuable addition to the larder (page 254). Crush shells of chicken eggs and store in cans under refrigeration. Still another neglected food is melon seeds. Many of the birds that eat sunflower will readily accept such seeds as squash, cantaloupe, and watermelon when we offer them as substitutes. If you are to have an adequate supply, you should begin saving melon seeds in early summer. There are still other leftovers that you may snatch from the garbage and use for bird feeding. But bear in mind that some will not keep well.

Most yards are too open and lacking in the tangles of trees, shrubs, and vines that are seen in natural habitats. But to have birds we do not have to let our yards revert back to the wild. The essential thing is to have a varied habitat—lawn and trees and shrubs of different heights and ages. Also we should try for a mixture of deciduous and evergreen trees and shrubs.

A good rule to follow when you have extra space for plantings is to use only varieties that are recommended for attracting birds. Pick some that are good food plants, others whose chief advantage lies in nesting sites or escape cover. Consult an author such as John K. Terres,* who provides detailed instructions on how to plant with the best interests of birds in mind. Also seek advice on what does well in your neighborhood from your county agricultural office and nearby nurseries. You will be surprised to find that most plants recommended for birds are also highly desirable from a landscaping and ornamental standpoint.

If there is a part of your yard that is swept by cold blasts of north wind, you can stop much of the force and create a sheltered place for birds with an evergreen hedge. Arbor vitae, hemlock, and pine are among the evergreens that can be used for this purpose. Evergreens are especially useful to birds in winter as they provide a safe hiding place when other trees are bare. One of the essentials of bird feeding is always to have good cover near feeders. There is nothing like a large sprawling tartarian honeysuckle bush to screen a feeder from the wind and at the same time supply birds with a haven and place to rest when not feeding.

Gardeners are sometimes rightfully suspicious of birds because of minor depredations to grapes, peas, strawberries, raspberries, and the like. Use of protective netting and scaring devices will keep such losses to a minimum. Birds in their turn keep many kinds of injurious insects under control. The good they do usually far offsets the harm. We can repay birds in some measure for their services by letting them have free access to flower beds and garden plots after we have gathered our harvest. Wait until birds have had a chance to feast before tidying up. The seeds, fruits, and half-rotten vegetables they find will keep them busy through much of the fall. Why spoil such a harvest for them? Garden produce is a good substitute for some of the foods we use at our feeding stations.

Songbirds in Your Garden, New York, Thomas Y. Crowell, 1968.

We should also be less energetic about removing dead tree stubs, dead branches, and brush piles. Woodpeckers will benefit if we are not overly zealous about pruning, and brush piles are a haven for such birds as wrens of all species, towhees, and song sparrows. A yard can be tidy and still contain enough wildness to meet the needs of most of our bird guests.

FIRST VISITORS

Having completed preparations and for the first time placed food at feeders, you will wait impatiently for the first bird to respond to your offerings. You may be surprised to find that resident house sparrows take longer than many other birds to make an appearance. This is likely to be true in spite of their reputation to crowd in wherever food is available. Despite an assertive nature, the house sparrow is basically shy and suspicious. It waits to see if any harm comes to the other birds before testing out a food supply for itself.

Usually tree-foraging birds like the chickadee, tufted titmouse, and blue jay are the first to sample our food. The cardinal, now a year-round visitor to feeders from southeastern Canada southward, may appear at about the same time. Not far behind, as a rule, are common species like the catbird, house finch, goldfinch, and song sparrow. If it is fall or winter, dark-eyed juncos and white-throated sparrows will quickly follow the example of the others. During invasion years, we may anticipate large flocks of seed-eaters, such as evening grosbeaks, pine siskins, redpolls, and purple finches. Sooner or later we can expect representatives of the blackbird family. Whether redwings, grackles, or cowbirds, they will assume control if we are not careful about what we feed and where (pages 64–5). Much the same applies to starlings, although these greedy eaters are seldom seen in numbers until snow and cold drive them to our premises.

The real test of our feeding effort is whether or not the chickadees, tufted titmice, nuthatches, and small woodpeckers put in an appearance. As we shall see, there are years when this important part of the feeding station company is absent because of better feeding conditions elsewhere. Once they do come, the tree-foragers are likely to stay with us the year round. Most of them are permanent residents. Few birds are more faithful to a food supply and few are more welcome. The one surprise is that they are sometimes so slow about finding us.

POOR SEASONS

What should we expect in the way of a feeding station company should the chickadees and their companions fail to find us? In the South one can almost always count upon a goodly number of visitors. But in more northern states the absence of chickadees can mean a poor season generally. This has been borne out by certain winters, such as 1957, when small woodland birds did not appear at feeding stations in parts of New England and other northern states. Aside from below-average temperatures in January, the weather was close to normal. Moreover, it was not one of those years when winter residents performed migrations southward. There was much speculation about what had happened and also a feeling of anxiety. Had the birds really disappeared?

Most birds, including house finches, will patronize a hanging hopper feeder with a spacious feeding platform.

That there had not been a disaster was apparent the next fall. Birds were back at feeders in normal numbers. It seems probable that the previous year chickadees and other winter residents had been diverted by an unusually plentiful supply of favored natural foods. Birds had remained farther afield instead of making their usual appearance in towns and about homesteads.

Events such as this can occur almost anywhere. Do not blame yourself or think that there has been a catastrophe affecting the entire bird population. Food is probably at the bottom of the trouble. Look for a possible return of birds to your feeders later that season; in rare instances, you may have to wait until the following fall.

LATE FALL

Weather is important in determining when birds will arrive at feeders. If it is a balmy fall, chances are that you will have few birds at your feeders. With a first snowfall or a sudden drop in temperature, you will be surprised at how quickly attendance picks up. Not only does the colder temperature whet the appetites of birds, but with each passing day the problem of finding enough food becomes more difficult. With fewer daylight hours there is less time for food finding, and usually by December the natural food supply is becoming depleted. Not only has some of this supply been used up by birds, but some has also been taken by insects and mammals. Decay is taking its toll, and many of the seeds are being washed away by rain or, as winter arrives, buried under the snow.

All through late summer and fall birds have been flying southward. Many people are not overly aware of this mass exodus of birdlife. Some of the migrants will travel only as far as more southern states; others will not stop until they reach the warmth of the tropics. For birds that spend the entire year in the same neighborhood, the departure of so many other birds does not necessarily mean any less competition for food. Sooner or later the place of migrants bound for sunnier climes is taken by seed-eating birds from farther north. The tinkling notes of tree sparrows and clicking sounds of juncos tell of newcomers that will be spending the winter with us.

Newly arriving birds from the north do not always immediately make their presence known. Not until a snowfall will many of them put in an appearance. If it should be a warm, open fall and winter, we may miss out completely on juncos, sparrows, and other open-country birds. On the other hand, with snow and cold weather, we will almost certainly have these visitors crowding in to our food supplies. Many know exactly where to go. This is not surprising as a fair number have spent other winters in our neighborhood.

Most writers warn not to begin feeding in the fall unless you can continue without interruption until the return of good weather. This is good advice, as many birds become so dependent upon our bounty that they would not be able to manage on their own if we suddenly discontinued our feeding at a critical time of the year.

Our main concern is for birds that establish winter feeding territories. No matter how hard-pressed they may be for food, territorial considerations keep such birds within a circumscribed area. The fact that you have initiated feeding in the fall means that many more birds than normal have settled nearby for the winter. Should you suddenly stop feeding, wide-ranging species will go elsewhere. Those with strong ties to winter feeding territories will be obliged to stay. Therefore, the greatest hardship will fall upon territorial species like the chickadees, white-breasted nuthatch, most of the small woodpeckers, and many of the sparrows and finches. Although such birds are for the most part hardy and self-sufficient, a sudden loss of food, particularly if coupled with heavy snow and freezing weather, could spell disaster. How serious a disaster will depend upon your neighborhood. If others have feeding stations that are not too far away, the birds may be able to adjust their daily routines sufficiently to make up for the loss of one feeding place. Nevertheless, it is best not to take chances with your guests. If you are obliged to be away for even a short time, try to make provision for your birds during your absence.

Before departing, fill hopper-type feeders as full as you can. The big advantage of the hopper-supplied feeder (pages 39–42) is that food is emitted only a little at a time. With several such feeders in use, it may be possible to tide seed-eaters over during the period of absence. For omnivorous feeders and birds that are dominantly insect-eating, provide suet and hard fat mixes at hanging feeders and other places where this food will not be covered over by snow. Since birds have to work harder for this kind of fare, the suet and mixes are likely to be long-lasting. Another long-lasting food, if any should happen to be growing in your neighborhood, is the Osage orange. Place the orange-like fruits where birds will find them. As they slowly disintegrate, the fruits will yield seeds that are well-favored by cardinals and other seed-eating birds.

Although you may be able to supply birds for a week or two by such measures, there is really no substitute for the small chores you perform daily. Removing snow, adding water to bird baths, putting out fresh food—these are details that should be attended to each day if you are going to be a good host to your many guests.

WINTER

Long before the full harshness of winter is upon you, you will begin to have an idea of what the season has to offer. One thing is certain: no two years will be the same. Some years our board is dominated by chickadees and their associates, other years we see mostly blue jays, juncos, and whitethroats. There will be occasional years when northern finches dominate our board. They are the most unpredictable visitors of all. You may decide by December that there is no chance that you will be playing host to these colorful visitors. Then, without warning, a few will appear. The flock will grow larger and before you know it, you will find that you are in the midst of an invasion. Your feeders and everyone else's will be inundated by colorful, scrappy birds whose tastes run heavily to sunflower.

Once they do appear, the northerners are likely to be around until May or even later. Not that the same birds will be steady patrons. Northern finches are so nomadic in their habits that they are seldom held in one place by a food supply. Usually, if one species puts in an appearance, other of the northern finches will not be far behind. Food failure in the north is the main reason for the erratic invasions that take place every few winters.

Forty or fifty years ago the arrival of a flock of evening grosbeaks was an event to talk about. Up until recently, we took the appearance of this most colorful of the northern finches much for granted. Spreading farther and farther south every few years and appearing in ever greater numbers, the evening grosbeak had become one of the most common winter feeding station visitors. But, as of 1993, there hasn't been a sizable invasion by evening grosbeaks in the East since 1984. Warmer winters and better food crops in the North would appear to be the answer.

Less well known are such other northerners as the pine siskin, common redpoll, white-winged crossbill, red crossbill, and pine grosbeak. It is a treat to have any one of these hardy seed-eaters at the feeder. They are much more unpredictable than the evening grosbeak, and several, including the crossbills, rarely come much farther south than our northernmost states. Still another seed-eater, usually regarded as a northern finch, is the purple finch. This handsome bird nests farther south than any of the other northern finches and also appears farther south in winter. Like others in this family, it has a habit of moving south in extraordinarily large numbers during some winters. This is usually during those invasion winters when the other northern finches come down as well.

Another unpredictable group are late migrants, or lingerers, as they are sometimes called. Many birds seem to wait too long and lose the urge to migrate. Others are trapped by early snowstorms and are obliged to stay behind. It is not that they are incapacitated. Low fat reserves and lowered vitality may simply mean that they are poorly fitted to undertake the long flight southward. Some birds have injuries or disabilities that prevent them from joining others of their kind as they move southward. Whatever the reason, the lingerers are poorly equipped for the winter ahead of them. Without feeding stations, few of them would survive.

So successful are northern orioles in over-wintering with the help of feeding stations that a whole segment of their population seems to have lost the urge to migrate. Almost unheard of outside the tropics in winter fifty to sixty years ago, the northern oriole is now almost a common winter resident throughout much of eastern North America. Few birds rely more completely upon feeding stations for survival.

Few other migratory birds have changed their habits quite to the degree that the northern oriole has. Nevertheless, there is scarcely a winter that we do not see a wide assortment of half-hardy species that rightly belong much farther south. They tend to shift for themselves until snow and cold weather bring them to our yards. Once bad weather has set in, they are almost completely dependent upon us for help. If we are good providers and the weather is not too harsh, the belated migrant stands a good chance of surviving. It is always a joy to see such a bird join its fellows as they return from their sojourn in the south.

If the weather has not been overly mild and natural foods too plentiful, your guest list by the end of December should be getting fairly long. Anywhere from twenty to thirty species is a normal quota at many feeding stations around Christmas time. Your list may be lengthened by a few additions in January and February. New arrivals are most likely to appear during or immediately after a snowstorm. Bad weather is synonymous with good attendance at feeding stations; mild, open winters see us with far fewer birds.

As January merges into February, there will be little perceptible change at the feeding station. The days are a little longer, and this will give birds more time for food finding. But the natural supply is more depleted than ever. Only sharp-eyed chickadees, kinglets, and brown creepers at this season seem capable of finding anything edible on the bark and twigs of trees. A few lonely yellow-rumped warblers look for the last remaining wax myrtle berries near the seacoast. Flickers and crows are reduced to eating sumac berries, and the small flocks of robins that have remained behind seek out bright red berries in the deepest swamps.

EARLY SPRING

Winter's long period of scarcity and uncertainty will give way in March and April to the most dramatic changes of the year. Even before the first deceptively warm days of spring there are signs of movement. Ducks, geese, snipe, woodcocks, killdeer, phoebes, and bluebirds seem too impatient to wait for thawing or signs of green to begin their northward flights. As the days lengthen and the sun's rays begin to eat away the snowdrifts, a certain restlessness appears among feeding station visitors. No longer as strict in their routine, they scatter to the countryside whenever the days are sufficiently mild. But a return to wintry weather sees them back at the feeding station in much the same numbers as before.

As long as spring progresses in a friendly fashion, without blizzards or bitter cold, feeding station attendance gradually diminishes. Juncos and sparrows of several kinds move northward while migrants from farther south pass through without showing much interest in feeding station fare. In more northern parts of the country it would not be a normal spring without periods of cold and snow. Such returns of winter impose one of the most serious hardships of the year upon birds that are not well adapted to severe weather conditions.

The one hope for the snowbound migrant is that the inclement weather will not last. Birds can depend upon fat reserves for a few days; thereafter they must find nourishing food or perish. A few find feeding stations, but many early migrants are birds that seldom recognize or use artificial food supplies. Rarely, if ever, do killdeer, phoebes, and purple martins come to feeding stations, and the same is largely true of robins, bluebirds, and most warblers. There are many birds that cannot be helped.

If it is disappointing not to be able to supply the needs of all, there is satisfaction to be had in the many that do respond. A late spring snowstorm may see the last of the winter visitors joined by mourning doves, red-winged blackbirds, towhees, various sparrows, and even meadowlarks. Once in a while an eastern phoebe that is particularly hard-pressed for food will take something at the feeding station. Other flycatchers, swifts, swallows, goatsuckers, and pipits, however, will remain completely aloof.

It is during these late snowstorms that you have one of your best opportunities to help birds. This is the time to put out more food than ever. Many of the snowbound migrants will not know where to look, so scatter food widely. Once the weather has improved, the birds are on their own again. Nothing in your larder will detain them. They are off to nesting grounds for the most vital time of the year.

WHETHER TO CONTINUE

Once the last of your winter visitors has departed, you may feel justified in closing down your feeding operation. After the last snow has disappeared and the spring buds are beginning to open, the feeling of crisis is over and you may decide that birds are safely on their own. In most parts of the country one can discontinue feeding without causing hardship in May; in the Deep South as soon as late March or April.

With winter feeding behind you, you may wish to turn your full attention to other facets of bird attracting. There will be birdhouses to occupy your spare time and the extra planting you should do for the birds. A year-round chore you should not overlook is keeping bird baths cleaned at frequent intervals and filled with fresh water. By feeding all year, you will have the pleasure of providing food for hard-pressed parents busy with nesting duties and the young that often come to feeders as well. Summer is the season to feed hummingbirds. Feeding in late summer and early fall serves notice that birds will always have a safe supply of food to come to. Whether to continue with bird feeding is a matter of personal taste. Do you miss having birds at your windows and do you miss the chores connected with feeding them? If so, you might as well continue with feeding and perhaps make it a year-round venture.

three

SELECTION, PREPARATION, AND PLACEMENT OF FOODS

The most essential part of a bird attracting program is *food*. Although everything else may be in perfect order, failure to provide the right foods can result in poor attendance. Birds can afford to be choosy now that bird feeding is such a popular hobby. They tend to congregate only where the food is to their liking. You can have an edge on your neighbors by using foods that are better liked by birds and giving special thought to preparation and placement.

The most basic foods in a bird feeding program will be seeds and grain, nutmeats, fats, bakery products, and fruit. No two or three kinds of food will satisfy the needs of all guests. Some foods are better from a nutritional standpoint, others are useful mainly because of taste appeal. The way to test the relative merits of different foods is to establish an experimental feeder. Build a tray with at least six compartments of equal size that birds can feed from. Place the tray on a feeding shelf. Fill each compartment with a different kind of food and see how quickly each compartment is emptied. The foods that disappear most rapidly will be the ones that have the widest appeal. After a series of such tests, you will know which foods are best suited to your feeding program. At the same time, do not overlook the special tastes you may find among your guests. Not infrequently, a food that has little popular appeal will suit a guest with more discriminating tastes.

After exhaustive tests at a home feeding station, biologist Verne E. Davison* came to the conclusion that taste is all-important in the selection of food by birds. Others maintain that it is not taste but size, color, and texture that influence choice.

* *Attracting Birds: From the Prairies to the Atlantic*, New York, Thomas Y. Crowell, 1967.

What makes birds choose a particular food is a difficult question to answer. Birds have poorly developed taste buds, yet they are highly discriminating in what they eat. It seems reasonable to believe that there is something closely akin to taste that rules their decisions when it comes to food.

You will discover some highly stereotyped tastes. The evening grosbeak will rarely leave sunflower to sample any other food. Cardinals, grackles, and house sparrows never seem to tire of the same daily offering of scratch feed (page 266). But blue jays, on the other hand, take a spell of eating this food or that one; then they lose interest altogether, and we do not see them for a while. Some of our visitors reveal rather unorthodox tastes. A wintering northern oriole at a Massachusetts feeder was seen to breakfast on pie dough, baked pie crust, and a little peanut butter and banana. In the afternoon the bird was back for strawberry parfait pie and even ate some of the whipped cream on top! A mockingbird at my feeder ate rotten banana that had frozen and thawed many times, and a downy woodpecker ate rotten pears. Other reported cases of taste peculiarities include a red-headed woodpecker with a special liking for potato chips, a catbird that breakfasted on a bowl of puffed wheat and milk, and starlings that liked sauerkraut.

Differences in food preference sometimes crop up between members of a mated pair. One chickadee of a pair coming to a feeder in North Carolina ate nothing but sunflower; the other nothing but nut crumbs or grated cheese. A male red-bellied woodpecker at my feeder ate cracked corn and suet, the female ate little else but sunflower. Many more observations along this line are contained in Len Howard's book *Birds as Individuals.** She became thoroughly acquainted with all the taste preferences of the birds that came streaming in through the windows of her Sussex, England, home to receive special food offerings.

A feeder with a compartmented food tray is useful for testing the merits of various bird foods.

*New York, Doubleday, 1953.

Another matter to consider in connection with food is economy. If we are going to give birds sufficient amounts of safe, wholesome food, we need to take extra care in both purchasing and handling. The first rule is to buy in bulk. This applies mainly to seeds and grain. We generally get a better product and at far more reasonable cost when we buy 50-and 100-pound bags. The handy smaller bags of birdseed that can be purchased anywhere often leave much to be desired. Frequently these bags contain only enough sunflower to give the appearance of a rich mixture. Much of the bulk is likely to be made up of millet, which may suit some of our customers but not others. A second rule is to buy each food item separately and not in mixtures. We do far better to mix our own instead of relying upon formulas that may not fit the needs of our clientele. When purchasing sunflower, try to get the smallest seeds available. Black oil sunflower, which has become by far the most popular variety to use in bird feeding, has the smallest seeds. It contains relatively more edible kernel and less worthless hull; at the same time it is easier for birds to open.

We can avoid one of the greatest waste hazards by storing food properly. Leaving seeds and grain in bags invites rodents and spoilage by weevils and mildew. I know of nothing more suitable for storage purposes than the 20-gallon galvanized metal trash cans that have tight metal lids. Before filling, first place a heavy-duty plastic trash bag in the can. After all of the seeds have been used up, it is advisable to remove the old trash bag and replace it with a new one. This will help eliminate any danger of insect infestation. Never mix old seeds with new ones. If seeds have gone bad during storage, discard them. In cool, dry weather it is safe to store seeds and grain for as long as three months. In the humid southeastern states, and again in the Pacific Northwest, it is not safe to store feed for longer than one month. This is particularly true of oil-bearing seeds, such as sunflower, safflower, thistle, and peanuts. The most serious pest of oil seeds is a grain moth, which may develop from worm to adult state in seeds stored a month or longer in containers or bags. Another danger from spoiled bird seed is a toxic fungus called aspergillus, which can infect birds.

If you would reduce wastage at the feeder, do not put out more food than birds can eat in a day. Try placing food at regular times at least twice daily. The amounts to put out can be judged rather closely in good weather. During bad weather keep up with the appetites of your guests by making frequent small offerings of food. In this way you will avoid much of the losses that result from wind, rain, and snow. It is helpful to keep some food in hanging feeders and a reserve of seeds and grain in hoppers that emit small quantities at a time. In this way birds will always have something to fall back upon.

Another way to save is to seek out special bargains at food stores and bakeries. Not infrequently you can get slightly damaged or spoiled food at no cost. This food may not be suitable for human consumption but generally there is no harm in providing it to birds. Among these bargains may be broken jars of peanut butter, over-ripe fruit, and stale bakery products. Also ask your butcher for pieces of fat and suet. When you add kitchen leftovers to bargains such as these, the cost of bird feeding becomes less and less.

Those who live in or near the country can take advantage of the natural produce of fields and woodland. By late summer begin looking for nuts, wild fruits and berries, and the seed heads of weeds. Store more perishable foods in a freezing compartment, the rest can be kept in appropriate containers until it is time for winter feeding. Natural foods can make a significant contribution to your feeding program. Sometimes these foods are the only ones that will gain the attention of birds that are not enticed by conventional feeding station fare.

One way to be a good host is to anticipate the need for a change in diet. Standard bird foods go a long way toward meeting the expectations of our guests. Yet there is always the possibility that we are offering too monotonous a diet. This will not bother certain of our guests, but others may begin to drift away if we do not make new foods available from time to time. Try spicing up your menu with occasional odd items—natural foods, for example, or leftovers from the kitchen. Whether you give these foods a permanent place on your menu will depend upon their availability and the enthusiasm that birds show for them. Probably less than half the foods you try will be worth a second trial. But keep on experimenting. This is a key to success in bird feeding.

Finally, in organizing your feeding program, you should give adequate thought to convenience. Food containers should be close at hand so that you do not have to trudge through cold and snow when feeders need replenishing. See if there is not a handy place to keep food on a side or back porch. Keep a ladle in the form of a scoop or tin cup in each metal storage can. Empty coffee cans make useful containers in which to carry seeds and grain to the feeders.

The cereal grains—corn, wheat, oats, rice, millet, canary seed, and grain sorghums—constitute the most important group of foods used in bird feeding. Rich in carbohydrates, the cereal grains are excellent suppliers of heat and energy. They are rather low in crude protein and mineral matter. For this reason it is desirable to supplement a cereal grain diet with foods that offer more in the way of protein and mineral matter. This can be accomplished with nutmeats, peanut butter, and suet mixtures containing peanut butter.

Corn has more taste appeal than most other cereal grains. In one form or another corn is eaten by practically every bird that comes to the feeder. It can be used on the cob, as whole kernels, cracked kernels, cornmeal, hominy grits, corn mush, corn muffins, and cornbread. If possible use yellow corn, since it contains Vitamin A, which is absent in white corn.

All of the cereal grains are cultivated members of the grass family. A number of seeds from other families are also useful in bird feeding, and many of them are more nutritious than the cereal grains. Some have only a limited appeal, while others,

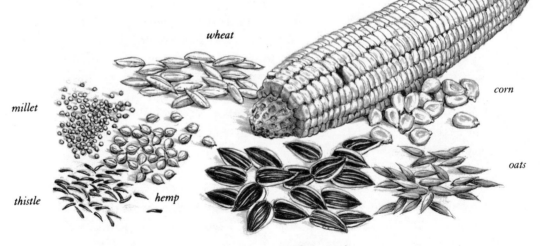

wheat

corn

millet

oats

thistle   *hemp*

sunflower seeds

like sunflower, find favor with every bird that is capable of using them. Sunflower is probably the best liked of any of the seeds or grains used in bird feeding. The rich, oily seeds are indispensable when it comes to feeding evening grosbeaks. The appeal of sunflower seems greatest with sparrows and finches and with small tree-foraging birds like nuthatches and chickadees. Virtually all our guests will take sunflower so long as they can find a way to penetrate the tough outer hull. Many birds depend upon the tidbits left by strong-billed birds that are more accomplished at cracking or pounding open the hull. Note the deftness with which each seed is handled by titmice, jays, and various finches.

Hemp seeds once enjoyed almost the same popularity as a bird food as sunflower. They, too, are oily seeds that supply needed calories during cold weather. However, the hemp seed has largely become a casualty of the drug traffic. Hemp is the plant that supplies marijuana. For many years now the seeds that are sold commercially have had to undergo parching. Hemp seeds are now harder to get and parching lessens their attractiveness to birds. This is too bad, for hemp had all the virtues of sunflower and far less of the seed was taken up by hull.

NUTMEATS

Nutmeats go a long way toward making up any deficiencies in protein or calories that may be present in our day-to-day offerings. All nutmeats rate highly from a nutritional standpoint and it takes only a few handfuls daily to round out a menu. Kinds to use will be governed largely by availability. The pecan, almond, and peanut are the only nutmeats that are sold as bird foods. Pecan meats ground to the proper size for bird feeding are available at many stores that supply bird foods. Peanuts can be used in any form. If you want to serve them in the shell, string a whole row together with needle and thread and then hang where titmice, jays, and nuthatches can work on them. There is no end of fun in the antics that birds will go through to get at the meats inside. The chopped meats of peanuts are sold as bird food, as are the hearts of the peanut, which are a by-product in the manufacture of peanut butter.

After exhaustive tests with various nutmeats at his feeders, Verne E. Davison came to the conclusion that the peanut is not too well liked by birds. Out of twelve kinds of nuts tested, only the pistachio rated lower in favor than the peanut. Certain of my tests bear out the results obtained by Davison. One winter scarcely any birds sampled chopped peanuts at my feeders. On the other hand, there have been times when I could not put this food out fast enough for the goldfinches and other birds that were feeding on it. Many others have also had this experience.

Davison found no difference in response by birds whether peanuts were cooked or uncooked, salted or unsalted. Although many birds seem to shy away from the peanut in certain of its forms, there is one way that the peanut is always popular. This is as peanut butter. There is scarcely a bird food that is more irresistible. However, this taste treat must be used with caution. A few instances have come to light of birds apparently choking on pure peanut butter. We can get around this difficulty by using peanut butter in bird food recipes of various kinds. For example, when mixed with cornmeal and suet, peanut butter is rendered completely harmless and birds still enjoy a tasty meal.

Among the more exotic nuts that appeal to birds are cashews, almonds, English walnuts, and Brazil nuts. Although most birds cannot possibly know these nuts in the wild, they accept them as eagerly as they do our native nuts. Normally too costly

*A tufted titmouse
takes pleasure in mastering
a string of peanuts
in the shell.*

to use in bird feeding, the exotic nuts have a place as occasional treats. Of our native nuts, black walnuts, butternuts, hazelnuts, and certain of the hickories are particularly well liked by birds. The cultivated pecan is another excellent nut for bird feeding. Whether we harvest nuts or buy them, the shell first has to be broken and meats chopped into fine pieces before birds can enjoy the contents. Where the nut kernel is much constricted as in hickories and walnuts, simply crack open and let the birds pick out the meats. They do this much more deftly than we could.

Nutmeats can be used in the same way as seeds or grain. Place at open feeders along with other offerings or use at small hanging feeders where there will be a more limited clientele. The flavor of nutmeats holds a special attraction for most woodpeckers, the titmice, nuthatches, jays, wrens, and yellow-rumped warblers. Nutmeats spoil rather rapidly, so do not put out too many at one time. When used in suet mixes, the meats stay fresh far longer. Simply stir them in when you are preparing a mixture and adding a variety of ingredients.

SUET AND FAT MIXTURES

The suet and fats you have been saving will come in handy when you start feeding birds in the fall. No longer do many people nail pieces of suet to trees or put chunks in wire holders. There are far better ways to use suet. A small cookbook has been written on how to make taste treats for birds using suet and various odds and ends from the kitchen.* Before trying your hand at any of these concoctions, be sure you have obtained suitable suet. The best kind is beef suet from the region of the kidney. Lamb or mutton suet is decidedly inferior as a bird food.

Before rendering, suet should be cut into strips and put through a meat grinder. Other fats, including lard, roast drippings, and bacon drippings, can be used either as a substitute for suet or as added ingredients. So long as these fats are free of rich seasoning or excessive amounts of salt, they appear to be perfectly safe for bird feeding. Suet makes a harder mix than other fats and one that better resists the weather. It is an energy-giving food that appeals to the appetites of birds whether they are dominantly seed-eating or insect-eating. By adding other ingredients to the

*Donna Suther, *Feed Your Feathered Friends*, Britton, South Dakota, The Britton Journal, 1971.

suet, we produce a food that is as nutritious and appetizing as almost any we can offer. Suet mixes go best in winter but can be used at any season.

BAKERY PRODUCTS

Whether in the form of doughnuts or stale white bread, there is something in bakery products that seems to have a special appeal for birds. White bread is one of the best foods to entice birds to a new feeder. Doughnuts and cornbread can be used in much the same way as suet and attract about the same clientele as does suet. Crumbs from cakes, biscuits, and crackers sometimes gain attention where other foods fail.

FRUITS

For the most part, fruits take second place at feeders. More often than not, the sliced apple, pear, banana, and orange we put out will get such little attention that we have to dispose of them before they rot. This is less likely if the feeding station is visited by mockingbirds, catbirds, robins, and starlings. In winter dried and fresh fruits are almost a necessity if you are acting as host to the northern oriole. This colorful visitor is partial to raisins, sliced apple, and orange. The same fare can be used with orioles in summer. As an experiment someone tried orange juice in a hummingbird feeder that was patronized by orioles. The orioles, which had been coming for sugar-water, liked the orange juice even better. If you are lucky enough to have scarlet or summer tanagers at your feeders in summer, try feeding them fresh fruit. There will be little waste when you have these bright-colored tropical visitors.

Dried fruits, such as raisins, currants, and small pieces of dried fig, are useful for feeding robins, thrushes, bluebirds, and waxwings, birds that are not receptive to most feeding station foods. Dried fruit is also well liked by catbirds and mockingbirds. This food has an advantage over fresh fruit in that it is longer lasting and not so messy. The best way to offer it is in a dish or shallow bowl. Raisins and currants are most readily accepted after they have been softened through steaming or cooking. Serve with the juice.

The fact that dried fruits are not overly popular with most birds is in a way an advantage. You can offer this kind of food with the expectation that it will be taken only by a few more discriminating guests and not gobbled up almost immediately.

On the whole, birds seem more receptive to fruit, whether dried or fresh, in summer. This is not surprising. Birds that are dominantly fruit-eaters are likely to spend the winter months in the tropics. Back with us for the summer, they miss the fruits they knew in more southern climes. We gain special favor with these fruit-eaters by supplying some of the fruits they knew in the tropics; they also accept apple and other temperate-zone fruits.

RECOGNIZING AND ACCEPTING FOOD

It is a common experience when feeding birds to have them completely ignore a food that from all accounts should be well received. Frequently the difficulty is not in the food but in how it is offered. I recall that birds at first totally ignored the doughnuts I had placed on feeding shelves. But when I crumpled a doughnut and offered the broken pieces, these were immediately accepted. Many other foods, including raisins, currants, sliced apple and orange, peanut hearts, and coconut, are likely to be ignored when first offered. Do not conclude too hastily that these foods are worthless at your feeder. Sometimes it is only a matter of waiting until a more inquisitive bird samples a food. I have had foods go two or three weeks before they were sampled. Once a food is sampled, other birds take note and soon begin to exploit the new discovery. However, if a food is consistently refused, there is no point in continuing with it. The banana is an example of a food that I have rarely had any luck with at my feeders. In view of the good results others have had with this fruit, I keep trying. Apple and pear are other fruits that are sometimes ignored at my feeders. But I have found that these fruits and others are often better received after they have become half rotten.

Slowness to accept strange foods is coupled with cleverness and ingenuity when it comes to retrieving food that has been purposely hidden or camouflaged in some way. On a number of occasions I have experimented with altering the appearance of foods in order to see if birds were able to detect my disguises. The birds usually succeeded.

Purple finches mastered some, but not all, of the disguises I attempted with sunflower seeds. Seeds coated with flour and placed on the feeders were quickly recognized and accepted. Seeds painted blue were also recognized. However, seeds that had been painted red went untouched no matter how long they were exposed. Also seeds hidden under a thin layer of sand remained undiscovered.

My next experiment was with pieces of bread that had been dyed different colors. The birds that were coming to my feeders at that time, especially blue jays, recognized and ate bread that had been dyed orange. Bread that had been dyed other colors, including yellow, pink, red, and green, remained untouched. I can hardly blame my visitors for not accepting most of the colored bread I offered. Birds have color vision, much as we do, and often seem partial to foods colored pink and orange.

Where food is placed is also a highly important factor in whether it is accepted or not. Even the most familiar foods sometimes go untouched for long periods when exposed at a new location. A peanut butter mixture smeared into bark crevices of trees near my feeding stations was always quickly discovered and utilized. The same mixture employed in the same manner on trees a hundred yards or so away went untouched. Much the same results would be repeated with any feeding station foods. Birds respond most readily to food when it appears at a place where they are accustomed to being fed; it takes time for them to find and accept foods at new locations.

FINDING HIDDEN FOOD

How do birds locate food? Is it always through vision or does the sense of smell or some other sense play a role? Sense of smell is poorly developed in most birds. Yet birds occasionally reveal an extraordinary ability to locate food that is hidden from view. Birds that store food for the winter have the ability to return to caches made months earlier. We occasionally see blue jays go to the exact spot in our lawns where a peanut, acorn, or sunflower seed had previously been buried. The Old World nutcracker is said to dig through as much as a foot and a half of snow to reach a spot where it had previously buried nuts. After a snowfall birds that come to feeders know just where to scratch or probe in order to obtain covered-over food supplies.

Still more intriguing is the apparent ability of birds to detect hidden food that has not been seen previously. A neighbor told me of an example of this kind at her feeder. She had removed the hanging peanut butter stick to which a downy woodpecker and other birds had been coming and instead placed some peanut butter in a cup on the feeding shelf. A bird could not see the peanut butter unless it happened to perch upon the rim of the cup. The downy, no longer finding the peanut butter at the customary place, began searching the feeding shelf. Sensing that the missing food was somewhere on the shelf, the bird spent the entire day in the vicinity. Finally it caught on to the container with its peanut butter.

In an experiment of my own, I placed a poultry mash that starlings were very fond of in a tightly closed paper bag. I left the bag at a place where they were in the habit of coming for food. It was not long before a starling had punctured the bag with its sharp bill. Soon this starling and others were dining upon the contents of the bag. A still more remarkable example of this kind is contained in Len Howard's *Birds as Individuals*. Readers who would delve further into this subject will enjoy her anecdote about Baldhead, the great titmouse that retrieved food from a paper bag concealed under two folds of a teacloth. According to Miss Howard, the bird had not seen her secrete the food, and the bag containing the food was located in an unfamiliar place.

four

DESIGN AND PLACEMENT OF FEEDERS

We need to advertise if we want to attract a wide variety of birds to our yards. And there is no better way to do this than to have plenty of food in view that can be had without mastering difficult feeding devices. Even if the supply is discovered by grackles, cowbirds, and starlings, this is not the disaster that some think it to be. Every guest has something to offer, and if we will only see this, it will greatly enhance our enjoyment and make the problems seem less imposing. If problems you do have, the way to remedy the situation is partly by manipulation of foods and partly by how you make use of your feeders. As we will see later, there are ways to dampen appetites by making changes in the menu. This can often be done by withholding some foods and making greater use of others.

And there is no reason to rely wholly upon bird feeders when it comes to supplying food. A slightly hollowed out tree stump, a large flat rock, a well cover, a roof outside a bedroom window, crevices in the bark of trees—all are handy places to stuff or scatter food. The ground itself is not a bad place at all if you have no serious problems with cats and if precautions are taken to prevent disease (see pages 45–6). To be sure, there are birds that rarely, if ever, feed on the ground. Therefore, if you are going to have a well-rounded feeding program, you almost certainly have to get some of the food up off the ground and into raised feeders.

By scattering food on the ground we cater to the feeding habits of the bobwhite, ring-necked pheasant, mourning dove, brown thrasher, blackbirds, and sparrows. Even the red-bellied woodpecker, which we think of as a tree dweller, does some foraging on the ground. Woodpeckers, nuthatches, tufted titmice, and chickadees will be equally at home at hanging feeders or small devices attached to tree trunks. Most birds will come to almost any kind of platform or shelf a few feet above the ground. Quite a few, including purple finches and evening grosbeaks, will come to second-story-window feeders.

Encouraging birds to feed at different levels and in enough places helps reduce friction. Birds that are out of their element, eating too high or too low, or under crowded conditions, are ill-at-ease. Some will show their insecurity by exhibiting excessively aggressive tendencies, others by being overly submissive. All of us who have fed birds have seen the single bird that plants itself squarely on a small feeding tray and denies feeding privileges to other birds for as long as it possibly can. Small feeders and not enough food encourage some individuals to become bullies. If we want to have our birds behaving in a reasonably courteous manner, we need to be generous with food and have it widely distributed.

More attention should be given to locating some of the feeders well away from the house. The tendency is to overdo the taming process. We lure all the birds we can to windowsills and close-by feeders. This is fine from the standpoint of watching birds and seeing exactly what they are doing. But in the process we attract such a mixed company that we end up having a few dominant species that crowd out the others. A more dispersed feeding arrangement—with food offered at different levels

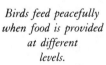

*Birds feed peacefully
when food is provided
at different
levels.*

and different distances from the house—makes for less mixing and much less friction. It is surprising how well birds will sort themselves out if we but give them the chance.

Friends of mine had difficulties with redwings and cowbirds that crowded into feeders close to their house. So they tried placing a hopper-type feeder mounted on a post farther out on the lawn in order to see if this would draw away the unwelcome guests. The results were even better than they had anticipated. The redwings immediately went to the elevated tray fed by the hopper, while the cowbirds went to seeds

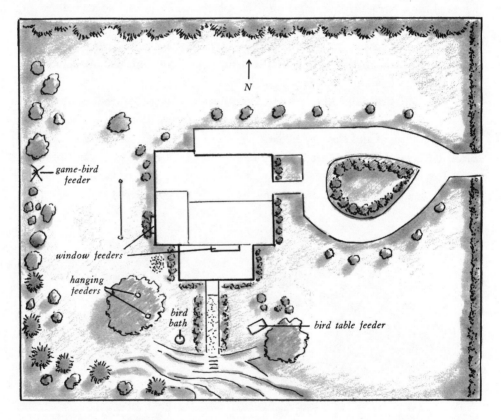

Plantings around this suburban home are inadequate to give birds all the protection they need from wind and possible enemies. Nevertheless, by placing most feeders on the south side of the house and near trees and shrubbery, the owners have offered birds reasonable protection, and feeders and bird bath are clearly visible from viewing windows.

and grain that spilled out onto the ground below. Similar results can be obtained with the common grackle, which, if anything, is even more willing to be lured away from the immediate proximity of the house.

Generally, if given a choice, the birds that rate lowest in our esteem will feed as far away from the house as they can. It would almost seem as though they are aware of our wishes and try to adhere to them. Or, more likely, crows, starlings, house sparrows, and problem members of the blackbird family have been subjected to more persecution than other birds that come to our feeders, and therefore it is wariness that keeps them at a distance. The gray squirrel, on the other hand, seems to have learned nothing from years of hunting pressure and persecution. Any relaxation on the bird lover's part and it is right outside his windows. Squirrel-proofing at some of the feeders will help to remedy the situation.

If there are cats in the neighborhood, it may be a good idea to keep feeders at slightly greater distances from cover than would otherwise be advisable. A cat out in the open where birds can see it represents no serious danger; it is another story when a cat is concealed under a bush near where birds are feeding. At the same time, we should not go to the other extreme and place food too far out in the open. It is true that exceptions can be made for open-country birds such as starlings, meadowlarks, blackbirds, and many sparrows and finches. In fact, several visitors, such as the horned lark, snow bunting, and Lapland longspur, would not come at all unless food was well out in the open. Birds that normally feed in the open are more accustomed to the danger of attack by aerial predators; hence they have developed evasive tactics that help them elude this kind of danger. Woodland birds also know how to elude danger, but they are much more dependent upon cover in the form of trees and shrubbery. If feeders are to be safe for most users, they should not be much over five feet from cover of some kind.

The feeders and bird bath in the modest suburban yard shown opposite have been arranged with a view toward overcoming crowding. With some feeders at windowsills and others at varying distances from the house, birds have a wide choice of places to select for feeding. A small thicket of natural growth along the rear property line is an ideal place to establish a feeder or two well away from the house. One might be a game-bird feeder and the other a feeder where troublesome birds can be lured with scraps and inexpensive foods.

Feeders have been located to take advantage of the trees and shrubbery that exist in this somewhat open yard. While there are dense hedges and scattered bushes, the yard needs more trees and bushes—especially kinds that produce fruits and berries well liked by birds. It is always helpful to have some nearby sources of natural foods so that birds do not have to rely so heavily upon our feeding station supplies.

Any natural growth, such as the thicket at the rear edge of this yard, should be carefully preserved during this day of complete land clearing for developments. Although newer plantings will in time reach a size adequate for cover and nesting sites, there is really no substitute for the diversity that is afforded by natural growth. If a property contains a spring or small pond with a marshy border, this is a haven to preserve at all costs. While much can be accomplished on a relatively open lot with foods, feeders, and bird baths, it is still *habitat* and not these other enticements that make a yard well suited to birdlife.

The feeders and bird bath should be located in portions of the yard sheltered from the wind. Usually the south side of the house, where many of the feeders are located in our plan, will have a good measure of protection because the house itself will block off cold northerly winds. When the south side, as in this instance, contains the windows where most bird watching will take place, we have all the right conditions for bird feeders on this side of the house. But even the north side can have its share if cold winds can be screened off by plantings, a fence, or a wall.

Another important consideration is escape cover to which birds can retire at any hint of danger. In the plan, wherever it is possible to do so, feeders have been located near suitable cover. The maple, apple, privet, lilac, forsythia, and other plants near the house furnish moderately good cover. The tartarian bush honeysuckle behind the bird table makes an excellent tangle where birds can congregate when not eating at the feeders.

SMALL HANGING FEEDERS

The trend in bird feeders for many years has been toward small, compact models that protect food from the weather and have features that reduce competition. Designers have been very successful in proofing these feeders against squirrels, starlings, blue jays, and still other visitors that to some may seem less desirable. The newer feeders are attractive looking and very much of an asset when it comes to improving the appearance of one's yard.

I have several of these small, modern feeders and find that they are particularly useful, when, if for some reason, I am not able to keep my other feeders well supplied. I have both small hanging and fixed feeders that operate on the principle of releasing only small amounts of food at a time. No matter how heavily birds feed at these devices, they cannot clean out the supply in a short time. This is something that happens all too frequently at my large, unprotected feeders. If my newer models are well filled, I know that there will be some food left if I should happen to be away for several days and unable to make the daily rounds. Also I can count upon my newer models during bad weather. Food is kept safe and dry and up where the snow cannot cover it over.

Droll Yankee

One of the most successful of the new feeders is a model called the "Droll Yankee," manufactured by Droll Yankees, Inc., of Foster, Rhode Island. The feeder is a cylinder of clear plastic—the hollow interior containing the food while birds eat at six outlets provided with perches. Food drops down to these outlets, which are circular and ¾ inch wide, as birds remove the food by eating it. This is the old-fashioned principle of the hopper feeder but superimposed upon a hanging cylinder. The hopper feeder,

*The Droll Yankee (right)
and an exclusive feeder
for small birds (left).*

long used in the poultry industry, keeps food protected until it is eaten and allows only a few birds to eat at a time.

When filled with a mixture of thistle and sunflower, the Droll Yankee is a good feeder for attracting a variety of birds, and, at the same time, exclusive enough to keep out a number of more dubious guests. The Droll Yankee caters to the feeding habits of small woodland birds like the chickadee and tufted titmouse, and finches, such as the goldfinch, purple finch, and pine siskin. Weather-proof and with a good capacity for holding seeds, the Droll Yankee will, as a rule, keep birds well supplied for several days without refilling. A newer model has three times the capacity of the older one and can be mounted upon a post or hung from a line. Several other companies have produced feeders modeled upon the Droll Yankee, which are basically hanging cylinders with one or more openings where birds feed.

One drawback to the Droll Yankee and these other feeders is that their superior performance may lull users into thinking no other kinds of feeders are necessary. If we intend to follow a policy of advertising our food supplies and, at the same time, making some of it easily available to our guests, we will want to make use of several kinds of feeders as well as a variety of foods. There are still other kinds of hanging feeders that are well worth trying.

Box-Type Hopper

Less of a departure from the poultry hopper are models that, like the Droll Yankee, can be hung from a line or tree limb; at the same time, these models can be placed upon a bird table or feeding tray. One, which is shaped like a box, is about a foot square, with a sloping roof, glass sides, and a small tray where birds can feed. Thanks to glass on one or two sides, it is possible to tell at a glance if more food is needed. No gymnastic feats are required of birds using this feeder. Mourning doves sometimes settle at the edge of even the hanging model. These feeders are reasonably weatherproof and economical. As with the Droll Yankee, we can fill the hopper and rest assured that there will still be some food for our guests if we should be gone for several days.

The lantern hopper looks very much like an old-fashioned kerosene lamp. It can be hung like an outside lamp on a bracket on the side of the house. Food is placed in a glass cylinder while birds feed at a tray below fitted with perches that stick out like the spokes in a wheel. Overhanging eaves provide birds with some protection from the weather.

The beehive hopper looks like a small beehive and can be hung almost anywhere. This feeder is designed for such a select group of customers that perches have not been added. In order to procure food from this feeder, birds must cling in a practically upside down position to the rim of the food outlets at the very bottom. At first glance this arrangement might seem to be asking too much of chickadees, nuthatches, and small finches. Yet, when one sees these birds feeding in the wild, they are very often clinging in a vertical or upside down position to seed heads, pine cones, catkins, or small twigs. The beehive feeder simply caters to the natural feeding habits of certain birds. At the same time, the sizable number of species that cannot perform these tricks cannot use this feeder. If anything, the beehive feeder is somewhat too selective. However, other feeders, using the same principle, have appeared, with better grips and more room, so that three or four birds can feed at a time. These models save food and can be used only by a very select clientele.

Hanging Coconut

One of the easiest feeders to make, and a handsome one too, is the hanging coconut. Either cut out a section of the coconut, as shown in the illustration on page 234, or cut a coconut in half at its widest portion, drill three holes at the edge for hanging with string or wire, and attach to a tree limb or line. The other half of the coconut may serve as a roof. If any coconut meat is left on the inside of the shell, this will

A hopper-type feeder is useful in reserving food for times of emergency.

provide a first food offering. However, birds sometimes ignore this food while squirrels take it eagerly. The main function of the hanging coconut is to serve as a dish for food that is out of reach of many would-be customers. Fill with a suet mixture or pour the mixture, while still warm, over seeds and grain at the bottom of the feeder. This is an excellent feeder for chickadees, tufted titmice, nuthatches, and small woodpeckers.

Hanging Log

The same clientele that uses the hanging coconut will come to holes bored in hanging logs or sticks which have been filled with a suet mixture. The logs, which are between a foot and a foot and a half long, about three inches in diameter, and with six or eight round holes for food, are attractive-looking as well as practical feeders. Insert a screw eye at one end and hang from a tree limb or line. If you cut your own logs, try to get pieces of wood to which the bark tightly adheres. Bark improves the appearance of this type of feeder and provides a surface that birds can cling to. With the addition of perches beneath each hole, the log feeder becomes usable to such species as blue jay, catbird, yellow-rumped warbler, northern oriole, dark-eyed junco, and tree sparrow. The starling sometimes obtains food at these feeders by hovering

*Suet-saturated pine cones
are popular with chickadees.*

before the holes like a hummingbird. Even though these attempts are clumsy, a substantial amount of food can be taken in this manner. Squirrels make for a still more serious problem. Not only do they clean out the food supply but they gnaw the surrounding wood as well. Squirrel-proofing (pages 50–2) may be advisable if many of these mammals are in your neighborhood.

Thistle Feeders

Some feeders have been designed exclusively for sunflower seeds; the same is true of thistle seeds. In thistle-feeders, the feeding vents, instead of being wide openings, are narrow verticle slits only one quarter of an inch high and located two inches above the perches. The feeder itself is a clear plastic tube with a cap at the top to open for refilling. The vents are small enough to keep the seeds inside until they are eaten. Birds are able to see the seeds through the plastic. I've had chickadees, pine siskins, and goldfinches come to a newly placed thistle feeder minutes after it was installed.

Because of heavy competition between house finches and goldfinches for thistle seeds, designers have produced an "Anti–House Finch Feeder," which is in deference to those who would rather have goldfinches. The feeder is exactly like the thistle feeder described above except that the feeding vents are below the perches, not above. Goldfinches, who hang by their feet from weed stalks while they feed, readily do so at these perches, reaching downward to feed at the openings. This is a maneuver that the house finch is almost incapable of performing, but it is within the capacity also of redpolls and pine siskins.

Commercially made hanging mesh bags are also available as thistle feeders, but I have found them to be too wasteful. Up to 35 percent of the seeds fall to the ground while birds feed at the openings.

BIRD TABLES

If it is our philosophy to encourage, rather than limit food consumption, we have an ideal feeder in the old-fashioned bird table. Almost any table will do. All that is needed is a flat, raised surface where seeds, grain, and other foods can be spread as if on a banquet table and where birds will have adequate room for feeding. A table

2½ feet high, 3 feet long, 2 feet wide, and with a rim at the edge ½ inch high (to prevent food from blowing away) is a convenient size. A peaked, detachable roof with overhanging eaves looks attractive and provides the protection from wind, rain, and snow that may be needed. During good weather the roof is not needed. Without it we get a better look at our visitors and they come more readily to the food.

Bird tables are not as popular as they used to be. This is largely because of the high cost of bird food. We are anxious to get most of our food up where it will not be spoiled by the weather or taken by less desirable visitors. Hence the popularity of small hanging feeders. At the same time, there are kitchen wastes and other foods that do not need to be preserved so carefully. It is a good plan to have some of these foods out in the open where birds can see them. In this way we advertise our feeding program and in the process probably get many more desirable species than we would otherwise. I use my bird table partly for advertisement and partly for bird watching. Birds are more at ease when they have a spacious place on which to dine.

Some of the foods that I offer at my bird table are over-ripe fruit, stale bakery products, nutmeats, scratch feed, and some sunflower. The guests that I entertain range from colorful cardinals and evening grosbeaks to the drabber, more plebeian starlings and house sparrows. There is little friction, as a rule, between these guests, because there is enough food and space for them all.

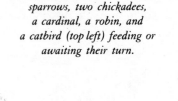

*A typical bird table scene with
a wood thrush (right), three chipping
sparrows, two chickadees,
a cardinal, a robin, and
a catbird (top left) feeding or
awaiting their turn.*

I give the top of the table a good cleaning every day or so, and I also rake the ground below. This chore is important if I want to keep the premises tidy and safeguard my visitors from the dangers of infectious disease that might be spread by moldy foods along with an accumulation of droppings.

GROUND FEEDING

Since some food always drops to the ground from elevated feeders, consideration needs to be given to the ground as a suitable place to feed birds. This is where gallinacious birds, pigeons, doves, thrashers, and many of the sparrows and finches do most of their feeding.

The same precautions that apply to bird tables are even more important on the ground. To forestall the danger of disease, food should be scattered only on well-drained sites (preferably sandy soil) and only in amounts that will be eaten quickly. Rake the ground thoroughly whenever debris begins to accumulate. As an added precaution to prevent disease, it is a good policy to rotate sites and even pour boiling water over areas that have been heavily used. Frozen ground or hard-packed snow offer the safest conditions for ground feeding. If cats are a problem, scatter food well away from cover.

The same rules apply on the ground as at elevated feeders. Food should be scattered near cover and in parts of the yard that are protected from the wind. We should be able to view ground-feeding areas from our windows. Also, ground feeding to be successful should not be a haphazard activity; food should be scattered regularly at well-drained sites. Not only is corn in its various forms the most economical food to use in ground feeding but it is one of the best foods for attracting desirable birds. Other seeds and grains are also well received on the ground. Food that is scattered on the ground is supplemented by sizable amounts that sift down from elevated feeders. It may be said that even without special offerings on our part, ground-feeding birds can always be expected to receive some portions of the feast.

Game-bird Feeders

If you have been patronized by game birds, such as the bobwhite, ring-necked pheasant, and in more northern states, the ruffed grouse, you may want to establish one or two game-bird feeders. These feeders will be nothing more than protected places on the ground where the force of the wind and drifting snow is blocked by a barricade of branches or a dense evergreen hedge. Evergreen boughs can be wired to a framework of poles that have been arranged in tepee fashion, as shown on the preceding page. Birds are attracted to the tepee by food scattered both outside and on the bare ground of the interior. Always provide plenty of openings so that birds can quickly escape in case of danger.

FEEDING SHELVES

Having gotten most of your birds in the habit of feeding from hanging feeders, bird tables, or the ground, you are ready to tackle the problem of the occasional bird or birds that may need special attention. The strategy with half-hardy lingerers and strays should be to get them feeding as close to the house as possible. At nearby feeding shelves they won't have as much competition from other birds and you can

*Bobwhites find corn
in a tepee-type
game-bird feeder.*

better look out for their needs. As a start, you should have a small feeding shelf or two fastened to the side of the house or nearby tree trunks. A shelf 18 inches long, 8 inches wide, with a raised edge, and held by brackets will be more than adequate to accommodate the several special guests you may have. A roof will be needed if you are feeding these guests during severe portions of the year.

After a time your guests may graduate to the more closed-in windowsill feeder. The standard windowsill feeder is about 18 inches long, 12 inches wide, 7 inches high, and topped with a removable glass panel. Not only are these feeders the coziest we can provide but they are easy to service. On cold, snowy mornings, we can replenish this feeder from our window rather than having to make a trip outside for this purpose. The fact that the glass-topped windowsill feeder is too closed in to appeal to many of our guests makes it more acceptable to birds that may be in dire difficulty. Nevertheless, these feeders are sometimes well patronized by bolder guests such as chickadees, tufted titmice, white-breasted nuthatches, Carolina wrens, mockingbirds, and any northern finches we may have visiting us. It is a real treat to see these guests only inches away.

*At window trays, birds—here a white-throat (left),
a black-capped chickadee,
two purple finches, a tufted titmouse (top),
and a rose-breasted
grosbeak—
feed only
inches away.*

A whole different side to bird feeding is revealed when we begin using suet and the various mixtures that can be made with melted suet. These foods call for different feeders and different techniques. The first rule is to expose such foods at elevated feeders where they will be well out of reach of prowling animals. The second is always to secure suet or small containers holding it, so that the food cannot be removed by mammals or bird guests.

Unlike seeds and grain, there is no need to protect suet from wet weather and it is solid enough to resist quick consumption by bird guests. Mixtures that result from melting suet and adding other ingredients are resistant to starling attack (pages 274–5). Suet and suet mixtures should be placed at a number of feeders so that all guests will have a chance at this energy-giving food. Unrendered suet can be placed in woven mesh bags such as those used to hold oranges or onions. Hang the bags from nails or tie to branches or a line strung between two posts. Pieces can be fitted into suet holders on posts or tree trunks, or used in holders in glass-topped windowsill feeders or certain of the hopper-type feeders.

Rendered suet, to which other ingredients have been added, generally makes for a better food than pure suet. Mixtures are more nutritious, longer lasting, and

In the late fall, a yellow-bellied sapsucker perches at a tuna fish can containing suet mixture. This is one of the easiest feeders to construct at home.

liked by more birds. Usually it is a sound practice to render a large quantity of suet
at one time. Then the question arises of what to do with the melted suet mixture in
the saucepans. The first step is to spread out newspapers and then pour the partially
cooled mixture into suitable containers and holes of hanging log feeders. As for

containers, you can use jar tops, aluminum foil dishes, plastic cups, milk cartons cut
down to suitable sizes, small cans, and even empty citrus rinds. Place the filled
containers in the refrigerator for storage; some may be used right away at bird feeders.
Small cans may be wedged into wooden frames on posts and tree trunks (as in the
illustration opposite). Empty tuna fish cans make receptacles that are well suited for
these holders.

DANGERS OF METAL IN COLD WEATHER

Some of us have had the unpleasant experience of finding that our fingers will freeze
to metal in very cold weather. Although birds have the protection of their feathers,
they do run some risk of having unfeathered parts freeze to metal surfaces. This is an
unlikely occurrence, but those of us who live in northern states should take a few
precautions if we are using feeders with exposed metal parts. The greatest hazard
seems to be in the narrow openings of wire-mesh suet holders. In order to reach the
suet inside the holder, birds may happen to touch against the wire with their tongues
or even their eyes. This risk can be avoided by using non-metal suet holders, such as
woven mesh bags or holders that are made with plastic-coated mesh instead of wire
mesh.

Suet itself helps insulate metal. By rubbing suet onto exposed metal parts, we
considerably reduce the risk of birds freezing to these parts in very cold weather.

A change in the design of a feeder may eliminate a hazard from exposed metal.
One case of a purple finch whose eyes froze to the sides of the metal feeding cups of
a Droll Yankee feeder was reported in Minnesota during a cold spell when the
temperature dropped to 20 degrees below zero. The designer widened the feeding
openings and since then no more such occurrences have come to light. Metal perches,
such as those of the Droll Yankee, do not seem to constitute a hazard. Even so, some
owners of feeders equipped with metal perches have switched to plastic ones.

Almost any hanging feeder or one fixed on a post can be squirrel-proofed. But due allowance must be made for the uncanny ability of these animals to tightrope walk, spring long distances from buildings or trees, or leap up in the air from a position on the ground. Two types of proofing have been used successfully against gray and red squirrels and the easiest of all to outsmart, the fox squirrel. One is shielding around the post to which the feeder is attached and the other is wobbly objects in the path of the squirrel trying to reach a hanging feeder.

Metal shields of various kinds have been used successfully to stop squirrels from climbing feeder posts. A smooth cone-shaped shield, the edges sloping downward and attached a few inches below the feeder, is usually quite effective so long as there is nothing on it that a squirrel can grip with its teeth or toes. A bell-shaped aluminum guard, 9 inches in diameter at the bottom and available at many supply houses, is well suited for round feeder posts about 1¼ inches in diameter. Simply slip the guard on the post before attaching the feeder. Shielding of any kind should be attached 3 to 4 feet from the ground. Some gray squirrels can jump upward from the ground to a height of about 3½ feet. It should be remembered that snow cover will necessitate installing feeders and shielding at higher levels than are ordinarily recommended because squirrels will take advantage of the shorter leaping distances that exist with deep snow.

Other methods of proofing are used with hanging feeders. One of the most

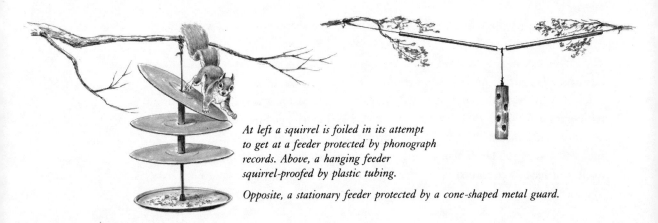

*At left a squirrel is foiled in its attempt
to get at a feeder protected by phonograph
records. Above, a hanging feeder
squirrel-proofed by plastic tubing.*

Opposite, a stationary feeder protected by a cone-shaped metal guard.

effective of these makes use of old phonograph records or aluminum pie dishes and discarded garden hose. Select three records with diameters of about 12 inches, cut the garden hose into three 4-inch sections, and assemble as shown on the facing page. If the topmost record, which tilts as soon as the animal places weight upon it, does not send the squirrel tumbling to the ground, the second or third almost certainly will.

Still another way to proof a hanging feeder is to cut 1-inch plastic tubing into two lengths of 36 inches each. Insert these two pieces of tubing onto a taut line as shown on the facing page. To reach the hanging feeder from either direction, the squirrel must venture out onto the uncertain footing of the plastic tubing. The cautious animal will back away, while the rash one will almost certainly take a tumble.

Squirrels are slow to give up. An observer reported a gray squirrel making thirty-three vain attempts in twenty minutes trying to get by a squirrel-proofing device; the animal fell to the ground each time. Failing to reach its goal, a squirrel, its tail twitching back and forth, will study the situation and then go on to try a different tactic. Squirrels sometimes gain access to feeders by making desperately long leaps from trees or rooftops. A gray squirrel was seen to jump 11 feet from a rooftop down to a feeder at least 8 feet away from the house. Such acrobatic feats sometimes make it necessary to move feeders still farther away from trees and roofs that can be used as springboards.

Still another approach is to make the feeder itself squirrel-proof. Designers have done this with varying degrees of success. Some of the anti-squirrel feeders are even hard for birds to use, and some leave a lot to be desired from the standpoint of appearance. But there are some good ones. For example, a pole-mounted feeder called the "Hylarious" was the first in a series of feeders that closes off the food supply as soon as a large bird or mammal places its weight on a treadle. Hylarious was a fitting name in light of the amazed look on a squirrel's face after it had triggered the closing device. As soon as the squirrel leaves, a shield, which closed off the food, rises and allows birds to resume feeding. Food is held in a metal container and, as birds feed, trickles down to feeding vents. A disadvantage is that it is impossible to tell how much food is inside without opening the container part of the feeder. But this feeder has enjoyed great popularity among those who feed birds and can be called 99 percent squirrel-proof. Nevertheless two squirrels have been known to work in tandem, one holding the shield up while the other eats!

There are now a number of other models on the market that employ the same features as seen in the Hylarious. A nice-looking one called "Double Trouble for the Squirrels" has feeding vents on both sides and clear glass panels that permit one to tell at a glance whether the container needs refilling.

It isn't easy to outwit squirrels; yet we must admit that they are clever animals, and if we will let them, they can give us as much pleasure and amusement as our bird guests. We would like them better, of course, if they did not eat so much and occupy so much space at bird feeders.

SPECIAL NEEDS AND CRAVINGS

Providing food for our guests is only a part of the overall plan we should have for attracting birds to our yards. Birds may seem self-sufficient when it comes to other bodily requirements. Yet there is much we can do to aid them in such vital functions as assimilation of food and care of plumage. The small extras we provide in the way of grit and water are in many ways as important as food; yet they involve very little effort on our part. Our biggest problem is remembering these details and faithfully performing whatever chores may be necessary.

GRIT

Birds must ingest sizable amounts of small hard objects as an aid to grinding food. The grinding agent may in turn be broken down and used for its mineral content. In a broad sense grit includes everything that a bird eats that has value in grinding food. Although small pebbles, especially ones composed of quartz, are the most common form of grit, many other objects are also used. Some are primarily grinding agents, while others like eggshell, pieces of charcoal, ashes, and dry earth are primarily ingested for their mineral content.

That birds do not always have ready access to grit is seen in the lengths they will go in order to obtain an adequate supply. It is not uncommon to see birds clinging to the sides of old brick buildings in order to obtain bits of mortar that lie between the bricks. The crumbly mortar of an old smokehouse near where I live is a constant attraction to house sparrows and other birds seeking their daily quota of grit. Roofing shingles covered with small pieces of gravel are also very inviting.

Grit requirements differ widely among birds. Doves need large amounts as an aid to grinding and digesting the soft vegetable foods that make up their diet. Mourning doves, for example, take from fifty to a hundred small pebbles a day. Proportionately large amounts are also taken by northern finches. Evening grosbeaks and other northern visitors seem continually to crave something that may be lacking in their vegetable diets. If it is not salt in some form that claims their attention, it is the minerals they find in ashes, charcoal, or soil rich in alkali or other substances. Birds sometimes exhibit even stranger tastes and sample snow or earth that has become impregnated with dog urine, discarded tea leaves, or soapy water. There seems to be much less eagerness for these substances when birds appear in more southern states during invasion years. It is possible that farther south they obtain diets containing more in the way of essential food elements. If this is true, it suggests that the occasional spectacular invasions southward by northern finches may be dictated in part by a need for mineral matter that is generally lacking in the north.

Birds that consume fruits and berries with hard pits seem to have little need for grit. The pits are adequate substitutes. When such birds change to other types of food, they are often obliged to go back to seeking grit again. Grit seems to be important to virtually all birds. If there is a time when grit is in short supply, it is winter. When the countryside is covered with snow, birds are hard-pressed indeed to find the grit they need. Their quest may take them to roadsides and other places where the snow has been cleared. Finding grit is often a hazardous occupation.

There are several ways of providing grit. I prefer to keep grit separate from food. This practice makes for less danger of contamination by droppings. Place grit separately in small containers or simply make a pile at a convenient place not far from the feeders. Provide some protection from the weather so that the grit will not be buried by snow. Although winter is the most important time to make grit available, birds may find an extra supply handy at any season. One of the best grits to use is seashore sand that is composed largely of quartz grains. Small pieces of oyster shell also make excellent grit. Oyster shell grit and other kinds may be obtained from poultry suppliers and pet stores. It is well to remember that most visitors to feeders are small birds that cannot handle large particles. For this reason coarse sand is probably the best all-around grit to use.

Though it serves as a grinding agent, eggshell is most important for its calcium content. No other mineral matter seems to be in so much demand, and this is particularly true during the nesting season. Jays and crows turn to nest robbing at this time of the year. This is not a form of depravity but a way of responding to an insistent need for more calcium. Birds find most of their calcium in insects, seeds, snail shells, bits of eggshell, and whatever meat that may find its way into their diets.

The best way we can help birds meet their calcium needs is to save the shells of chicken eggs. Every week or so I grind up a supply that will go into suet or grease mixes. A meat grinder is invaluable for this purpose. During the nesting season many of my visitors cannot seem to get enough food containing eggshell. On the other hand, crushed eggshell by itself is not always recognized and may go unused. This is good reason to mix the shell with foods that are being taken at the feeder.

Eggshell is the only offering that proves successful with purple martins. Many people who have martin colonies put supplies of crushed eggshell on the ground below occupied houses. The martins have no difficulty in recognizing the shell.

Mourning doves coming to grit.

It is a common belief that salt is harmful to birds. While there may be some truth in this (page 265), there is little or no harm in the modest amounts of salt contained in many feeding station foods. The salt in bakery products, peanut butter, salted peanuts, and bacon grease is probably a desirable addition to the diet. Some birds show a craving that goes well beyond the saltiest foods we offer. Northern finches, especially pine grosbeaks, pine siskins, and crossbills, will go to almost any lengths to obtain salt. A taste for salt has been observed among other birds as well.

If we provide pure salt for birds at feeders, it is almost always ignored. The best way to make salt available is to mix it with some other substance such as snow, earth, or ashes. In the wild, birds seek out salt or salt-impregnated earth at salt licks, salt blocks for cattle, and highways where salt has been used to melt ice. The descent of birds to highways for salt is fraught with danger, and there are occasions when heavy mortality ensues.

WATER

It is likely that no part of the bird attracting program is so often neglected as that of providing birds with a supply of fresh, clean water. Most people take water for granted and do not realize how hard-pressed birds may be for this vital commodity. John K. Terres in his *Songbirds in Your Garden* states that at his home on Long Island birds would have to make a round trip of four miles to reach water if he did not keep his bird baths properly supplied. In more arid parts of the country absence of water severely limits the numbers and distribution of birds.

Historically, bird baths have been used as decorative features to grace the lawn and garden. Little thought was ever given to their utility so far as birds were concerned. Usually bird baths were placed in the hot sun and in a part of the yard far removed from cover. The cat problem, which was particularly acute during the early 1900s, seemed to dictate that the bird bath be in the open and on a pedestal.

Only in fairly recent years has it been discovered that bird baths, when properly used, bring an even greater variety of birds to the yard than feeding stations. A bird bath that I maintained in my yard in Virginia over a period of several years attracted some seventy-five species, or thirty more than came to my feeding stations. Many of the users were feeding station customers that found the baths convenient places for stopping off between trips for food. A long list of others were birds that stopped by only briefly, attracted solely by the sight of water. Among the occasional visitors were flycatchers, thrushes, vireos, and warblers—all birds that are hard to attract with food but that come readily to water.

If you have an old-fashioned bird bath, the first step in improving it is to remove the pedestal, then locate the bath near the ground in a shady or semishady part of the yard. This will make for a fresher, cooler water supply and also give birds a greater sense of security. As with feeding stations, it is essential that cover be reasonably close-by. This is doubly important for birds that have been bathing. In a wet, bedraggled condition, birds are slow of flight and therefore depend upon a safe haven where they can dry their feathers and await turns at the bird bath. A dense American holly that partially overhung two baths at my Virginia home was an ideal haven for birds in between baths. Cover of some kind is a necessity near bird baths and the thornier the better if it is going to be a protection to birds and, at the same time, exclude cats.

The old-fashioned bird bath was usually too deep and the sides too steep for the safe accommodation of birds. Birds take to the water rather gingerly. If there is the slightest suspicion of insecurity, they do not come at all. The sides of the bath should slope gradually toward the middle and the average depth should be no more

A ground bird bath is especially pleasing to warblers.

than 1½ inches. The deepest portion could be up to 3 inches, but generally it is better to provide a bath that is too shallow than one that is too deep. Also birds must have secure footing. Some of the plastic bird baths on the market today are much too slippery, and few birds ever gain the courage to use them. A rough cement finish is well suited to the needs of birds, and there is no objection to lining the sides with natural stones of various shapes and colors.

The tendency today is to make the bath look as natural as possible and have it blend into an appropriate natural background. A bird bath can be combined very effectively with the stonework and plantings that go into a rock garden. I surround my rock-bordered bird bath with plantings of ferns and mosses—plants that suit a moist environment.

Birds are slow to recognize water. There is no more effective way to overcome their reluctance than by installing a water-drip. This is nothing more than a hose or other outlet above the bath which is regulated to supply a slow drip or patter of falling water. This will be all the invitation that is needed to bring warblers and other more diffident guests to our bath. The most important time to have a water-drip in operation is during the periods of spring and fall migration. Our regular customers are on to our water offerings and do not need any added inducement.

If there is any time of the year when water is at a premium for bathing, it is winter. Birds are eager for water for drinking purposes in winter, and, if anything, they need to bathe more often in cold weather. The reason is not hard to discover. Birds bathe to keep warm! It is especially important that the feathers be keep clean and well groomed during the colder months. A feather contains interlocking webs known as barbules. When in place, these shut out the cold and thereby provide proper insulation from the rigors of the weather. Using the bill, much as we would use a comb, the bird carefully grooms its feathers and anoints them with oil from a special gland at the base of the tail. The first essential requirement in this routine is that the feathers be clean. This is why bathing is so important in winter and that even with the mercury hovering slightly above zero, birds sometimes insist upon bathing. The attendance at my bird baths in Virginia was twice as great in winter as in summer. However, in summer, birds, like people, drink to keep cool. Domestic poultry are said to drink twice as much water at $100°$ F as they do at $70°$ F. Therefore, during very warm weather, as during very cold weather, attendance at the bird bath can be expected to pick up considerably.

Keeping bird baths open and in use all winter is easy with an electrical appliance called an immersion water heater. This is a heating element that is placed in the bath and that can be attached to an electrical outlet by means of an extension cord. In very cold weather an immersion water heater is not likely to supply enough heat to keep the entire bath open. Therefore there may be occasions when you will need to break the ice and pour in hot water. The warmer water will be appreciated by birds both for drinking and bathing. Wild birds, like domestic poultry, hesitate to drink very cold water. Tests with poultry show that water consumption is increased by about 25 percent when the water is heated from near freezing to around 50°F.

Whatever the season, bird baths should be cleaned frequently and kept filled. John K. Terres recommends cleaning and refilling baths daily. This is good advice. Baths should be scrubbed or hosed out at frequent intervals if birds are to be safe from exposure to salmonella and other disease organisms. On busy days, when birds are drinking and bathing a great deal, it may be necessary to refill the bath several times daily. Even in rainy weather, it is a good idea to clean baths occasionally in order to rid them of leaves and other debris.

OTHER BATHING

Birds do not limit themselves to water bathing but indulge in a variety of other kinds of baths that seem to be associated primarily with care of the feathers. The most common kind, aside from water bathing, is sun bathing. We may witness birds sun bathing at any time of the year and usually in a protected place, like a porch roof or a window feeding tray. Normally the sun has to be quite hot before birds will indulge in this habit. A bird offers itself to the full effects of the sun's rays by spreading its wings and tail and opening its feathers as fully as it can. Sprawled on its side with head cocked, the bird seems to be in a trance and to be totally oblivious to whatever is going on around it. However, the spell can be quickly broken, and we may shortly see the bird preening itself or eating.

Not to be confused with sun bathing, but involving some of the same postures is a strange behavior known as anting. A bird may be seen picking up ants and rubbing the crushed remains through parts of its plumage. In another form of anting, a bird will squat in an ant hill and let ants crawl through the feathers. Birds appear to gain various benefits from these bizarre performances. It has been pointed out that anting is indulged in more frequently during the periods of molt. This suggests that it may be a way to gain relief from irritation caused by newly emerging feathers. Birds also rub other mildly irritating substances against the feathers and parts of the body. The effect may be soothing although it is difficult for us to judge. Anting will probably always remain something of an enigma.

Dusting is still another form of bathing that birds sometimes indulge in. Whenever it is sufficiently dry, certain birds may be seen scratching in dusty places and throwing the dust over their feathers in much the same way that they splash water when at the bird bath. The house sparrow is by far the busiest dust bather of any of the birds that come near our homes. Dusting is a communal activity among house sparrows and half a dozen birds may be seen indulging in this habit at one time. House sparrows will often break up soil with their bills; then they will squat in the dry soil and begin going through the motions they use when they bathe. Many small craters appear in the soil wherever house sparrows conduct their dusting activities.

The only other frequent dust bathers we may see in our yards are wrens, ring-necked pheasants, and bobwhites. Dust bathing seems to be primarily for the purpose of ridding feathers and body of external parasites. It also seems likely that birds derive pleasurable sensations from this activity. In bathing, song, and other of their activities, birds seem to gain a fair measure of pleasure as well as practical advantages.

Bowl-shaped Ground Bath

The cement ground bath is well suited to the needs of the birds that come our way. Many birds that won't come to the ground for food will do so for water. Pick a location near cover and within easy view of your window. Line baths with rocks so that birds will have a place to perch. If one bath seems inadequate, place one or two more nearby. The most important requirements are to clean baths frequently and keep them filled with fresh water.

The old-fashioned pedestal bath had the merit of keeping birds up off the ground, where they would not be so easily preyed upon by cats. However, these baths are often poorly designed—too deep, too steep-sided, too slippery. Far superior is the shallow basin. The sides slope gently and even in the middle the water is no more than 3 inches deep. Birds prefer baths that are low to the ground and have escape cover nearby. The bath should be in partial shade so that the water won't become too warm in summer. It is advisable to place bird baths several feet away from bird feeders so that seeds and debris will not fall in them. The cat situation should be well under control before installing a ground bath of any kind.

Water-drip and Circulating Water Systems

The water-drip serves two purposes—it helps keep the bath filled and provides a pitter-patter which lures many birds that would otherwise not find their way. The water-drip is especially effective in getting the attention of thrushes, vireos, and warblers when they pass through on migration. The best way to bring water to the bath is with a hose made of ⅜-inch plastic tubing. A hose of this size will require a special coupling if it is to fit the conventional outdoor faucet. The arrangement shown

The steady drip drip of water acts like magic in bringing birds to the bath, and the extra water helps keep the bath full.

here is fine except in below-freezing weather. Sometimes we can keep a flow going in freezing weather by turning a hose or faucet on full force. A bird bath can be kept open in cold weather through the use of a good electrical immersion water heater. A safe, reliable one, with a weatherproof electrical cord attached, can be obtained from a poultry supply store or a wild-bird supply center. Do not attempt to rig up a device of your own!

There are still other ways to advertise the bird bath: with the help of a spray or of flowing water. Ask wild-bird centers and garden stores about sprinklers, misters, bubblers, and recycling systems. The latter keep water in constant circulation through tubing with power from a small electric pump. The system can include one or more bird baths connected by waterfalls. Debris is removed by filters. Combined with a rock garden, the bird bath becomes a place of charm and beauty. Flowing water is irresistible to birds.

THINGS THAT GO WRONG

It would be remarkable indeed if you did not find a few flaws in your operation after you have been feeding birds for a while. The biggest problems will usually come from overly hearty eaters. There is no rule saying that this species or that one is troublesome. Much depends upon circumstances. Favorite guests sometimes surprise us by being bullies or eating more than their share. We ourselves may be partly to blame by offering food in ways that invite trouble. By making changes in the menu or using more selective feeders, we make for a smoother feeding operation. A more difficult problem is that of birds striking windows. A good share of your efforts should go into eliminating hazards and making sure that there is nothing unsafe about your feeders or the foods you offer.

UNRULY GUESTS

Care must be taken not to confuse the harmless bickering and jockeying for position that is seen so frequently at feeders with more unruly kinds of behavior that upset the feeding routine. If sizable numbers of birds are being prevented from eating, you may have to step in. Try a change in menu, a shifting in position of feeders, or more feeders of one kind and fewer of another. These tactics usually work. We become arbitrators, settling each dispute we see with a minimum of fuss and without harsh measures. The wasteful and unnecessary solution of getting rid of "undesirable species" was discarded by all thoughtful persons many years ago.

Blackbirds

All but absent from feeders during the early days of bird feeding, blackbirds are now among the most common visitors to feeders—sometimes in such flocks that they crowd out other birds and consume all the food.

The common grackle is generally regarded as the most annoying of the blackbird visitors. We frequently see it strutting about our premises as though it owned the place. Other birds are intimidated by its size and aggressive manner; moreover, it takes up space at feeders and consumes a disproportionate amount of the food for its numbers. We might not mind occasional visits by grackles, but all too often a flock settles down in our neighborhood and we see these hulking birds daily for months and months. The grackle population has increased greatly during recent years, and, along with other blackbirds, grackles have been quick to take advantage of opportunities found around suburban residences. There is no easy way to discourage these birds unless you are willing to make fairly drastic changes in your feeding menu.

Withhold corn, bread and other bakery products, and most seeds, including sunflower. Substitute thistle and safflower and offer them in a hanging feeder such as the Droll Yankee. Continue with fruits, such as apple, orange, and raisins. Suet and fat mixtures are taken sparingly by grackles so that you may be able to continue with these foods and still discourage your grackles. If the grackles do not leave, they will at least cease making a nuisance of themselves after you have made these changes. As the situation improves, gradually return to your former menu; but be prepared to switch back. Grackles never seem to forget a location where they have enjoyed good fare. One should also bear in mind that grackles are easily scared and will usually leave the yard if a person appears at the door or bangs on windows.

The other blackbirds—red-winged blackbird, brown-headed cowbird, rusty blackbird, and two strays from the West, the yellow-headed blackbird and Brewer's blackbird—do not settle in to quite the degree that grackles do. We have no quarrel with the last three as they are not common at feeding stations anywhere in the East. The first two are not as omnivorous as the grackle and therefore are more easily discouraged.

Red-winged blackbirds and brown-headed cowbirds can be discouraged by withholding bakery products and most seeds and grain, including sunflower. As with the common grackle, substitute thistle and safflower for the other seeds and grain. Add all the fruit you like to the menu, including apple, orange, and raisins, and continue with suet, suet mixtures, and any mixtures based upon peanut butter. Scaring tactics work fairly well with redwings but not so well with cowbirds.

Blue Jays

In the jay is found a mixture of mischievousness, jauntiness, and color. Many of us like the bird, but others complain about its hearty appetite and tendencies toward nest robbing. Whatever its faults, the jay helps as much as any bird in turning the feeding station flock into a well-organized unit. Some members of the feeding station company are quicker than others to recognize food, others are more proficient at opening food and, as they eat, leave tidbits that the whole company can enjoy, and still others are quick to spot danger and give warning calls that all the others recognize and heed. The blue jay is the quickest to give an alarm and always the boldest when danger is near. These traits alone are enough to make us forgive various shortcomings. If we want to dampen the jay's considerable appetite, we can make it more difficult for the bird to carry off food. Rarely does a jay eat anything at the feeder. Food is crammed into a throat pouch until there is no more room; then the bird takes more in its bill. Off it flies with as many as twelve sunflower seeds at one time. Other seeds, grain, suet, pieces of fruit, and bread are transported in the same manner. The birds usually disappear from sight so that we do not know if the booty is eaten or buried. Many times it is buried.

If you want to slow down the food-carrying-off process, you can do so by grinding larger food items into small pieces. Even sunflower can be conserved by grinding it, husk and all. And to keep jays from carrying off suet, make sure pieces are fastened or in secure holders. Blue jays are too omnivorous to discourage solely by making changes in the menu. But if you substitute thistle for sunflower, this will definitely dampen their appetites.

There is general agreement among those who know the jay that the nest-robbing habit has its basis in calcium deficiency during the nesting season. Provide a source of calcium to which they can go and you have all but cured them of this destructive habit. One of the best ways to do this is to crack or grind up shells of chicken eggs every nesting season. Place where jays can find them.

Crows

To let crows have free rein at the feeders would see suet, fat mixes, and other foods disappear much too quickly. However, crows rarely appear except under stress of bad weather. When they do come, they are constantly on guard and ready to fly away as soon as someone appears near the window. Years of persecution have instilled a profound mistrust of man in this bird. I try to make amends by having a special place where crows can come for food during bad weather. The birds respond well to corn, kitchen scraps, and suet. I discourage them from coming to feeders near the house by banging upon windowpanes.

Doves

*Mourning
dove.*

Both mourning doves and domestic pigeons are greedy eaters. Also doves are suspected carriers of several avian diseases including trichomoniasis. Normally the only step needed to discourage these otherwise desirable visitors is to stop supplying the few foods that attract them. A temporary halt in handouts of grain, seeds, and bread should bring an end to steady patronage by doves. Doves can be kept out of roofed-over grain and seed feeders by installing vertical bars, spaced an inch and a half apart, around all openings. Most tubular hanging feeders are out of reach of pigeons and doves.

House Sparrows

An addition to our avifauna that dates back to 1850, the house sparrow soon became so abundant that it posed a serious threat to native birdlife. Anyone attempting to feed birds around 1900 usually got swarms of this sparrow and few others. The situation was particularly acute in cities and agricultural regions devoted to grain. By 1915 a decline in numbers had begun. Today the house sparrow is not as numerous or pestiferous as it was even a decade or two ago. Our main complaint is that this persistent little bird takes up room and consumes food that we would rather see go to more distinguished guests.

To solve the sparrow problem, develop your feeding program around small hanging feeders. Do not feed on the ground or use shelves or bird tables. House

sparrows tend to shy away from feeders that are tipsy or that offer insecure footing.
For this reason, hanging log feeders and coconuts are not much to their liking. Place
popular house sparrow foods, like cracked corn, wheat, oats, and bread, in the small
hanging feeders. This should also apply to thistle and sunflower which are mildly

popular with house sparrows although sometimes scarcely taken at all. Ordinarily
fruit, raisins, suet, suet mixes, and peanut hearts have very little appeal and can be
supplied at any convenient feeders. Strict adherence to this routine will almost
certainly discourage your house sparrows and perhaps force most of them to go
elsewhere. There is a risk in this method, however, in that you may be discouraging
some of your other customers. For example, you will have poor luck with such birds
as towhees, juncos, tree sparrows, and white-throats unless you sprinkle liberal
amounts of seeds and grain on the ground. In the end you may decide that house
sparrows are not enough of a nuisance to bother with trying to discourage them. It
is often the best policy to welcome them and hope that their presence, along with
an abundance of easily obtainable food, will attract a wide variety of other birds.

Mockingbirds

No one knows why some mockingbirds are perfectly peaceful and others seem determined to chase every other bird from the yard. Midwinter is the season when an
occasional mockingbird (often a first-year male) shows greatest irritability. Not only
do such birds guard sources of well-favored foods, such as fruit-bearing trees and
shrubs, but feeders containing little or nothing that a mockingbird would eat.
Occasionally mockingbirds are so persistent and ferocious in their attacks that feeding
station attendance falls off to almost nothing.

Mockingbirds differ from most other birds in that individuals may guard a
feeding territory against every intruder that comes along. This may include cats,
dogs, birds of all kinds, and *above all* other mockingbirds. One way to come to terms
with such a bird is to provide a special feeder where your mockingbird will come for
choice tidbits. This will be a feeder exclusively for mockingbirds. If the scheme
works, your mockingbird will eat here and stop molesting birds at other feeders.
Among the foods that have special appeal to mockingbirds are raisins, grapes, sliced
apple, orange, banana, nutmeats, cheese, suet, peanut butter mixes, bread, and cake.

Seeds and grain have little or no appeal to mockingbirds. It may take time to find out which foods your mockingbird likes best. Tastes vary considerably from one bird to another. Offer choice foods at a windowsill several times daily, and you will soon have the mockingbird eating there and perhaps even taking food from your hand.

You make your yard attractive to mockingbirds when you plant holly, grape, Virginia creeper, crabapple, flowering dogwood, elaeagnus, privet, and pyracantha. Often mockingbirds will patronize food plants such as these and stay away from feeders. However, be sure not to place feeders too near natural sources of food. An aggressive mockingbird will interpret visits by other birds to feeders as trespassing upon its natural food supply.

It is not easy to outwit a mockingbird, but do not give up. If one ruse fails, try another.

Robins

Who would ever think that this self-contained bird would be troublesome at bird feeders! Yet, now and then, a robin takes it upon itself to dominate a feeder in much the same manner as a mockingbird. One winter a lone female robin stopped by at a feeder I maintained in northern Florida. The bird immediately set out to chase off any bird that came near this feeder. Sometimes the robin would pursue another bird far beyond the confines of the yard. It was not long before all use of the feeder by other birds ceased. The ever-victorious robin made herself at home on a perch near the feeder. Rarely did she accept a morsel but she frequently came to a nearby bird bath. Slowly the irritability wore off, and first one species and then another was allowed to return to the feeder. After about two weeks the robin had accepted a lower status in the hierarchy and was sometimes chased by other birds.

If a domineering robin should happen to settle in your yard, the best thing to do is *wait*. Sooner or later the bird will tire of its belligerency and let other birds feed without molesting them.

Starlings

The large starling populations we have with us today resulted from the release of one hundred birds in New York City's Central Park, during the years 1890 and 1891.

Now the starling is found nearly everywhere on this continent and, like the house sparrow, has not been slow to find its way to feeding stations. Unlike the house sparrow, the starling does not settle down to become a steady boarder; instead it is chiefly a cold-weather visitor that turns up in greatest numbers when snow is on the ground. Neither starlings nor house sparrows pay the slightest heed to the rights of other birds, but crowd in wherever they can, totally ignoring threats and protests of others. Starlings are by far the more unruly of the two. When many are about, the feeding station soon becomes a mad jumble of fighting, screeching birds. Fortunately, starlings save most of this fury for each other and reserve outside attacks—for reasons we cannot fathom—mainly for woodpeckers. Medium-sized woodpeckers, such as the sapsucker and red-bellied woodpecker, seem to bear the brunt of this grudge. Sometimes the woodpecker is turned over on its back and given a severe pummeling.

Starlings are easy to discourage if you will withhold a few of their favorite foods. You can do this without seriously inconveniencing your other guests. Keep on supplying thistle, safflower, sunflower, whole kernels of corn, orange, and a hardened suet mixture (page 274), and you can continue to accommodate most of your other guests while discouraging starlings. You can also try a starling-proof suet feeder sold by many suppliers. At the same time, there is a long list of appealing foods (given

*Whenever starlings take over a feeder,
it is time to change the menu.*

on page 275) that should not be offered during your anti-starling campaign. It should be borne in mind that under stress of hunger, during very bad weather, starlings will eat almost anything. Luckily, these periods do not last. Starlings always seem to welcome the opportunity to get back to a diet of natural foods.

Northern Finches

Most of us are only too happy to have these colorful birds board with us. We may complain of the cost of supplying them with their favorite diet of thistle and sun-flower, and we may disapprove of the way they sometimes crowd out other birds. Nevertheless, we go right on feeding them and are delighted when there is a return visit the next year.

The way to cope with crowding is to increase the number of feeders; it is especially helpful to install one or two at second-story windows. Goldfinches, and especially purple finches and evening grosbeaks, tend to go to higher feeders whenever they are available. This effectively relieves congestion at lower levels.

Domestic Fowl

Those of us who live in the country often have problems with domestic geese, ducks, chickens, and other farmyard animals. They too like the foods we offer to our wild bird guests. If domestic animals cannot be kept where they belong, we may find it necessary to raise feeders higher off the ground and use more small hanging feeders. Chickens, for example, are poor flyers and cannot utilize a feeder that is partially closed and can be reached only by flying. Second-story-window feeders are safe from all domestic fowl.

Squirrels

What can be done when feeding programs established for birds are taken over to a large degree by squirrels? This is one of the most vexing problems that many of us have to face when we take up bird feeding. Squirrels occur nearly everywhere in the East and they react to feeders as though we had placed them especially for their benefit. They are omnivorous animals that like almost everything we offer, especially

the more expensive bird foods. Squirrels are skillful enough to reach most bird feeders
and so bold about it that they scarcely react to our shouts and imprecations.

The gray squirrel is the most fearless. Because of its numbers and wide range,
it is also the most troublesome of the several squirrels that visit yards. Fortunately,
it is frequently diverted by natural foods. When nuts, berries, tree buds, mushrooms,
and other natural foods are in good supply, gray squirrels generally leave us in peace.
March and April are lean months when we see all too much of these bushy-tailed
visitors. They usually give us a respite during the summer, but unless there is an
exceptionally good nut harvest, we are likely to find them back with us through the
fall and winter.

Although preferring some foods over others, gray squirrels find practically
everything on the bird feeding menu acceptable. Among the foods most favored are
sunflower, coconut, nutmeats, including walnuts, pecans, and peanuts, and such
other foods as peanut butter, bread, jelly, and grapes. Suet is one of the few foods
that is not overly popular with this omnivorous animal.

The more northerly ranging red squirrel has all the taste preferences of the gray
squirrel and a few special likes of its own. The red variety takes a wider range of
fruits than the gray and is more carnivorous. Suet offerings will not escape its notice.

Fortunately, the red squirrel is a rather solitary little animal that cannot abide
the presence of others of its kind and would, if it could, chase off all the gray squirrels
in the neighborhood. Its life seems given over to constant conflicts. So occupied are
red squirrels with questions of priority that there are long periods when we do not
see them at our feeders. Whatever their faults may be, they are engaging creatures
that are endlessly fascinating to watch. And we are forced to admit that the same
statement holds true to a large degree for the much more common gray squirrel.

The fox squirrel, with a wide range through the East, is not particularly skilled
at getting to hanging feeders; moreover it is uncommon or absent over wide areas.
There is still a fourth squirrel which we sometimes suspect of robbing feeders but
whose presence we seldom verify by seeing one. This is the flying squirrel, a dainty
nocturnal visitor that unbeknownst to us may be taking food at suet holders and
feeding trays. The chipmunk, a ground squirrel, as distinguished from the above-
mentioned four, which are tree squirrels, is usually a welcome guest.

The biggest problems with squirrels are in suburbs and country districts where
they have become too numerous for their good and our own. Not only do squirrels

make a nuisance of themselves by taking space and undue amounts of food at feeders but they are sometimes destructive to the feeder itself. Wooden parts that have soaked up oils are especially subject to being gnawed.

The usual approach to discouraging squirrels is to move feeders away from the house and into the open where squirrels cannot gain access by jumping. At the same time, posts or supports can be equipped with metal shields or other devices that will prevent squirrels from reaching the feeders (pages 50–2). Proofing can often be very effective. Bird feeders are spared while squirrels, if we wish, can be offered food on the ground or at unprotected feeders.

Still another solution to the squirrel problem is to call upon the services of a yappy dog. The same one that chases cats out of your yard will almost certainly turn its attention to squirrels if you give him a little encouragement (see pages 75–6). Once squirrels know they are under the watchful eyes of a dog, they will begin going elsewhere for their meals.

PREDATORS

Even the predators have been getting a much-needed respite these days. No longer does the appearance of a snake, hawk, owl, or small mammal predator seem to represent a serious threat of some kind. Most of us are happy to have such visitors. The role of the small bird-hawk, for example, is an important one if our songbird populations are to be reasonably free of disease and as vigorous as we would like.

The secret of keeping predation within reasonable limits lies in having a well-planted yard. When a predator appears, some birds go to the tops of tall trees, others to evergreen hedges, still others to brush piles or dense tangles. So long as there is a diversity of cover and the warning notes of such sentinels as blue jays, few birds will fall victim to predation. Those that do, will, in all probability, be ones whose reactions have been slowed by disease or other infirmities.

Still another side to predation is the loss that occurs to eggs and young during the nesting season. These losses are counteracted to a degree by second and third nesting attempts and in most songbirds, by the sizable numbers of eggs (five to ten) in each clutch. In spite of the fairly high reproductive rate, a number of species seem to be in trouble. Little wonder that they are when we recall that birds not only face expected losses in the form of disease, predation, and severe weather, but that man has done much that is harmful to the environment, which in turn has had an adverse effect upon many forms of life.

The way to deal with predators is not by the outdated methods of poisons, traps, and guns, but through better management of the land, including the immediate surroundings of our houses. Proper pruning of shrubs and small trees, for example, makes for suitable nesting sites that are relatively safe from damage by predators. Excellent information on how to improve the nesting capacity of your yard is contained in Rupert Barrington's book *The Joys of a Garden for Your Birds.*

Hawks

The fast-flying Cooper's and sharp-shinned hawks prey upon small birds and are often attracted by the flocks that visit feeders. The sparrow hawk, or kestrel, rarely takes a bird, and even less likely to do this are large *Buteo* hawks, such as the red-shouldered and red-tailed hawks.

There is no harm and much good in the occasional forays that bird-hawks make into the midst of the feeding station company. They weed out the unfit and thereby reduce the incidence of such crippling diseases as foot pox. When a small bird-hawk makes its appearance, every bird in the yard seeks cover or "freezes" wherever it

*By weeding out the unfit,
the sharp-shinned hawk
performs a useful
if seemingly
cruel service.*

happens to be. A sharp-shinned hawk sitting impassively in a tree near the house can close down all activity at feeders as long as it maintains its vigil. If the hawk keeps birds away for an unreasonably long time, it may be necessary to go out and try scaring it off. Sometimes the only way to deal with a particularly stubborn hawk is to live-trap it and carry it in a cage to a location many miles away where it can be safely released. Bird banders are usually only too glad to carry out this chore for us. The numbered bands they put on the legs of birds are of potential value in determining migration patterns, ages to which birds live, and various other facts about the lives of birds.

Owls

Much that has been said about hawks applies equally well to owls. For the most part nocturnal hunters, owls help keep down populations of small rodents; they also prey upon other birds, and larger owls sometimes prey upon smaller ones.

As with hawks or other birds of prey, never destroy or molest an owl. The birds are much too valuable and in most states are protected by law. You attract owls to your yard when you provide cover in the form of large evergreens. In the South, dense clumps of bamboo afford cover to owls. If you do have an owl or two, this is nothing to worry about. As many birds as ever will still use your feeders.

Shrikes

The northern shrike commonly preys upon small birds. The smaller, more southerly ranging loggerhead shrike is primarily an insect-eater and rarely preys upon birdlife. Our attitude toward shrikes should be the same as toward hawks and owls. The shrikes have become greatly reduced in numbers in recent years and need all the help we can give them.

Snakes

Over many years of bird feeding, I have never seen a snake at or near one of my feeders. The only reason a snake would make a special visit to the vicinity of feeders would be for insects or small rodents. You can forget about snakes as constituting any menace to the free-flying birds at your feeder.

House Cats

Birds make up between 4 and 25 percent of the diet of the stray house cat. Except for an occasional animal that has an obsession about killing, cats that are household pets take a toll much less than that of the feral cat. Depredations by cats upon birdlife are most severe during the nesting season. This is when cats have an advantage because of the ease with which they can get to low nests or catch young birds that are not yet accomplished flyers.

Rarely does a cat catch a bird at a feeder. This is particularly true if feeders are off the ground and on posts or hanging lines with squirrel guards. Outside the nesting season, cats are a nuisance but not any more destructive to birds than most native predators. The main objection is that they make themselves at home in the yard and thereby keep the birdlife in a state of agitated excitement.

If you have a cat, try to keep it indoors during the nesting season. At the very least, keep it indoors at night. As added precautions, clip the cat's claws and attach a bell to its collar. These simple steps will make your cat a much less efficient bird catcher. As for your neighbors' cats and strays, you have an effective solution if you do not mind keeping a dog. The dog is one animal that cats respect. Such breeds as poodles, terriers, dachshunds, and boxers produce persistent cat chasers. If you would like a barkless dog that is as tenacious as any, try a basenji. This long-legged, long-necked African—somewhat larger than a beagle—will not only keep cats away but will make life miserable for squirrels, rats, or any other nuisance mammals that may appear in your yard. In addition, the basenji is an excellent pet.

To carry your crusade one step further, join the humane society nearest you. Only through organized effort can headway be made against the difficult problem of stray cats and other homeless animals.

Dogs

Many people needlessly worry about the effect that noisy, romping dogs have upon birdlife. If anything, birds are better adjusted to this kind of disturbance than we are. A passion for chasing cats and squirrels makes dogs far more of a help than a hindrance to birds. One thing to watch with dogs is that food, especially suet and bakery products, be kept in feeders that are out of their reach. An occasional dog will chase birds and sometimes even catch one. This is a problem that calls for better training and discipline of the dog by its master.

HITTING WINDOWS

When a bird flies into a window, the reason is usually because it is bewildered. Sometimes windowpanes catch the reflections of nearby trees. Birds may mistakenly try to fly to these reflections much as they would to the branches of a tree. Or birds may simply blunder into windows. Certain species more than others are deceived by the transparent quality of glass and never seem to learn not to fly into it.

Fatalities rarely occur unless birds hit window panes with great force. The most violent collisions occur when birds are being chased or when they are responding to an alarm. There is evidence that mockingbirds intentionally chase other birds into windows. A mockingbird in Florida was accused of having caused the window deaths of eleven catbirds over a period of a few days. Window deaths of cardinals at a

*Silhouettes
of small hawks
help prevent
window
strikes.*

Virginia home were blamed upon a mockingbird. Small bird-hawks scare other birds so that they fly into windows.

Prevention

It would be impossible to eliminate all the sources of danger that send birds into panicky alarm. Nevertheless, there is much we can do to make windows safer. The first step is to draw a floor plan of your house and number each window. Wherever a bird has forcibly hit a windowpane a few feathers will remain sticking to the glass. Use this evidence to compile a bird-strike list for each window in the house. You will probably discover that nearly all the casualties are at one or two windows.

Now to determine why these windows are so much more dangerous than the others. Step outside and get a bird's-eye view of these windows. Can you clearly see the panes or does light from another window or open door in the room blur the panes and make it seem as though you were looking through an opening? If you are somewhat confused, you can be sure that the effect is doubly confusing to birds.

Try closing a door or pulling a shade. This may help. But chances are that you will have to do more. Something in front of the window that tinkles, glitters, or flutters will serve as a warning so that birds will slow down and not go crashing headlong into the panes. If you do not mind a premature touch of Christmas, try hanging bells, ribbons, tinsel balls, or almost anything you would use on a Christmas tree, *outside* not inside the window. Another approach, especially where you have a problem at a large picture window, is to attach a paper silhouette or two of a small bird-hawk in the act of diving on the inside of the glass. If your hawk is at all lifelike, you will have made the window much safer for your bird guests.

Windows that are unsafe because of reflections or light conditions are the poorest possible locations for bird feeders. Bringing more birds to the vicinity of such windows by having feeders in them or nearby only compounds the problem. If, in spite of all precautions, casualties persist at a window containing a feeder or one with a feeder nearby, by all means move the feeder to some other part of the yard. On the other hand, many windows of the house, perhaps all of them in some houses, may contain no special hazards and therefore are safe for bird feeders. There are many windows with feeders where a bird casualty has never been witnessed. By placing bird feeders in, on, or very close to safe windows, we greatly reduce the risk of bird strikes. Birds feeding close to windows learn to recognize the glass as a barrier, and, if disturbed, do not gain enough momentum to fly into the window with enough force to harm themselves.

John K. Terres in *Songbirds in Your Garden* recommends putting screens of the sheerest nylon marquisette available in front of windows that are particularly hazardous to birds. Such screens do not obstruct the view and may last from two to three years. A screen of this kind is one of the best ways to prevent birds from damaging themselves. Other materials that can be used for such screens include gauze, dacron, and netting. The nearly invisible Japanese mist nets, used by bird banders to catch birds, make excellent screens for windows and the material is long lasting.

While devising suitable precautions, you can keep birds from flying into windows by dabbing the panes with a cleanser or simply by splattering them with soapy water. Once you have installed proper protection you can have clean windows again.

First Aid for Victims

Some species almost never hit windows, others are highly accident-prone and hit so frequently that we are obliged to take all the precautions we can think of. House finches and purple finches are chronic window hitters, and we are apt to find frequent casualties among doves, chickadees, thrushes, warblers, juncos, and fox sparrows. A purple finch that I had hospitalized for a window injury survived another hard bang and one or two lighter ones before it departed. The tenacity with which house finches and purple finches fly into windows can be matched only by members of the dove family. Margaret Millar, writing of window strikes at her Santa Barbara home, stated that mourning doves and band-tailed pigeons made up only 10 percent of her feeding station clientele, and yet the two species supplied over 90 percent of the considerable number of window casualties she had at her home.*

If you find a bird lying below a window it has hit, never assume it is dead unless it has obviously been there a long time. Many times the bird is only stunned and will recover if you handle the case properly. First of all, do not leave the bird lying there. A cat or dog may find it. Pick the bird up gently and put it into a darkened container. A paper bag will do. Twist the top and leave the bag in a safe place. Darkness will keep the bird quiet should it awaken, thus preventing fluttering

***The Birds and Beasts Were There*, New York, Random House, 1967.

and possible further injury. If the bird seems active and wide awake when you look in at it, release it at once if it is still daylight. If the bird appears listless, you may have to hospitalize it and hope that it will eventually recover after a period of quiet.

A good rule to follow when we find that something is adversely affecting the bird population around us is *Do everything possible to help if we humans are at fault*. On the other hand, if it is a natural loss—something that has been taking place over the ages—it is generally best to maintain a hands-off policy. We help when we remove artificial hazards; we needlessly interfere when we try to change the ways of nature.

seven

HOW TO HAND TAME

Most of us find enough pleasure in watching birds from our windows without inviting them to come to us when we are outside or, as some have done, having them come flying into our houses to become special guests. Taming birds is not just a stunt, however. In *Birds as Individuals*,* Len Howard, the noted British student of bird behavior, discovered that taming birds brings out the real personality of a bird and allows us to better understand its mental processes. When gripped by fear or uncertainty, a bird does not reveal its true self. According to Miss Howard, "At the slightest suspicion of fear a bird alters its natural behavior; it becomes hesitant, its actions cautious and guarded, thus often creating false impressions about the bird."

Len Howard, through her studies of hand-tamed birds that came thronging daily into her living room, opened up a whole new area of understanding and appreciation about small garden birds of England. Birds on our side of the Atlantic are a little less responsive perhaps because they have not undergone taming as long as their Old World cousins. But with the taming that takes place at feeding stations, our birds are becoming more and more responsive to any overtures that we may make. We too can become better acquainted with our birds if we conduct taming experiments. We need not go to the extreme of having birds come into our homes. For many of us, it will be enough to have birds recognize us as the agents responsible for providing food. The first step in achieving their confidence is to establish a familiar routine with certain cues to which birds will respond.

*New York, Doubleday, 1953.

How do birds respond to the common noises they hear when they visit our yards? Sharp, loud noises like the slamming of a door, a car back-firing, or the report of a gun send them darting off in a moment. Once the sound has drifted past, birds are back at their former occupations almost as quickly as they departed. Many other noises do not seem to be upsetting and are ignored. Birds do not fly off at the sound of loud music, the barking of a dog, or the hum of traffic. Similarly, they are not bothered by human speech unless it happens to be particularly loud or raucous. Sound is ever present in the natural world in which birds live and therefore is not something they try to avoid. The only exception is when the sound carries with it a warning of possible danger.

Many of those who have been successful in taming birds advise speaking to them in low conversational tones. Birds seem to understand the inflections in our voices and are reassured when we speak to them gently; likewise they are frightened if our tones should happen to be shrill or angry. Although Len Howard usually spoke to her birds in the friendliest manner possible, there were occasions when she felt it necessary to restrain a bird that was too forward in its actions. A mildly stern "no" would cause a bird to desist from a forbidden activity but was not enough to make the bird fly away. An angry "no," on the other hand, caused instant flight. The bird's reaction always corresponded very closely to the forcefulness with which Miss Howard issued her command.

We are not always aware of the fact that sound is as effective as sight in bringing birds to food. In opening a window or door or rattling the lid on a food container, we make noises that announce our intention of putting out more food. Birds have been waiting for sounds such as these, and this is one reason they assemble so quickly when we put out a new supply of food. However, some of the sounds we make are likely to be repeated many times during the day without the expected appearance of food. When an auditory or visual cue proves to be unreliable, birds become much less responsive.

If you want to have birds come flocking every time you refill the feeders, try conditioning them to a cue that is unmistakable and always associated with the appearance of food. Being conditioned is learning to accept a particular signal as a stimulus for certain behavior. Pick a distinctive sound which is loud enough to alert the birds near your house whenever you start to put out more food. Two methods that I have found to be successful are ringing a bell and banging upon a tin pail with a metal object such as a knife. This is easier than calling up your birds by shouting to them every time you are about to put out food. Shouting is effective if you always use the same words, such as "Come and get it," and apply the same pitch and volume. It also helps to have regular feeding times. Birds are creatures of habit and respond best when we establish a schedule that they can rely upon.

COMING TO THE HAND

Once you have established yourself as the one who provides the food, you may want to go on to the next step, which is hand taming. This is a pursuit not to be taken lightly. Hand-tamed birds can be a nuisance by coming to us whenever we go outside. Also, as in bird feeding in general, we should not change the habits and routine of birds unless we are prepared to continue with our practice. If we are willing to accept the responsibilities, hand taming can be a rewarding experience, and one that gives us a much better insight into the minds of our small visitors.

The first step in hand taming, according to Alfred G. Martin,* is to remove all the food from your feeders except a small quantity at the corner of one tray. Go to this corner, Martin advises, and, either standing or sitting, lay your hand flat on the tray with a large portion of the food in it. Wait patiently, and when a bird arrives, observe three important rules:

1. Speak softly to the bird.
2. Avoid sudden movement and do not turn your head to look at the bird.
3. Do not swallow.

Sooner or later a bird, probably a chickadee, will come hesitantly to the edge of the tray and after several false starts will gain courage enough to come to your hand and pick up a piece of food. In your excitement over this conquest do not make the mistake of looking intently at the bird or swallowing. According to Martin, swallowing warns the bird that you may be a predator intent upon a meal. Also keep

Hand-taming Wild Birds at the Feeder, Freeport, Maine, Bond Wheelwright, 1967.

your hand as flat and rigid as you can. Roy Ivor* explains that of all the parts of the body the hand is most feared by birds. They regard hands as traps and therefore are suspicious of any sudden movement of the hand. They also object to being cuddled or stroked.

Hand taming can be accomplished in other ways than those described by Martin. I find it helpful to condition birds to my presence by first standing or sitting somewhere near the feeder for ten or fifteen minutes a day over a period of several weeks. If I am sitting, I will gradually move the chair closer. My only purpose in doing this is to get birds used to me. When I have taken up my position by the feeder, I follow the procedures described by Martin, and with luck I'll soon have a bird or two feeding from my hand.

Others try hand taming from the window. If you would like to try this approach, place your hand, with food in it, on a window feeding tray; to get birds conditioned beforehand, start with a food-filled glove on the feeding tray. Once birds have accepted the glove, they will be quicker to take food from your hand. Of course, taming from a window is not the same as being outside and having birds recognize you. However, window taming is a good way to begin winning their confidence. It is also a more comfortable way when the weather is cold.

Hand taming is not necessarily something that has to take place at home. Many of the birds that live in city parks are already so tame from feeding that they will quickly respond to friendly overtures. This, of course, is overwhelmingly true of the domestic pigeon. Sometimes when I am in the woods miles from home, a chickadee

*Redpolls are already tame and need little urging
to accept food from the hand.*

* I Live with Birds, Chicago, Follett Publishing Co., 1968.

or bird of another species will appear on a perch close by and eye me in a way that tells me it expects food. Perhaps the bird has been tamed by someone else or it may simply be a bird that naturally has little fear of man. Be prepared for such occasions by always carrying some seeds or nutmeats in your pockets.

Tameness varies greatly from species to species. Some of our visitors never give in to our overtures; others, like chickadees, tufted titmice, and white-breasted nuthatches, are already semi-tame and need very little encouragement before certain individuals accept food from our hands. This is especially true of northern finches— birds that ordinarily show surprising confidence. Northern birds on the whole are tamer than those of middle and more southern parts of North America. There is no ready explanation for this fact other than that northern birds are obliged to be bolder about finding food. They live in a region where food is scarce and hard to find over a large part of the year. I tend to discount the theory that in wilderness regions birds are tamer because they have fewer contacts with man and hence less reason to distrust him. Many of the contacts that birds have these days are reassuring and should, if anything, build up their confidence in us.

As might be expected, northern birds are the easiest to hand tame. The gray jay, or "whiskey jack," is an uninvited guest at northern campsites, and here it is in the habit of helping itself without qualms to food that is on the cookstove or already in dishes from which campers are eating. Not far behind in brashness is the northwoods black-capped chickadee. Considerably bolder than the same chickadee that lives farther south, the northern black-cap is also an unbidden guest that will at times take food in much the same way as the gray jay. Martin found that he could hand tame about half the black-capped chickadees that appeared outside the door of his Maine woods dwelling. He had even greater success with several of the northern finches—60 percent of the redpolls and nearly all the pine grosbeaks that came to his feeding station responded to hand taming.

RECOGNIZING PEOPLE

One of the pleasures of bird feeding is that birds quickly learn to recognize you as the one who supplies food. You need only open the door and step outside and birds will come flying toward you. A stranger, on the other hand, is rarely greeted in this way. Even though the stranger may go on to offer food in exactly the same way you do, birds will usually remain aloof for a while. Moreover, should you appear wearing unfamiliar clothing, you will be greeted as though you were a total stranger.

In summer the wife of a friend of mine used to take food with her to the garden, where there was always a tame female cardinal to receive it. When cold weather returned, she noticed that the cardinal no longer responded to her offerings. What could account for the sudden change? Recalling that she had always worn shorts in summer and that she was now dressed differently, she decided upon a new strategy. She returned to her summer garb and the cardinal once again accepted her food offerings. She was obliged to wear shorts whenever she went out-of-doors to feed the bird during the cold months that followed.

As a rule, birds will accept a stranger *only if the person they know is along.* It sometimes happens that a host will take a guest outside without forewarning him about his birds. The startled guest may suddenly find a bird perched upon his head or shoulders. Usually, however, a hand-tamed bird will go to the host who has done the taming and no one else. This may happen even when the host is surrounded by a group of other people.

Do birds recognize their human friends after a period of absence? Len Howard reported many instances of birds recognizing her after long intervals. A great titmouse, for example, remembered her after an interval of two years. Alfred G. Martin reported that four hand-tamed pine grosbeaks, out of a flock of fifteen, returned after a two-year interval. One of the birds announced its presence by looking in at him through the windowpane, all the while flapping its wings and tapping upon the pane. Still another example of a bird recognizing a person after an absence was given to me by Lawrence Zeleny, who writes as follows of his experience with a tame catbird: "One summer I hand tamed an adult catbird to take raisins from my hand. For seven successive years on either April 29 or April 30 the catbird reappeared and immediately came to my hand for raisins!"

The fact that birds learn to recognize us and come to us alone for food is a lesson in the adaptability that is so conspicuous in birds that come to feeding stations. The person who is a stranger is not accepted until his actions prove that he means no harm. No matter how tame they may seem, the birds that come to our yard never lose a natural wariness. Always uppermost in their minds is the necessity of avoiding danger.

Once birds have come to recognize you as a provider of food, you can expect them to worry you a bit whenever the supply becomes low. One tactic is to tap upon windowpanes. A bird will simply peck repeatedly upon a pane with its bill; sometimes this action is accompanied by fluttering up against the pane and making piteous calls. Hand-raised orphaned bluebirds when hungry would peer in every window of the Zeleny residence until they saw someone. Then, on seeing a person, they would raise a clamor and peck at the windowpanes. They never pecked the windowpanes of a room that was empty.

No one can resist such obvious requests. You either rush out and replenish the feeders or open the window and give your imploring guest the immediate attention it demands.

Unlike the ability to recognize people, window tapping seems to require a fair amount of intelligence on the part of the bird that engages in it. First of all, the bird must know that its benefactors reside inside the house. Moreover, the bird is aware of the part of the house its friends happen to be in. No energy is expended tapping the window in a barn, garage, attic, or empty room; it is a room where the bird knows it will get our attention. In addition, the bird has a special motive for engaging in this activity. It is always to let us know that the feeders are empty and that more food is needed.

*Chickadees watch us
and let us know it is time to put
out more food.*

Is this habit one of the rare examples of insight or reasoned learning in birds or the much more common trial-and-error learning? Probably the latter. A bird that has already associated us with the replenishing of food, and that knows we are in the house and which room we are in, has before it the problem of gaining our attention. It goes about the solution with a characteristic trial-and-error approach that is so often used by birds and other higher animals. At first the bird attempts to gain our attention by means of repetitious call notes uttered from a vantage point near our window. Failing in this effort, the bird may try tapping upon a resonant surface with its bill in order to gain our attention. An observer in Wisconsin reported black-capped chickadees and white-breasted nuthatches tapping "indignantly" upon the floor of the feeding shelf and a nearby window frame when the supply of sunflower seed was gone. A red-bellied woodpecker in South Carolina tapped upon a metal awning when the feeder was empty and a downy woodpecker in New England expressed its disappointment by tapping upon shingles on the side of a house.

Still not getting the desired response, the bird may at last stumble upon a better way to gain our attention. This will be tapping upon the windowpane of the room we are in. The success that the bird achieves through this method will cause it to repeat the performance every time the feeders are empty. Although not a common habit, window tapping has been observed in birds on both sides of the Atlantic and the participants have represented such families as woodpeckers, titmice, nuthatches, mimic thrushes, thrushes, and the sparrows and finches.

GETTING ATTENTION IN OTHER WAYS

Still other methods of getting attention are used by birds and some of them are as effective as tapping upon windowpanes. A female cardinal at my home in Virginia used to stare in at me when the feeders were empty. All the while the bird would pick up and drop the empty hulls of sunflower seeds. Domestic pigeons went through an equally effective pantomime outside my window when the bird baths were empty. Two or three pigeons would stand at the edge of a bath, dip their bills in as though there was water, and then look up, staring expectantly in my direction.

This last example of attention getting should not be confused with displacement activity which is the scientific term for acting out a frustration. Unable for some reason to carry out a purpose, a bird may react by engaging in an altogether different kind of activity. Although this activity may have no functional value, it does serve a purpose in being an outlet for pent-up feelings. When my bird baths are not filled or are too crowded for some birds, the disappointed candidates will sometimes go through all the motions of bathing at a nearby shallow dry hole which is a depression in a rock surface. Similarly, a bird unable to eat at feeders because of crowded conditions may begin elaborate preening operations. This may occur even though the bird has earlier seen to its plumage.

Birds have still other methods of letting us know of their needs. A mockingbird at a home in a Washington, D.C., suburb used to dash madly from window to window to follow a housewife as she did her chores. This was to let her know that it was time to provide more raisins. Needless to say, this tactic always elicited a prompt response. After hand taming black-capped chickadees at her northwoods Ontario home, Louise de Kiriline Lawrence found herself constantly being importuned by her spoiled guests. They would follow her from window to window. Clinging to eaves or icicles, they would look in at her and if this didn't bring a response, they would begin tapping upon the panes.

IDENTIFICATION, LISTING, REPORTING

Identification is one of the most difficult parts of bird study. For most of us, a long period of intensive use of a bird guide is necessary before we can safely recognize this species or that one. Luckily, there are a number of excellent bird guides available. More popular ones are well illustrated, and the species descriptions give the reader the important points to look for in making an identification. The only drawback of most present-day bird guides is that they do not come down to the level of the beginner, who often does not have any knowledge of bird classification. Not knowing family characteristics, the beginner is frequently obliged to page through the entire guide in making a search for the bird he has seen.

A bird guide should be studied carefully and the illustrations gone over again and again. It is surprising how often a bird will be recognized because of frequent past thumbing in a well-used bird guide. Then, once proper skills have been learned, the student should go on to a more advanced guide. There are several that should be kept readily available for reference.* Try each guide and see which one you like best. Many find it is helpful to have them all.

Identifying birds at the feeder is quite a different feat from telling birds in the field. Since a bird can be counted upon to make return visits to the feeder, there is, as a rule, more than enough opportunity to study the bird carefully and note every detail of its plumage and other features. In the field there are seldom good opportuni-

---

* Roger Tory Peterson, *A Field Guide to the Birds*, Boston, Houghton Mifflin Company, 1980; Chandler S. Robbins, Bertel Bruun, and Herbert S. Zim, *Birds of North America*, New York, Golden Press, 1966, 1983; *Field Guide to the Birds of North America*, Washington, D. C., National Geographic Society, 1983; and *The Audubon Society Master Guide to Birding*, 3 volumes, New York, Alfred A. Knopf, 1983.

ties to study a bird at leisure. Only too often the bird flies away or disappears in the foliage. This does not necessarily hamper the field expert. He can often swing his binoculars into position quickly enough to catch a glimpse of the bird, which is usually enough for identification. The flight pattern, the bird's relative size, its shape, and a distinguishing mark or two are all that is necessary.

When watching birds at a feeding station, especially at window feeders, binoculars are not always needed. A simple field glass that magnifies three or four times is adequate for most needs around the home. However, when one makes trips farther afield, a 7X35 prism binocular becomes a necessity. This binocular magnifies objects seven times and is highly popular with bird watchers.

Do not overestimate the advantages of identification at feeding stations. Sometimes you see the bird too well and note details that are not present in bird guide illustrations. This point is best illustrated when a bird is seen for the first time in the hand. Even common species like the house sparrow and starling are so strangely different when held that we sometimes fail to recognize them. Many of the mistakes in identification made at feeding stations are a result of noting too much in the way of detail. The observer must learn to omit some of the fine points and try to remember, for the most part, only features that will be helpful from the standpoint of the bird guides.

WHAT TO LOOK FOR

One of the most important steps in identifying a bird is to write down at once the information that will help when you look up the bird later on. It is surprising how quickly we forget vital details. So make a habit of carrying a pocket notebook and putting in it information that might otherwise be forgotten. You should not confine your note-taking entirely to the bird's appearance. Observe everything you can about the bird and what it is doing. This is by far the best way to arrive at the correct identification.

One way to begin learning to recognize a few species well is to concentrate upon those that visit your feeding stations. These birds will be less difficult to learn because you see them so often and so well. Only after you have become thoroughly familiar with the birds that are close by should you begin trying your luck farther afield. Always start with the easiest species first. This is a second important rule to follow.

Size

How large was the bird? The best approach to this question is to compare the bird's size to that of a well-known bird you are familiar with. Many bird watchers are in the habit of using the common crow, the robin, and the house sparrow as standards of comparison. A small bird can be compared to the house sparrow's length of 6 inches, a medium-sized bird to the robin's 10 inches, and a large bird to the crow's length, which is between 17 and 21 inches.

Shape

Is the bird slender or stout? Is its tail long, short, or stubby? Is the head large or small in proportion to the body? What does the bill look like? These are some of the most important characteristics to look for in making an identification. Look for a short upturned tail in wrens, a crest in the pileated woodpecker, blue jay, tufted titmouse, cedar waxwing, and cardinal, and a stout body and short tail in the nuthatches. In flycatchers, and especially owls, the head is proportionately large in respect to body size.

The shape and length of the bill are always important clues. Is the bill long and slender, short and thick, thin and sharply pointed, straight, slightly upturned, or curved downward? Bill characteristics are especially useful in separating one species from another and also in deciding which family a bird belongs to. Many of the birds that visit feeding stations have very distinctive bills that are helpful in making the correct identification (see illustration, page 120).

Color

This is one of the most obvious and most helpful clues. Not many birds, for example, are largely or wholly blue in color. Any blue bird in your yard would almost have to be either an eastern bluebird, blue jay, male indigo bunting, or male blue grosbeak. Also there are not many nearly all red or gray birds. Red is a color that is largely monopolized by the male of the species; good examples of dominantly red males are seen in the cardinal, summer tanager, and scarlet tanager. The more somber gray is seen in the tufted titmouse, mockingbird, female cowbird, and dark-eyed junco.

Where there is more than one color in a bird, draw a rough outline of the bird and mark in areas that have a solid color of one kind or another. Sometimes a vivid color is limited to a small area. The scarlet crown patch of the ruby-crowned kinglet and the yellow rump of the myrtle warbler are examples. The rump patch in the myrtle warbler is the one yellow marking on this bird that can be counted upon regardless of age group or time of the year. The name of this common warbler has been changed quite appropriately to yellow-rumped warbler.

Distinguishing Marks

Birds that have no prominent markings are called nondescript. These are the hardest birds of all to identify. Anyone who has tried to identify an orange-crowned warbler, a greenish-yellow bird without distinctive markings, will appreciate this fact. In certain families, such as the hummingbirds, many of the warblers, orioles, tanagers, and certain of the finches, the females and immatures are dull colored if not nondescript in appearance, while the adult male is brightly colored. In such cases, the biggest problem is always in identifying females and immatures.

More often than not—and this is true of most feeding station visitors—there are few, if any, obvious differences between adult males and females and first-year immatures. Note the sameness that is found in crows and jays, titmice, wrens, catbirds, mockingbirds, brown thrashers, and most thrushes.

Luckily there are many species that have such prominent distinguishing marks that we should have little trouble with them. Note the black band across the breast in the flicker, the black "V" imposed upon a yellow breast in the meadowlark, the flaming red crest in the crow-sized pileated woodpecker, the white line over the eye in the Carolina wren, and the black face mask in shrikes and male yellowthroats.

Even the sparrows are not as nondescript as they may at first seem. Many have fairly prominent distinguishing marks. The vesper sparrow with white outer tail feathers, the adult white-crowned sparrow with its prominent white crown stripe, and the song sparrow with its black central breast spot are examples. In sparrows, as with other groups, learn the easiest ones first and the others will fall in place as you get to know them better.

Flight

Distant wing beats are often a useful clue to a bird's identity. Little difficulty will be had in recognizing the massed flight movements of the cedar waxwing, a species noted for swiftness and precision. Much the same can be said of the starling. An undulating flight is characteristic of redpolls, pine siskins, goldfinches, and snow buntings. In these species you cannot be sure of identification by flight alone. You also need to see something of the bird. The flight of woodpeckers is undulating but not the same up-and-down of the aforementioned finches. Woodpeckers rise on a series of wing beats and then slide downward with wings partly closed. This labored flight instantly sets them apart from other birds.

The art of recognizing families or species by their flight characteristics is important if you are going to do much observing of birds in the open.

Mannerisms

Those who watch birds at feeding stations are in a position to learn more about the individual habits and mannerisms of birds than almost anyone else. Birds reveal distinctive mannerisms in countless ways. Look at the way birds approach the feeder, search for food, eat, bathe, dust, or sun themselves. Try making a list of some of the most distinctive traits you observe among birds at your feeding station.

*Tufted
titmouse.*

No one can overlook the white-breasted nuthatch's unusual approach to the feeder. It is always headfirst down a tree trunk; then perhaps a short flight to the feeder itself. Woodpeckers also make use of tree trunks as they approach a feeder. They move up or down the trunk, staying upright and bracing themselves with the tail, which has unusually stiff feathers. Some individuals almost always approach a particular food supply from the right, others from the left.

Most birds do all their eating at the feeder and do not fly off with food except when they are taking it to young. But nuthatches, chickadees, tufted titmice, and blue jays almost always fly off with food. Note the way chickadees, titmice, and jays wedge a piece of food between their toes and a perch and then how they pound with the bill until the food is broken apart and consumed. Doves never fly off with food but move about a feeding area on an uncertain course, all the while picking up food with rapid jabs of the bill. Certain sparrows and the towhee do a lot of scratching while they eat. This is true even when there is such an abundance of food that scratching would seem to be superfluous.

It should be pointed out that habits and mannerisms such as those mentioned are rarely treated in bird guides. For more detailed information one must go to A. C. Bent's *Life Histories* or such reliable sources of information as Forbush's *Birds of Massachusetts*.

Habitat

This is as useful a clue as any in deciding if a bird should rightly belong in your yard. Near the coast, gulls and especially herring and ring-billed gulls are more and more in the habit of coming to yards that are close to water. Small yards that are far from water cannot be expected to attract water birds, although we sometimes do have surprises in this regard. The American woodcock, known by its large head and grotesquely long bill, occasionally wanders to almost any yard that supports a large earthworm population. Larger yards with wide lawns attract such open-country birds as killdeer, water pipit, horned lark, meadowlark, Lapland longspur, and snow bunting. If the yard is at all closed in by trees and shrubbery, we would not expect to find these birds. Even so, there is a strong tendency on the part of many open-country birds to invade yards in residential districts. The red-winged blackbird is an example of an open-country bird that was formerly all but unknown in densely populated districts but that now makes itself at home in yards of all sorts.

Do not be confused by the placement of hawks, fowl-like birds, doves, and owls in the front part of your bird guide. These families have been placed near or among the water birds, not because of habits but because of close taxonomic relationships. You will find nearly all visitors to your yard, with the exceptions already noted, among the land birds and the four families just mentioned.

The value of sound as an aid to identification depends largely upon the ear of the observer. Many persons find descriptions of bird songs or notes too difficult to be useful. This is understandable. It is almost impossible to put the musical notes of most birds into meaningful words or phrases. The Golden Field Guide, *Birds of North America*, describes bird songs by means of sonagrams. But a proper understanding of these sonagrams requires some knowledge of music. Other aids are the many song recordings, such as those of the Cornell Laboratory of Ornithology. It is particularly helpful to listen to a bird song recording after a session of hearing birds in the wild.

Luckily, there are a few calls and songs that are easy. Who is not familiar with the "chick-a-dee-dee-dee" song of black-capped and Carolina chickadees and their spring "phoe-be" calls? The "yank-yank" notes of the white-breasted nuthatch are easily learned and so is the catlike mewing of the catbird. The eastern phoebe says its name, "phoe-be," and the yellowthroat can be recognized by its "witchity-witchity" notes.

FINAL DETERMINATION

After a process that is partly elimination and partly the accumulation of bits of information, you will have an identification that you can place your whole confidence in. This will give you the incentive to go on with the identification of still other birds. The process will become easier and easier. And finally there will be only an occasional bird that will give you trouble.

What to do if you find a bird that defies all your efforts and remains unidentifiable? This is not an uncommon problem and it is helpful to know that even the most expert field observers cannot always identify every bird they see. Sometimes the bird that gives us the most trouble is a common species that we see every day. The difficulty with this particular bird may stem from a plumage stage that is not shown in the bird guides or some other characteristic that gives the bird an odd look. A trace of albinism is a frequent cause for confusion. While complete albinism is something we rarely see in birds, the partial albino is almost commonplace. I can nearly always count upon one or two such birds at my feeders.

When you do see an odd bird that you cannot find in your guide, you should pay less attention to appearance and more to what the bird is doing. A bird's actions are sometimes the best giveaway to its identity. Also observe the company the bird keeps. Although albinos are occasionally ostracized from a flock, it is normal to expect a bird to stay with others of its kind. Many of the most interesting observations we make at our feeders pertain to birds that have abnormalities of one kind or another. So do not be overly disappointed if the bird you could not identify proves to be a cowbird, grackle, or member of some other common species that did not happen to look like its fellows. It is always rewarding to follow such birds and note their behavioral quirks.

Birds, as everyone knows, are capable of covering vast distances, and it is not at all unheard of for a bird that should properly belong several thousand miles away to appear in the eastern part of the United States. Many of these strays, as they are called, are western birds that perhaps became confused while on migration and strayed far off course. The prevailing westerly winds on this continent seem to favor displacement of western birds eastward. However, many eastern birds also stray off course and some of them appear in the West far outside normal range limits. It must be admitted that little is known concerning the mechanisms that keep birds on course when they are migrating. The stray that appears at our feeders is an admission that something went wrong.

Strays make up a small but sometimes conspicuous feature of our bird population in the East. Largest numbers are apt to appear in the fall. If a stray finds its way to your feeding station at the advent of cold weather, it is likely to remain the rest of the winter. Such birds, however, are not always to be relied upon. A stray may visit other feeding stations besides yours and perhaps desert yours altogether. The trick is to find the food that will hold this bird to your feeding station.

What to do about the positive identification of such a bird? Since this is a matter of scientific interest and not solely personal curiosity, you should immediately get in touch with others. There should be someone with expert ability in bird identification near you. Bird watchers have a habit of banding together to exchange information and help each other with identification problems. Once you are part of such a group, you no longer need to worry about identifying every bird on your own. Any strange bird that comes to the attention of anyone in the group is certain to stir up a flurry of phone calls and visits to the home of the person who has seen the bird.

There is no such thing as giving up on the identification of a bird. In the days before good field glasses and bird guides it was customary for eager enthusiasts to shoot a bird in order to be positive about its identification. Today this approach is much frowned upon, and indeed is illegal except for the few who have scientific collecting permits. The approved technique today is to study the bird as carefully as possible, noting every feature that might in any way be an aid to its identification. In a few cases, it may be deemed necessary to capture the bird in a banding trap, and then someone who is competent in such matters will examine the bird in the hand and take detailed notes and measurements. The captured bird is released as quickly as possible and usually with a numbered aluminum band on one leg. With its identity assured, should it be found again, the bird is on its way and oblivious of the stir it has caused.

KEEPING A LIST

Nearly everyone who has a feeding station keeps a list of some kind. One of the most popular types is the yard list. Entered are all the species seen in the yard or observed from the yard. Ducks and geese flying over are as much a part of the yard list as birds seen at the feeding station. Many bird watchers find this kind of listing more rewarding if they have a system to indicate exactly where the bird was seen. One way to do this is to add an asterisk after each species seen in the yard and omit the asterisk for those seen outside the yard. This system can be applied to the feeding station, bird bath, or any other part of the yard you have a special interest in. Your lists will be more accurate if you make sure the bird at the feeding station was eating something and the one at the bird bath was drinking or bathing. Many times birds join the throng out of curiosity but do not participate in the activity that is taking place.

The joy of keeping a list is in seeing it grow. The first winter I fed birds at my home near Leesburg, Virginia, I attracted only fifteen species or so. All were kinds that respond readily to food offerings—red-bellied, downy, and hairy woodpeckers, blue jay, Carolina chickadee, tufted titmouse, white-breasted nuthatch, Carolina wren, house sparrow, cardinal, dark-eyed junco, tree sparrow, white-throated sparrow, and song sparrow. Eventually the word gets around, though. Old customers come back and new ones make their appearance. By the end of my second year of bird feeding, I had a list of about thirty species. The following several years the list did not grow so rapidly and the arrival of a newcomer became an event that was always looked forward to with keen interest. Some years were more exciting than others. The northern finch years were always rewarding and brought such new customers as purple finch, evening grosbeak, and pine siskin. One of the most recent additions to my feeder was the house finch, a bird from the West that was introduced to the New York City region and is now rapidly spreading out in several directions. By the end of five years, my feeding station list had grown to forty-five species. I consider this a fair number for the heavily wooded area where I live. Friends and neighbors who live in somewhat more open country have attracted a greater variety of birdlife than I have. I know of several who have feeding station lists of sixty species or so.

The longer bird feeding is continued in one place, the longer your list becomes. You will also begin to notice that you are attracting a greater proportion of birds that are unusual to your region. This is because your food supply has become well known to all the birds of the neighborhood. A stray or rarity of any kind that happens by is simply drawn along with the others.

If your list is going to be as helpful as possible and provide a record that you can always refer back to with confidence, make sure that you get off to a proper start. First of all, do not be content with just a list. Keep a notebook or diary in which you record such details as dates, species, numbers seen, weather conditions, unusual observations, habits, and the like. A detailed description, the date, and other appropriate data should accompany the report of a rare or unusual species. Also describe albinos or any bird with unusual plumage pattern or coloration. Finally, you should make a habit of recording birds in A.O.U.* checklist order. This is not an alphabetical listing of birds but a system that takes into consideration the evolution of birds from primitive fish-eating species to our present-day songbirds that are believed to represent the highest development so far attained in the bird world. Loons and grebes come first on the 1983 A.O.U. checklist; finches and weaver finches last. Once you are used to the checklist order, you will find that it is one of the handiest methods of listing birds.

Still another way of listing birds is to use an alphabetical arrangement. This I

---

* American Ornithologists' Union, a scientific society that publishes the ornithological journal *The Auk* and periodically a checklist of North American birds.

have done in the appendix where my interest is in helping readers find birds quickly. However, elsewhere in this book I have, with few exceptions, used the standard A.O.U. or phylogenetic arrangement of listing birds. An exception to this approach is found in Part II, where I treat individual species that come to feeding stations. Instead of beginning with the most primitive family that visits our feeders, which is the fowl-like birds, I begin with the sparrows and finches. I hope I may be excused for this rearranging. The purpose was to bring into focus the birds that supply by far the greatest number of visitors to feeding stations and also many of the best known visitors. Placing these birds first gives more emphasis to their importance. At the same time, I agree with those who would put sparrows and finches at the top so far as evolutionary progress is concerned.

Bird listing, while often a serious pursuit, also has its more frivolous side. Many bird watchers try to see how many species they can list in a day, a year, or a lifetime. The late Ludlow Griscom, well-known ornithologist and field expert, had a life list of over 2,500 species. Included were birds he had seen on his world travels. Most of us restrict our life list to a smaller geographical unit: North America, the United States, or the state where we live. Whatever boundaries we establish, it is always a thrill when we pass a goal that we have set for ourselves. Although listing of this kind is largely a form of recreation, it does develop skills and the list enthusiast cannot help learning a lot about birds.

REPORTING

How can we turn our observations into information that is useful to others? This is one of the questions that confronts the enthusiast soon after he has begun watching birds at his feeding station. A new species has appeared for the first time, another has failed to return, a habit never seen before has been observed. Are these events worth sharing with others? If so, how does one get started in reporting observations about birds?

So far as importance is concerned, the only safe rule is to assume that nearly all the details you see are worth noting. Many of us, for example, see common grackles taking bread and other food to the bird bath, wetting the food, and then eating it. The fact that this habit has already been reported upon in ornithological literature does not make further observations unnecessary. We may note details that have not been carefully recorded. How does the grackle hold the food while wetting it, how long is the food kept submerged, what happens after the food has been retrieved from the water—these are all appropriate matters to investigate and perhaps write upon.

Someday you may want to write an article about birds for a magazine or newspaper, or even an ornithological journal.* This is when you will need all the help you can get from your notes or bird diary. So do not put off the task of keeping a detailed record of what you see. And do not be overly concerned about duplicating observations others have made. So long as you have recorded the details more accurately and precisely than ever before, you can be sure you have made a worthwhile contribution. Many of the most exciting and informative books about birds are by persons who have recorded the small details they observed in watching birds around their homes. This is the secret of such writers as Louise de Kiriline Lawrence and Len Howard.

There is also a conservation side to keeping bird records. More support is needed in monitoring this nation's birdlife. It is vital to know which species are doing well and which need help. The task of supplying this information falls to many hundreds of volunteers who keep a close watch upon the birdlife of their neighborhoods. Many limit their observations to their home grounds; others cover wider areas. There are also organized activities such as breeding bird censuses and winter bird counts. The Christmas Bird Count, an annual event since 1900, is a continent-wide attempt to arrive at population figures when birds are not moving about as much as usual. The thousands of volunteers that participate in this count enjoy themselves thoroughly and, at the same time, provide vital information concerning the status of the hundreds of species that are recorded each year.

Only through careful census work can we know in time if a species is in trouble. Ever since the publication of Rachel Carson's *Silent Spring*, there has been growing concern over the damage that pesticides of many kinds have done to our environment. Birdlife in many instances has been adversely affected. Now that some of the more damaging pesticides have been banned, we can hope for signs of improvement. Other problems remain, and we are still beset by the dislocations caused by the unwise introduction of foreign bird species during the last century.

*Leading scientific journals devoted to ornithology include *The Auk, The Wilson Bulletin, The Condor*, and *Journal of Field Ornithology*.

The eastern bluebird is only one of a number of species that has declined alarmingly. Bluebirds are vulnerable to cold weather and to loss of their cavity nest holes to more aggressive intruders. The cold winter of 1957–1958 saw heavy losses in the bluebird population. But steady competition for nesting cavities, first by the introduced house sparrow and presently by both the house sparrow and starling, has been the greatest obstacle that this bird has faced. Fortunately, the public became aware of the bluebird's plight early enough for the adoption of helpful measures. The bluebird's housing difficulties have been relieved by the establishment of hundreds of nest-box trails that are carefully monitored to keep out house sparrows and starlings.* Nevertheless, the bluebird's status remains precarious and not enough can be done to help this beautiful bird.

Are other of our familiar birds in trouble? This we do not always know for certain. Probably cavity nesters, such as the woodpeckers and crested flycatcher, are experiencing difficulties similar to those faced by the bluebird. The red-headed woodpecker, for example, was once common throughout the East; now it is rare to see this bird in most parts of its eastern range. Although flycatchers, thrushes, vireos, and warblers, with few exceptions, are not regarded as members of the feeding station company, we do often see these birds in our yards; this is especially true during migration. There have been reports that indicate drastic declines in these families

We help bluebirds by providing much-needed housing.

*If care is taken to limit the diameter of the entrance hole to 1½ inches, the opening will be too small for starlings but large enough for bluebirds.

and in still other species that visit our yards. Deforestation in the tropics has been given as a reason for these declines.

Are we being overly pessimistic about some of our birds or are drastic declines in numbers actually taking place? This is a question that very much needs answering. We can assist in supplying the answer by sending reports to the local Audubon Society or naturalist group and to *American Birds* (formerly *Audubon Field Notes*), a journal devoted to field ornithology, and to Project FeederWatch, a continent-wide survey whose participants send in reports on numbers and activities of birds seen at their feeders. Editors do not insist upon polished or scholarly accounts; emphasis is upon an accurate appraisal of the trends you see in your neighborhood.

If you begin to find, as many do, that birds are your one absorbing interest, that you watch them at every opportunity and read everything you can find about them, you might as well go all out and become a full-time bird watcher and conservationist. The two pursuits go hand in hand, for without conservation we cannot have the rich birdlife that is our heritage. You will find yourself attending meetings, giving talks, leading bird trips, joining organizations, and taking part in conservation efforts. Many participate in such activities and find it a very rewarding way to spend their time. Thinking back, many recall that their involvement began with watching birds at a feeding station.

BENEFITS TO BIRDS

Since World War II, bird feeding has developed into such a popular hobby that surveys are conducted to determine how many people feed birds annually. According to a 1988 survey by the U.S. Fish and Wildlife Service, 82 million people feed birds in the United States during the winter and buy 1 billion pounds of bird seeds. At least 3 million people feed birds in Canada. It can be seen that from small beginnings a hundred years ago, bird feeding has developed into a pursuit that is enjoyed by millions of people and that supports an industry that supplies every need from food and feeders to bird baths. Today nearly every sizable community has one or more garden stores or wild-bird centers where these products are sold.

Bird feeding is a hobby that has taken hold almost everywhere. The enthusiasm of bird-conscious New England has reached other parts of the country as well. Bird feeders are found from the semitropical southern Florida to remote northern outposts in Alaska and Canada. Birds respond well wherever feeding is conducted. Nearly everywhere bird feeding is a winter hobby, and more and more it is becoming a year-round pursuit.

Benefits to us come in the form of the excitement over the small events that take place daily at our feeders. We find a peace of mind and inner joy that is lacking in so many of the artificial distractions of our time. For birds more food means greater security during the winter and again in spring when natural food supplies are likely to be at their lowest ebb. The needs of the nesting season are eased when we make suitable foods available in summer (see page 269). Help in the way of extra food has undoubtedly been responsible for some dramatic population increases among many bird species during this century. There have also been changes in range and migratory habits that can be attributed in large part to bird feeding.

While some changes due to bird feeding probably go back to the first several decades of this century, it was not until around 1950 that bird feeding was conducted on a large enough scale to make for many differences. By 1950 the most important differences were more and more half-hardy species wintering in the North, a loss in migratory urge among several species that formerly wintered exclusively in the tropics, and a pronounced movement by field-foraging birds into towns and cities and about homes. Also birds were becoming noticeably tamer, and in winter more and more birds were occurring about homes with feeding stations and not in wilder districts.

The trends that were first being noticed forty-five years ago have continued. At the present time, species that commonly visit feeding stations are doing well. This is an encouraging development at a time when many forces seem pitted against birds and other wildlife. Benefits that have come to birds during this century have often been canceled out by adverse factors. Among these are pesticides that are harmful to wildlife, air and water pollution, monocultural practices in farming and forestry, clean farming, intensified land use together with large-scale construction projects, and drainage and filling of ponds and marshes. We have also inherited the after-effects of the nineteenth-century mistakes of bringing over the house sparrow and starling. Added to all this is the destruction to birdlife that comes when birds collide with onrushing vehicles, fly into windows, hit tall buildings and television towers, and fly into lighthouses at night. That many species of birds have held their own or have prospered in the face of these adversities is a tribute to the more positive things that have been taking place.

It would be a mistake, however, to attribute the present favorable circumstances surrounding some portions of our birdlife to the one factor of more food being available. Improved landscaping and plantings have also had far-reaching effects that have generally been beneficial to birds. Also of great help to birds have been changing attitudes on the part of the general public. Most of us today look upon living birds as valuable assets to be appreciated for aesthetic reasons as well as for a number of important economic reasons. We show our good will by doing more to help birds.

Finally, warmer winters in recent years have been one of the greatest boons to many of the small birds that frequent our yards. The first evidence of a warming trend goes back to 1850.* At first the change to warmer temperatures was slow and irregular. But after 1900 it was more rapid. Today we have the warmest winters this country has experienced in over one hundred years. Warmer temperatures coupled with the extra food supplies at feeding stations have made the lot of many small birds easier. Some of the most striking changes that have taken place are listed below.

MORE BIRDS LINGERING IN THE NORTH IN WINTER

A sizable number of species, including both water birds and land birds, can be termed half-hardy. This means that although the species as a whole migrates to a warmer portion of this country or farther southward, some individuals stay behind in the North. Feeding stations as well as any lessening in the severity of the winter climate greatly improve the outlook for half-hardy birds that stay behind. Unlike chickadees and other northern residents, birds that fall under the half-hardy category are not well adapted to northern winters. Many perish with the first snowstorms and intense cold. But the fact, as deduced from bird census figures, that the number of such birds spending the winter in the North has greatly increased, suggests that a great many do survive. Species that seem to have benefited most from feeding stations and warmer winters are the bobwhite, mourning dove, common flicker, yellow-bellied sapsucker, Carolina wren, gray catbird, brown thrasher, hermit thrush, ruby-crowned kinglet, orange-crowned warbler, yellow-rumped warbler, pine warbler, red-winged blackbird, rusty blackbird, common grackle, brown-headed cowbird, rufous-sided towhee, chipping sparrow, field sparrow, white-crowned sparrow, white-throated sparrow, fox sparrow, and song sparrow.

Bobwhite.

Mourning doves did not begin wintering in the North until 1920. Now they are common in winter as far north as the Great Lakes and middle New England. Hundreds take up residence near towns where bird feeding is a popular pastime. The white-throated sparrow did not make its winter debut in the North until about 1930. Now it is a common winter resident in coastal districts of New England and far inland as well. The white-crowned sparrow, appearing in the North about 1950, has

*C. E. P. Brooks, *Climate Through the Ages*, New York, Dover Publications, 1970.

followed exactly the pattern of the whitethroat. Still more recent has been the appearance in winter of the fox sparrow as far north as New England.

REDUCED URGE TO MIGRATE

The northern oriole was the first of the tropical migrants to begin to stay behind in conspicuous numbers. There were occasional winter appearances by this bird in the North during the first half of this century. By 1950 the northern oriole had begun to appear regularly every winter in New England and nearby areas. The trend has spread to other parts of the East so that now this colorful oriole is almost commonplace in winter in coastal states and occasionally farther inland. It is significant that northern orioles are most common in towns and cities in winter and that they almost invariably take up residence near homes with feeding stations.

Around 1936 a few dickcissels were being noticed in winter in New England. Normally this species was as much of a migrant to the tropics as the northern oriole before the days of bird feeding. As with the oriole, the tendency by the dickcissel to over-winter grew and spread to other regions, including the West Coast. The dickcissel now has much the same winter distribution in eastern North America as the northern oriole.

The over-wintering pattern of first becoming established in New England and then appearing in a much wider geographical area is also seen in the yellow-breasted chat. This warbler, which normally winters in the tropics, made its winter debut in New England about 1950. Following the example of the northern oriole and dickcissel, the chat began making appearances farther south as well. Presently it can be expected in small numbers in winter in coastal states from New England to Texas.

That New England seemed to be the center from which the over-wintering habit was first observed can be explained partly by more feeding stations in New England and partly by more observers. But by 1960, New England had partially lost these advantages. Bird watching was becoming a popular hobby everywhere and feeding stations had become commonplace throughout the East. So it is not surprising that after 1960 reports were beginning to come in of changing habits of still other birds, and these reports were mostly from outside New England. Beginning about 1960, indigo buntings were first noted spending the winter in sizable numbers along the coasts of southern Florida. Formerly almost the entire population went to the tropics. The indigo bunting was apparently finding a congenial winter home in Florida. Many were appearing at feeding stations. When, as frequently happened, the bright-colored males appeared together with the even more gorgeous male painted buntings, it was one of the most thrilling sights in the history of bird feeding.

The rose-breasted grosbeak is still another migrant to the tropics that is beginning to stay behind in small numbers. During the winter of 1972–1973, this colorful grosbeak was reported from widely scattered localities all the way from southern California to the Atlantic coastal states. There seemed to be no one focal point for this species. It was turning up almost anywhere and almost always taking advantage of feeding stations.

Two other tropical migrants were making their debuts at about the same time as the rose-breasted grosbeak but in smaller numbers. A scattering of reports during the winter of 1972–1973 of blue grosbeaks and summer tanagers at feeding stations from about Kentucky and Virginia southward suggests that still other neotropical migrants may be following the examples of those already mentioned.

These occurrences do not mean any general breakdown in migration patterns is taking place. The vast majority of individuals in the species mentioned leave for the south as promptly as ever and go all the way to their ancestral wintering grounds. Somehow a few individuals are not so well oriented and remain in the North. Each winter there seems to be a tendency for more such individuals to stay behind. The habit appears to grow in proportion to the number that survive.

SOUTHERN SPECIES EXTENDING THEIR BREEDING RANGES NORTHWARD

A number of southern birds have been pushing northward since sometime during the last century. The outstanding example is the cardinal, whose range expansion over the last one hundred years has taken it from the Ohio River to central Ontario and from the vicinity of New York City to northern New England. This movement northward was almost certainly a response to the already noted warming trend in winter climate. That feeding stations have helped is seen in the momentum that this movement has gained since about 1960. During a period of ten years—from 1960 to 1970—the cardinal has gained as much new ground approximately as was gained during all the preceding decades of this century. The presence of food at feeding stations makes it possible for the cardinal to get by in winter at northern limits where otherwise it would almost certainly fail to do so.

Other southern species that are benefiting in much the same way as the cardinal are the mourning dove, red-bellied woodpecker, tufted titmouse, Carolina wren, and mockingbird. These last five have not matched the cardinal in its rapid strides northward, but the tufted titmouse and mockingbird are not far behind.

RAPID POPULATION INCREASE

Although exact figures are lacking, it seems likely that many species that patronize feeding stations are more common today than fifty years ago. Several species have made such striking gains that there is no doubt about their improved status. The three species that have shown the most striking gains are Anna's hummingbird, evening grosbeak, and house finch. All three are common visitors at feeding stations: Anna's is common in the far West, and the other two are widespread.

The success of Anna's hummingbird is a tribute to the benefit of sugar-water in hummingbird feeding and should offset fears of those who suggest that partial dependence on this food may be harmful to hummingbirds.

From a little-known bird of the Canadian wilderness, the evening grosbeak has within the past one hundred years erupted into an abundant species that has reached feeding stations as far south as northern Florida and the Gulf coast. Since 1900 an expansion of the breeding range has taken the evening grosbeak into the easternmost provinces of Canada and southward into our more northern states. It seems likely that sunflower seeds from feeding stations have contributed substantially to this success.

The house finch, with an entirely different background, is also in the midst of a spectacular population boom. From small numbers released near New York City in 1941, the house finch has spread everywhere in the East and may soon join the western population from which it was derived. Wherever this colorful little finch appears, it avails itself of food at feeding stations. It seems likely that feeding stations have been a major factor in helping this finch become established in the East.

Although the western states are not covered in this volume, bird feeding is popular in this part of the country as well. A spectacular increase in range and numbers of Anna's hummingbird has been correlated with increased numbers of feeding stations as well as the planting in yards of flowers well liked by hummingbirds. The success of Anna's hummingbird is a tribute to the helpfulness of sugar-water in hummingbird feeding and should offset the fears of those who suggest that partial dependence on this food may be harmful to hummingbirds (see pages 168–9).

WINTER BIRDS SEEKING OUT FEEDING STATIONS

How different the situation is today from a hundred years ago when John Burroughs commented upon the wildness and indifference of the birds that he saw near his woodland cabin. The efforts of the early bird attractors have borne fruit. Birds are now so acclimated to our yards that we often look for them in vain when we go farther afield. It is in northern states in winter that the birdlife is most largely concentrated in areas where people live. The winter woods in northern states often seem bleak indeed. But look for a return of birdlife to wilder areas in good weather. Even in midwinter birds get the urge to roam and do so on bright, sunny days.

BIRDS BECOMING TAMER

Thanks to food and protection, birds have become much tamer since the early days of this century and many more are now nesting in yards. Some of the biggest differences are seen in such species as the mourning dove, northern flicker, blue jay, common crow, American robin, and wood thrush—birds that were once much more distrustful. These birds and many others have shown their confidence in us by seeking out the close proximity of our dwellings for food or nesting sites, or sometimes both.

The mourning dove is still a wary bird where hunted, but once given protection it settles down to such tameness that it seems a different species altogether. On the sidewalks of some southern towns and cities, mourning doves scarcely get out of the way when people approach. This confidence is carried over to our yards, where mourning doves are now common feeding station visitors and place their flimsy nests in trees and bushes close to houses. If you have any partially rotten trees in your yard, you may find a pair of northern flickers drilling a nesting hole. The male flicker may also beat out a resounding tattoo upon the gutter during the nesting season. Although more confident than formerly, the flicker is still a bit wild when compared to such other members of its family as the downy, hairy, red-headed or red-bellied woodpeckers.

The once wary blue jay has progressed much farther in its metamorphosis. Early in this century it was a suspicious and wild bird in much the same way that the crow was. Slowly the blue jay began to move into towns and cities and began to accept trees in yards for its nest sites. It did this first in the South, but by the 1920s the blue jay was well established as a yard bird almost everywhere. It seems questionable if the common crow will overcome its suspicion to the extent that the blue jay has. Too many centuries of persecution by man are behind its wariness. Nevertheless, the crow is seen in yards much more often than before and sometimes is a nuisance at feeding stations. It may yet take to nesting in close proximity to homes.

The American robin is so much of a yard bird that we tend to forget that many nest in the wild as well. It has taken the robin many decades to overcome a basic suspicion of man, and the process is still not completed. Nevertheless, the robin is one bird that seems perfectly at home when nesting close to houses. The wood thrush has taken much longer to adapt to such surroundings. But since 1950 wood thrushes have taken to nesting in yards in much the same manner as robins.

The movement to well-planted yards continues apace. Many species, like the house wren, Carolina wren, gray catbird, northern oriole, cardinal, chipping sparrow, and song sparrow have made their abodes in our yards ever since people have been keeping records. Other species are only now getting established. These changes in birds' habits are all part of the taming process which has been going on since the early days of bird attracting and in which bird feeding has played an important part.

FIELD-FORAGING BIRDS COMING NEAR HOMES

The appearance of crows, blackbirds, and, in the West, magpies in yards and close to homes is not to the liking of everyone, but it was an expected event in view of the taming process that has reached so many segments of our bird population. As early

as 1920 and before, field-foraging birds had begun to appear about homes. But not
until about 1950 had large flocks of them become a common sight on our lawns.

The red-winged blackbirds, common grackles, and brown-headed cowbirds that
appear in large numbers, especially in the fall, are mainly in search of acorns, insects,
and other natural foods. The flocks descend briefly like a swarm of locusts and are
then gone. If the flock has found our feeding stations, gone too is most of the food.
The common crow fortunately appears in only small numbers. Seldom will we see
more than ten or fifteen at one time.

In many parts of the East, field-foraging birds have found feeding stations to
be a handy substitute for the food they used to find in grain fields. Now that so much
agricultural land is disappearing before developers or reverting back to forests, there
is beginning to be a dearth of the kinds of food that appeal most to crows and
blackbirds. This is particularly true in New England and adjacent New York State,
where so much of the agricultural economy has disappeared. In this part of the East,
necessity as much as tameness has brought crows and other dark-colored birds to our
doorsteps.

BIRDS THAT VISIT FEEDING STATIONS

Along with the increased number of feeding stations and growing popularity of bird feeding, there has been a corresponding increase in both numbers and species of birds that take advantage of our food supplies. Fifty-five species were recorded at feeding stations in the East during the years prior to 1910.* Since then the number coming to feeding stations in this same region has more than doubled. My list, which like the earlier ones does not include water birds, strays from the West, or escaped cage birds, contains one hundred twenty species. Therefore sixty-five species have taken up feeding station habits since the first decade of this century for an average of about one a year. Not all of these one hundred twenty species are well adapted to feeding stations. Many are casual visitors that we rarely see and others are only beginning to take up feeding station habits.

Including both casual and regular visitors to feeders, we have before us a broad segment of the birdlife of eastern North America. Hawks and owls are visitors along with such familiar guests as chickadees, titmice, and nuthatches (complete list on pages 276–8). Any one feeding station plays host to only a third or fourth of this total, and this much variety is usually achieved only after recording every visitor seen during several years of bird feeding.

Besides the species we normally expect through the year, we may play hosts to strays—that is, birds that have wandered in from great distances. Fall and winter are seasons to expect strays from the West. Over twenty western species are occasional visitors to feeding stations in the East (pages 279–80).

*Gilbert H. Trafton, *Methods of Attracting Birds*, Boston, Houghton Mifflin, 1910.

116

*Birds
That
Visit
Feeding
Stations*

As though we did not already have enough in the way of variety, feeding stations, especially in cities, are sometimes visited by escaped cage birds. A number of these colorful foreigners have now become established and therefore are much in evidence. This is particularly true in cities of south Florida. Exotics to look for at feeders range from newly introduced game birds to parakeets and mynas (pages 281–3).

If you wish for still more variety in your bird feeding, all you have to do is take food to city park ponds and other water areas where birds are fed. Almost always there will be a clamoring throng of domestic geese and ducks that practically trample you in their uninhibited importuning for food. During the winter you will be greeted by such visitors as coot, Canada goose, mallard, and herring gull. At the seashore gulls, always hungry and adept at catching food in midair, will be very much in evidence. Two shore birds that are winter visitors along our coasts have also learned the art of asking for handouts. The sanderling and ruddy turnstone have tastes that run to meat scraps, fishing bait, bread, and popcorn.

Wherever you go, the best food to gain attention will always be white bread. Take along enough bread to get the banquet started and then offer something more substantial. After all everyone else has been offering bread. For waterfowl there is nothing that is more universally appreciated than corn and other cereal grains. Gulls disdain grain but respond readily to fish, meat scraps, bakery products, and almost any kitchen leftovers.

So long as we give birds time to get used to our offerings, they will respond and begin to recognize us as the providers. When away from home, we should try to accustom birds to receiving food at certain times and places. Birds are creatures of habit, much as we are, and respond much better if we establish regular feeding routines.

If food seems to be greatly emphasized in the species biographies that follow and elsewhere in this book, there is good reason. Food is the drawing card that brings birds to us. Much of the success in bird feeding lies in taking pains to choose the right food or combination of foods. Not everything sold as bird food will do. Only through testing many foods at our feeders can we arrive at the foods that best suit us and our clientele. And since food needs change with the seasons, the menu should never become too fixed. Also, we may suddenly find ourselves hosts to unexpected guests with special food needs.

117

Birds
That
Visit
Feeding
Stations

Foods listed after each species in the biographies that follow are ones that the species in question normally utilize. However, individual birds sometimes vary widely in their reactions to food. The food that is accepted by a northern oriole one winter in Massachusetts may not appeal at all to a bird of this species the same winter in South Carolina. If the first two or three foods tried do not meet with a bird's approval, do not give up. There is always another food to try. Sometimes the best food for an unexpected guest is one that other birds will not eat. In this way there will be fewer problems from competition. Food is something we have to keep experimenting with.

Feeders are also important. They serve a purpose in distributing food at different elevations and in different ways so that birds will separate themselves according to where they normally feed. The best rule is to use a variety of feeders, space them widely, and offer food on the ground. By doing this, you make for less congestion and better opportunity for all visitors to have a chance.

Feeders have decorative value and usefulness in bringing birds within full scope of our vision. Also feeders save on the food bill. Food in suitably constructed feeders is protected from the weather, and many times from the ravenous appetites of squirrels and large eaters among our bird guests. Covered feeders give birds protection from the elements. This is important where wind, rain, or snow may interfere with feeding activities.

Then there is the problem of when to expect certain species at our feeders. Very often the information we obtain in bird books does not agree with what we see at our feeders. A number of species are in the process of changing their habits. Some of the changes are occurring very rapidly. The northern oriole, for example, is now probably more common at feeding stations in winter than in summer. A great deal of ornithological history is being made at feeding stations and some of it is occurring because birds are being fed and therefore are better able to withstand northern winters.

After getting a feeding program established, our next goal should be to learn more about our visitors. Not only do we want to know what they eat and what they are doing when we have them in view, but we are also curious to know what they are doing when out of our sight and hearing. In the biographies that follow occasional reference will be made to activities other than those that take place near or at the feeding station. Birds always seem to be busy about something and much of the fun is in finding out how they pass their time.

Eighty species out of one hundred twenty that visit feeding stations in the East have been selected for special treatment in the sections that follow. Not all of these eighty are common visitors or even ones that most of us are likely to see at our feeders. Several, like the pileated woodpecker and meadowlark, have only recently taken up feeding station habits. Others, like the gray jay, boreal chickadee, most of the northern finches, and the snow bunting, we can expect only during some winters and generally only in more northern states. Other species, like the downy woodpecker, blue jay, and cardinal are wide ranging and can be expected at feeding stations almost everywhere in the East.

Every species has habitat preferences. Where you live and the type of plantings you have in your yard determine to a large degree the kind of birds that you will have at your feeders. Much depends upon whether you live in city, crowded suburb, wooded residential area, wooded countryside, or open farming country.* Luckily, some birds are not overly choosy and will visit you wherever you happen to live.

---

*Readers should consult Thomas P. McElroy's *The Habitat Guide to Birding*, New York, Alfred A. Knopf, 1974, for information on the kind of habitats to visit for any particular species.

SPARROWS AND FINCHES

In treating sparrows and finches, I have followed the older classification, which placed them in the same family with buntings and grosbeaks. This group is well represented at feeding stations. Of the over seventy species found within our borders, at least three-fourths of them find their way to feeding stations. In the East we can count upon twenty-five members of this group. Some are old standbys like the cardinal, junco, and white-throated sparrow. Others are invasion species that appear only in years when shortage of food or other conditions compel northern finches to come southward. Still others like the dickcissel and blue grosbeak are chance visitors that may happen by if we are lucky. The distinguishing characteristic of members of this group is a short, heavy conical beak, which is ideally suited for cracking open seeds. The conical beak is developed to almost grotesque proportions in the evening grosbeak. Other grosbeaks, including the cardinal, have the same heavy beak structure but their beaks are not quite so large. Juncos, sparrows, and goldfinches, on the other hand, have relatively much smaller conical beaks. This does not prevent many of these birds from opening sunflower seeds. The most bizarre beaks of all belong to the crossbills. The overlapping scissors-like beaks of these northern birds are ideally suited for extracting seeds from pine cones. Their crossed beaks are not a handicap when used upon sunflower seeds.

Members of this group are not exclusively seed-eaters. Finches take readily to insects during the summer and most species begin feeding their young on an insect diet. At feeding stations finches show varied tastes and can be attracted to much the

120

*Birds
That
Visit
Feeding
Stations*

same fare that appeals to woodpeckers and titmice. Some finches have unconventional tastes such as the liking for salt shown by northern finches.

The finches contribute more than any other family to the numbers and variety seen at feeders. Some are among the most colorful of our visitors, others are the plainest. All are highly welcome guests that rarely give us any cause for complaint.

CARDINAL

This is one of the best-known feeding station visitors and also one of the easiest to recognize. Everyone knows the brilliant red male cardinal with its crest and black face. The female is only a little less vivid, but more a yellow-brown than red. A southern bird, which in Audubon's day was rare as far north as Philadelphia, the cardinal has unceasingly pushed northward. Within the last few decades cardinals have become common in middle New England. Range expansion in southern Canada has been equally spectacular. Ability to adapt to a variety of habitats, and especially to advantages offered by man, is a prime factor in the cardinal's success.

Expansion northward has largely been made possible by the availability of food at feeding stations. Few birds respond more readily. Throughout the South the cardinal is usually the first bird that comes to food offerings; in the North it is much shyer, taking food on the ground, as a rule, instead of coming to windowsills or bird

Conical beaks of seed eaters:

cardinal

red crossbill

pine grosbeak

junco

goldfinch

tables. In any event, we no longer think of the cardinal as a strictly southern bird. The bright red of the cardinal is now a familiar sight at feeding stations throughout the East. It is *the* bird more than any other that has come to symbolize bird feeding.

Cardinals sometimes strike us as cantankerous birds. This is the impression we get when we see one or two males trying to keep all the others from a feeding tray. This kind of jockeying for position is commonplace among the finches and should not be taken too seriously. Sooner or later every bird gets its turn. Even the despotic male cardinal that won't let his mate eat with him all winter eventually relents. With the return of spring weather, he begins to regard his mate in a new light. Instead of chasing her from the feeding tray, he now begins to offer her shucked sunflower seeds and other choice tidbits. When he brings these offerings, she crouches appreciatively with her beak open and wings vibrating. Her posture and actions are exactly the same as those of young birds begging food from parents. A pair that are in residence continue to come to feeders through the summer. Brood after brood of young are brought to feeders and taught how to feed themselves. Cardinals sometimes rear as many as four broods during a nesting season.

The cardinal is one of the earliest birds to arrive at feeders in the morning and one of the last to remain at dusk. In winter birds sometimes feed so late that we have difficulty distinguishing them. Thanks to these extra early and late feeding sessions, cardinals do not seem compelled to eat as long or as intensively as visitors that confine their feeding to the bright hours of daylight. As a result, cardinals seem to have

*Cardinals never tire of
sunflower seeds and scratch feed.*

122

*Birds
That
Visit
Feeding
Stations*

more time for other activities. Even in midwinter cardinals take time out for song.Sometimes we hear a male begin a song and some distance away his mate will complete it. These duets, known as antiphonal singing, are heard more and more often with the approach of the mating season. Cardinals also do a fair amount of traveling during the non-breeding season. The flock that comes to our feeders may spend part of the day searching hedgerows and field borders where favorite natural foods grow. Verne E. Davison,[*] in noting that cardinals are as a rule absent from feeders in the South for a period of three to six weeks in the fall, states that the birds at this time are busily searching for pine seeds. Pine mast is so well liked by cardinals that in the fall it offers serious competition to feeding station fare in many parts of the country.

The ground seems to be the preferred feeding place of the cardinal. However, to protect food from the weather and also give birds protection, sheltered raised feeders provide a distinct advantage. This is particularly true in the North, where heavy snowfalls are often a problem. As a rule, cardinals are not slow about coming to bird tables, trays on posts, window trays, and hanging feeders with perches. Now and then they also visit hummingbird feeders.

We sometimes get the impression that all cardinals need or will eat is sunflower and cracked corn. This is far from true, as cardinals will eat almost everything offered at the feeding station. That there is a wide taste range in cardinals has been demonstrated in tests conducted by Verne E. Davison. Besides sunflower, scratch feed, corn, and wheat, we can offer cardinals suet, suet mixtures, sorghum, barley, millet, peanuts, peanut hearts, nutmeats of all kinds, melon seeds, raisins, banana, cornbread, and white bread.

ROSE-BREASTED GROSBEAK

Lucky indeed are those who have this appealing bird at their feeders. From Pennsylvania and Nebraska northward, the rose-breasted grosbeak is an uncommon summer resident that we are more likely to hear than see. The brightly colored male and his more subdued mate have a way of staying out of sight. Food is the one way to get to know this bird. If you have not discontinued your bird feeding, you may have a

[*] *Attracting Birds From the Prairies to the Atlantic*, New York, Thomas Y. Crowell, 1967.

chance visit by one of these birds along about late May or June. Once onto food supplies, rose-breasted grosbeaks become surprisingly tame and can be taught to eat from the hand. In my experience the male tames more quickly than the female. Sometimes we are lucky enough to have three or four pairs at our feeders. With this many pairs, there is almost a mob when later on the young join their parents at feeders. We begin to see the offspring along about late June or July. Beginning with the winter of 1972–1973, a few rose-breasted grosbeaks have been seen at feeders during the winter.

The two feeding station foods most popular with the rose-breasted grosbeak are sunflower and peanut hearts. This grosbeak also takes suet, scratch feed, millet, canary seed, raisins, and melon seed. As to feeders, the preference seems to be for trays at first- and second-story windows. This bird also comes to bird tables, suet holders, hanging feeders with perches, hanging logs, and occasionally hummingbird feeders.

BLUE GROSBEAK

The vision of a nearly all-blue bird with a heavy "grosbeak" beak materializes when we see the male of this species. The female, on the other hand, is a drab bird that is sometimes mistaken for a female cowbird. We look for blue grosbeaks in summer throughout the southern states and as far north as Nebraska, Illinois, and New Jersey. This species has shown a modest tendency to extend its range northward. A few individuals have a way of appearing north of the breeding range in spring and again in early fall. Beginning with the winter of 1972–1973, blue grosbeaks, like so many other tropical migrants, began to show up in some numbers in this country in winter. Feeding stations seem to have been a factor both in making us aware of birds such as this one in winter and in supplying food needed for survival. Although May through August is the season when this vivid bird is chiefly with us, there is now a chance of finding it at almost any season.

Our expectations are sometimes dashed when the blue grosbeak that appears in our yard in late spring moves on after a short stay. Usually such guests are migrants. A male that visited an improvised feeding station of mine on the Texas coast in late May stayed only four days. The first two days the bird was constantly about and fed

124

*Birds
That
Visit
Feeding
Stations*

at length at the feeder, which it shared with house sparrows. The next two days its visits were much less frequent.

Blue grosbeaks have made appearances in fall at feeding stations, particularly ones near the coast in New York and New England. Birds this far north seem to be misguided stragglers. Foods taken at feeders include sunflower, scratch feed, sorghum, peanut hearts, and pecan meats. Many times food is taken almost exclusively on the ground. Occasionally, however, these birds feed at bird tables, trays on posts, or window trays.

INDIGO BUNTING

This is the most likely all-blue seed-eater at feeding stations. A smaller edition of the blue grosbeak, the indigo bunting can be told by its size and much smaller bill. The female indigo bunting is an unexciting brownish bird that is hard to place unless the male is nearby. We look for these small buntings from about late April on. The males, which arrive first, may sometimes be seen flocking over lawns. It is an indescribable sight when male indigo buntings join evening grosbeaks and cardinals at feeders. This is a combination occasionally seen at a few privileged feeders in the Northeast.

Most indigo buntings retire to the tropics for the winter. But beginning around 1960, sizable numbers have been observed in Florida in winter. Winter flocks of up to sixty birds have been seen at single feeders in Sarasota and other nearby Florida west-coast communities. It is a colorful sight when these flocks appear at feeding stations at the same time as painted buntings. The two species get along well together. Formerly the indigo bunting was unheard of in winter in more northern states. Now such an appearance is not so unlikely. The indigo bunting can be included on the growing list of tropical migrants that do not always journey southward. Many now stay behind in Florida, while an occasional bird may appear in winter at feeding stations in more northern states.

The most likely time for indigo buntings to visit feeding stations is during spring migration and again in the fall as birds start southward. The early spring flocks that consist entirely of males are one of the sights we look forward to each spring. These flocks are an annual occurrence at a number of well-favored feeding

stations in coastal regions of New England. After nesting gets underway, indigo
buntings tend to drift away from the vicinity of human habitations and therefore at
this season are much less common at feeders.

Food preference of the indigo bunting runs heavily toward millet; other foods
taken include canary seed, peanut hearts, pecan meats, and, in the tropics, banana.
Most of the time the indigo bunting seems to feed on the ground, but it is versatile
enough to take food at bird tables, trays, and hanging feeders.

PAINTED BUNTING

There are several dominantly blue or red birds that visit feeding stations, but only
one of these visitors has a combination of colors that includes both red and blue. The
male painted bunting is a red and blue bird with a golden-green back. The female
is so nondescript that we would be completely baffled by her plain green if the male
were not nearby.

The time and place to look for painted buntings to best advantage is from late
fall until late spring along both coasts of Florida. There are many feeding stations,
particularly in more southern coastal communities, that play host to large numbers
of these birds and often to many bird watchers as well who come to see them. One
requirement is plenty of dense foliage where birds can retire after feeding. The
sprawling, introduced Brazilian pepperbush, found so widely in South Florida, serves
this need very well.

Still another productive area for the painted bunting in the East is the coastal
region of Georgia and the Carolinas. Here the painted bunting is a summer resident
and extremely rare or absent the rest of the year. Feeding stations in this area begin
to be patronized by adult painted buntings in May and June. After young leave the
nest, they, too, frequently join parents at feeders. The occasional appearances of
painted buntings during the fall in states still farther to the north may be related to
storms sweeping up from the south. Almost annually, painted buntings are reported
in coastal states as far north as New England and are usually seen at feeding stations.
These occasional stragglers create a lot of interest and nearly always end up being
well photographed!

Once this small bunting starts coming to a feeder, it is a persistent visitor and

126

*Birds
That
Visit
Feeding
Stations*

sometimes seems to rely too much upon whatever we have to offer. In this respect, the painted bunting is similar to the house sparrow, a bird that we should hardly mention in the same breath with it. The freeloading tactics of the house sparrow and the frequency with which it visits our feeders do offer parallels, however. Another characteristic is that once painted buntings find a feeding station, they come back year after year. There are feeding stations in Florida that have been patronized steadily every winter for over thirty years by painted buntings.

Although in winter a good-natured bird, the painted bunting may become extremely quarrelsome during the mating season. Alexander Sprunt, Jr., in his account of the painted bunting in the Bent series, tells of battles that are "frequently bloody and often fatal." Such battles are part of a fierce rivalry seen between males in late spring and early summer. If males are coming to the same feeder at this season, there are either frequent battles or the birds learn to time their visits in order to avoid confrontations. At a South Carolina feeding station, if the same two males happened to arrive at about the same time, one would linger in bushes some distance away while the other fed. As soon as the first bird had finished its meal and departed, the second would take its place at the feeder. Painted buntings at this feeder were intolerant of birds of other species and harassed the much larger cardinals.

The painted bunting is partial to elevated feeders such as bird tables, trays on posts, and window trays and accommodates itself well to small hanging feeders. It sometimes feeds on the ground. Like the indigo bunting, the smaller painted bunting likes nothing better than millet. Other foods that are well received are sunflower, suet, scratch feed, canary seed, rape, peanut hearts, and bread crumbs.

DICKCISSEL

The recent adaptation of the northern oriole to northern winters and feeding stations has a close parallel in similar behavior by the dickcissel, also a migrant to the American tropics. Around 1936 it was first noted that a few dickcissels were beginning to stop off in New England states to pass the winter instead of flying on to the tropics. This trend has continued and presently dickcissels, like northern orioles, can be found in winter throughout most of the eastern states.

That dickcissels reach the Atlantic coast in early fall, after making a roundabout trip from a breeding range in the Mississippi valley and westward, has been a matter of interest to ornithologists during recent years. Now this small grasslands finch is seen more and more in winter and nearly always associated with flocks of birds coming to feeding stations. Numbers of dickcissels at any one feeding station vary from one to five or six. Their closest associate at feeding stations is the house sparrow. In fact, the dickcissel becomes such an integral part of the house sparrow flock that we have difficulty separating the two species. Our only clues with female and immature dickcissels are yellow on the breast and a somewhat trimmer appearance.

The dickcissel flies off in the same abrupt way as the house sparrow and usually at the same instant that the house sparrows depart. If anything, the dickcissel is a little more timid than its companions and slower about returning to the feeder after it has made a hasty departure. The striking feature of these mixed flocks is the perfect way that the dickcissel becomes integrated. It goes everywhere with the house sparrow flock, eats the same foods, and dines at the same times.

By mid-April the last lingering dickcissel has normally departed for the breeding range. In Atlantic coastal states we see no more of this bird, as a rule, until late summer. During their fall appearances dickcissels accept the same foods and feeding stations as house sparrows. They are generally seen at bird tables or on the ground, but make infrequent visits to hanging feeders. Their tastes run to sunflower, scratch feed, wheat, oats, sorghum, and millet.

EVENING GROSBEAK

There is wide misunderstanding concerning the history of this bird at feeding stations. Many consider it a comparative newcomer and tend to regard its appearance as a novelty. While the evening grosbeak does surprise us by its numbers and the way it is forever expanding its range, it is not a recent visitor by any means. In his *Life Histories*, A. C. Bent reported that winter invasions of this bird in northeastern states go back to 1890 and that even as early as this, there were reports of visits to feeding stations. Therefore the evening grosbeak was on hand during the earliest days of bird feeding.

Prior to 1890 the evening grosbeak was a little-known bird of the northern wilderness. The first specimen known to science was a bird shot with a bow and

128

*Birds
That
Visit
Feeding
Stations*

arrow by an Indian boy in 1823, which came into the hands of Henry R. Schoolcraft of Sault Sainte Marie, Michigan. The fact that this bird began to be seen in winter in New England states after 1890 suggests a shift in population together with a population increase that occurred about this time. Since the appearance of the evening grosbeak in New England, there has been an enormous population increase and range expansion. The breeding range has moved both eastward and south. In recent years the evening grosbeak has appeared as a nesting bird in many parts of the Northeast, where formerly unknown during the summer. Recent pioneers sometimes visit feeding stations together with the young that have left the nest.

The most spectacular feature of the evening grosbeak's rise to prominence has been its winter invasions southward. It began to be taken for granted that the evening grosbeak, after reaching Virginia and the Carolinas in 1951, would continue to appear ever farther southward during some winters. For a while this proved to be true. During some winters, the grosbeaks reached northern Florida and the Gulf coast. But as of this writing (1992), there hasn't been a large-scale invasion southward in the East since 1984.

When evening grosbeaks do appear far south on their invasions, there is usually no dearth of birds in the north either. During some winters the evening grosbeak is found at feeding stations all the way from the Great Lakes and Maine to the Gulf coast. If there is a scarcity of evening grosbeaks anywhere during such years, it is within the vast northern wilderness that comprises the breeding range.

Part of the evening grosbeak's glamour is in its appearance. The huge parrot-like beak, and, especially in the more vivid male, the contrast of yellow, black, and white, make this a startling bird and one that surprises us because we do not expect such color in a far northern bird. The other part of our interest lies in this grosbeak's habits. Because of its tameness and habit of appearing at feeding stations in large numbers, the evening grosbeak is a species that lends itself well to study. Thousands are banded each year and a great deal has been learned about movements and habits.

Much of the information that has been obtained about the evening grosbeak comes from detailed observations made at feeding stations. I am indebted to John K. Terres for providing me with a letter from a Canada correspondent who tells of her experiences with evening grosbeaks during the winter months in a suburb of Quebec. As far north as Quebec, according to Mrs. Owen Carter, the evening grosbeak does not desert feeding stations during the later hours of the day; rather, birds feed pretty much continuously. This observation is in contrast to the experience of observers in this country who generally note that evening grosbeaks stay at feeders during the morning but desert them soon after noon. But there is a tendency for birds to feed later and later in the day as the season progresses.

Mrs. Carter noted that on cloudy days the flock that comes to her feeders may take out an hour between feedings to go to roost in nearby trees. On bright days there are often gatherings on rooftops exposed to sunshine. Here birds spread their wings and sun bathe. Also they drink some of the water that accumulates from melting snow. There is less dependence upon feeding stations on warmer sunny days. Birds vary their diet by feasting on fruits of highbush cranberry and flowering crabapple. Another activity in good weather is to fly "for the sheer joy of it." Flocks on such days make the rounds of other feeding stations and seek out fruiting trees and shrubs through a wide part of the suburb.

On very cold days, when the temperature falls to somewhere between five and thirty degrees below zero, the evening grosbeaks do not depart at all from the immediate vicinity of the bird feeder. Birds arrive when it is not yet daylight and continue feeding with little respite until shortly after darkness has set in. The amounts of sunflower seeds that are consumed on such days are prodigious.

During the large-scale invasions southward, evening grosbeaks seem only partially dependent upon feeding station fare and in many instances scorn it altogether. Birds accept a wide variety of natural plant foods and these often seem in sufficient supply to sustain them. Evening grosbeaks, in contrast to other birds, frequently reject the fleshy parts of cherries and other fruits and eat only the kernel that lies inside the pit. The huge bill is an effective tool for reaching such fare. Other favorite foods are the seeds of the widely planted box elder and those of other maples and the ashes.

Grit is an essential ingredient in the diet, and evening grosbeaks spend much time during northern winters in foraging for small pebbles and other grit on open ground that has been cleared of snow. Ash heaps are also an attraction for the small cinders and pieces of charcoal they yield. In much the same way, these birds seek out salt. Large flocks at times descend to highways and their edges where salt has been used to melt snow and ice. Mortality is sometimes heavy when birds fail to get out of the way of onrushing vehicles. We can assist by mixing salt and ashes and stirring them into a pail of water. Pour the solution at intervals over a block of wood or a

130

*Birds
That
Visit
Feeding
Stations*

rotting stump. The crystals that form will provide a much safer source of mineral matter for this grosbeak and other northern finches.

When large flocks of evening grosbeaks are present, it is advisable to scatter food widely—on the ground, on bird tables, and at first- and second-story window feeders. When there is adequate elbow room, evening grosbeaks feed much more peacefully among themselves and at the same time are not so likely to disrupt the feeding activity of other birds. Although they will feed almost anywhere, higher feeders seem most appreciated and particularly ones at second-story windows. While showing a preference for bird tables and trays, including second-story-window trays, the evening grosbeak has the ability to master many small hanging feeders, including the Droll Yankee. The main requirement is that sunflower be present. The ground is also readily accepted as a feeding place.

Sunflower is standard fare for evening grosbeaks. They will take vast amounts if we let them. As a rule, these birds will leave a feeding station as soon as the supply of sunflower seeds becomes exhausted. No other food approaches this one in appeal. Among the few that occasionally serve as substitutes are suet, safflower, peanut hearts, peanuts, pecan meats, wheat, sorghum, millet, melon seeds, and apple seeds.

In summary, these are the common habits of the evening grosbeak:

1. Visits by one or two individuals, usually females, precede the appearance of a flock at a feeding station. Birds may arrive at feeding stations in more

*Evening grosbeaks
are beautiful
but cantankerous.*

northern states in October, but over most of the East arrivals are as late as December or January.

2. Birds are more likely to appear at feeding stations in towns and cities than at feeders in rural districts.

3. There is much visiting back and forth between feeders in a given neighborhood. Early flocks are likely to move on and are sometimes replaced by flocks coming in from somewhere else. Exchanges in makeup of flocks are likely to go on all winter.

4. It is rarely possible to estimate the number visiting a feeder by counting birds present at any one time. Since other flocks may arrive off and on through the day, the total number attending may be much greater than we think.

5. From the time of arrival to early spring, birds restrict their feeding station visits almost entirely to morning hours. The last month or two of the stay visits are extended later and later into the afternoon so that by May it is not unusual to see some birds eating as late as 5:00 p.m. As far north as Quebec these changes are not apparent. From the first, birds tend to stay at feeders throughout much of the day.

6. Shoving, pecking, and tugging are routine in a flock of feeding evening grosbeaks. Birds seem little inconvenienced by this. But under densely crowded conditions, irritability grows and fighting becomes more intense.

7. Birds are relatively tame so far as people are concerned. A flock will feed unconcernedly when we watch from the other side of the window only inches away. Birds take alarm at sudden noises and become jittery for days at a time if the feeding area is visited by a small bird-hawk or shrike.

8. Evening grosbeaks are not wholly dependent upon our food supplies and many times pass them up in favor of natural foods.

9. The final departure of the last of the evening grosbeaks from our feeders in spring can be as late as the end of May or early June.

10. Evening grosbeaks make frequent use of bird baths for drinking; however, it is exceptional to see one bathing.

Not so long ago this was *the* northern finch that was most likely to be seen in winter at feeding stations. This all changed a few years ago when the evening grosbeak began coming south in ever greater numbers. Not only has the purple finch been overshadowed by its larger, more colorful relative, but the house finch, a close relative from the West, has suddenly exploded into prominence. Within a radius of one hundred miles of New York City, the house finch is now the more expected of the two birds.

This is not to say that the purple finch is losing out to competition. It is still a common bird and most winters it appears as far south as northern Florida and the Gulf states. It is also a summer resident in northern states. From Pennsylvania, West Virginia, and Ohio northward the purple finch is a common breeding bird that favors us with its song and frequent visits to feeding stations.

Like the evening grosbeak, the purple finch eats prodigious amounts of sunflower seeds. Seeds are picked up and opened one at a time. Each seed is maneuvered by the tongue into position between the cutting edges of the upper and lower mandibles. The grinding action of the two mandibles causes the hull to split open. The bird is left with the edible kernel, which is quickly consumed. Sometimes birds will feed steadily for as long as half an hour. Allowing five seconds per sunflower seed, a bird feeding for half an hour would consume three hundred and sixty seeds.

When occupied in eating, birds are quiet, with little moving about. Except for occasional hot-tempered arguments, the purple finch is one of our more mild-mannered guests. Alfred G. Martin tells of bitter duels he has seen at his feeders. He has sometimes seen two birds go straight up in the air to a height of 30 feet and then, still locked together, fall to the snow where the struggle is continued. Tempers seem shortest when there is not enough food to go around. To keep our flock feeding peacefully we should be good providers.

Unlike a good many of our visitors, purple finches do all of their eating at the feeding trays. There is no carrying away of food to eat elsewhere. If there is any preference for a place to feed, it is a second-story-window shelf. Purple finches accommodate themselves to most feeding devices. Larger trays and bird tables seem best suited to their needs. In addition, purple finches have adapted well to the newer hanging feeders. The Droll Yankee is within their abilities, as are other small hanging feeders. Purple finches also come to food on the ground and sometimes to hummingbird feeders.

Not nearly as limited in its tastes as the evening grosbeak, the purple finch will go on to other foods after exhausting the sunflower supply. It will accept suet, suet mixtures, sunflower, safflower, scratch feed, canary seed, millet, thistle, buckwheat, flax, rape, peanut hearts, pecan meats, and melon seeds.

HOUSE FINCH

A comparative newcomer to the East, the house finch is now one of our most widespread native birds. It is now present in southern Canada, Hawaii, and all of our lower states. The eastern population started with the release of a few birds on Long Island in 1941. This population has spread so rapidly that it is expected to link up with the western population by about 1995. Help from feeding stations and the ability to occupy the same niche as the house sparrow contribute to the house finch's outstanding success.

Wherever this newcomer has appeared, it has taken readily to feeding stations. Frequently mistaken for its close relative the purple finch, this successful small finch is usually given a warm welcome. Sometimes, however, it seems too much of an opportunist. The way it adapts so easily to urban life makes us compare it sometimes to another successful import, the house sparrow. The two species do seem to have much in common. Luckily the house finch is not so aggressive and has a pleasing song and colorful attire. Whether the house finch will be a good citizen remains to be seen. In the West the house finch displays a weakness for soft fruits—a taste that has often brought it into conflict with agriculturalists.

Whatever food tastes the house finch may develop in the East, we know that it exhibits an astonishingly omnivorous appetite when at western feeders. Equally at home on the ground, at bird tables, and at hanging feeders, the house finch tries a little of everything at western feeders and is not particular as to whether it is seeds, grain, fruits, or kitchen scraps. The long list of foods that are taken in the West includes sunflower, suet, suet mixtures, peanut butter, peanut hearts, nutmeats, scratch feed, rape, millet, canary seed, thistle, raisins, dates, grapes, apple, orange, peach, plum, apricot, fig, loquat, watermelon, banana, doughnuts, and white bread.

134

Birds
That
Visit
Feeding
Stations

In the East the house finch seems to limit itself at feeders largely to seeds and grain, with sunflower and thistle being favored above everything else. Like the purple finch, the house finch has adapted to newer hanging feeders. It frequently feeds at length at Droll Yankee feeders or thistle bags and is also at home on bird tables, trays on posts, window trays, and the ground. It takes readily to hummingbird feeders.

PINE GROSBEAK

Each of the northern finches is a distinctly different bird. Many are seen rarely if at all, and therefore we have only a vague impression as to habits and appearance. To those of us who live south of the Canadian border, the pine grosbeak is as little known as are the crossbills and as much a mystery as any of our northern visitors. Those who have been fortunate enough to have the pine grosbeak at their feeders are impressed by its beauty and tameness. Ernest Harold Baynes* writes of being able to sit down in the middle of a flock and have the birds feeding in his lap. Birds awaiting their turn perched on his head and shoulders. The most extraordinary part of this experience, according to Baynes, was being able to pick up a bird in each hand.

Others who have been visited by pine grosbeaks call them dull-witted or dumb. They point to this bird's characteristic slowness to catch on to our food supplies. Probably it would be more appropriate to blame the pine grosbeak's slowness on its self-sufficiency. When it can find ample supplies of natural foods, it has no need or taste for our fare. Only when there are failures of food crops in the North does the pine grosbeak come southward in winter. During occasional winters this bird reaches Maryland, Virginia, and Kentucky.

One way to get the pine grosbeak's attention is to offer foods that it comes to in the wild. Donald J. Lennox of Whitefield, New Hampshire, lures pine grosbeaks to his feeders with bunches of mountain ash berries, fruits of highbush cranberry, samaras of ash and maple, and sliced apple. Even with offerings such as these, the grosbeaks do not normally come to his feeders until after natural supplies have become depleted. Other foods known to attract the pine grosbeak are sunflower, flax in the

*Wild Bird Guests, New York, E. P. Dutton, 1915.

head, hemp, and cranberries. Feeders must be out in the open to get very much attention from the pine grosbeak. Preference is for bird tables or food on open ground.

COMMON REDPOLL

This heavily streaked subarctic finch with its red cap and black chin is little known at feeding stations except during rare invasions. There are winters, however, when this small finch is seen as far south as Virginia, the Carolinas, southern Ohio, and Kansas. For the most part, invasion flocks rely upon natural foods. But when drawn to feeding stations by the example of other birds, redpolls reveal a keen appetite for many of our foods and a remarkable tameness. Those of us who live south of New England will be lucky if we see this species one year in eight or ten.

During the course of a winter in Massachusetts, I became intimately acquainted with this engaging little finch through a flock that came to my feeding stations. I first became aware of their presence in late February. As many as three hundred were feeding in a weed field near the house. Here the flock moved restlessly from place to place, feeding for a time by clinging to weed stalks and then moving on as though impelled by an innate rhythm. When the signal came for an abrupt departure, the whole flock immediately responded; in contrast, when the flock later found my

*Redpolls feeding
at trolley feeder.*

136

Birds
That
Visit
Feeding
Stations

feeders, there was a breakdown in discipline. Individuals no longer under the control of a common will stayed at the feeders as long as they pleased.

During the month that the redpolls were in attendance, I became well acquainted with the tameness that is so characteristic of this species. In collecting birds into a gathering cage prior to banding them, I noted that many still free sought to enter the banding traps. Some of the outsiders would peck through the mesh of the gathering cage at the birds imprisoned within. Individuals would often feed calmly within the trap while every effort was being made to scare them into leaving through the exit. Another bird bander, Mrs. Kenneth B. Wetherbee, actually captured redpolls by hand at her window feeder.

Alfred G. Martin, with a lifetime of experience feeding birds in Maine, answered without hesitation when I asked him which was the tamest bird he knew. His reply was the redpoll. As far north as Mr. Martin's home near Bangor, Maine, the redpoll is seen only one year out of every four or five.

Redpolls are adept at clinging to suet holders and hanging feeders. They do very nicely on the ground or on bird tables and window shelves. Sunflower is a favorite food, but the redpoll seems to be one of the few members of the finch family that is unable to cope with the outside hull. Redpolls sometimes get their share by gleaning tidbits left by other birds. Foods that are to the redpoll's liking include sunflower, suet, suet mixtures, canary seed, flax in the head, thistle, and white bread.

PINE SISKIN

Of the smaller northern finches, this is the one that is most often expected at feeding stations and it is also the greatest traveler. During occasional winters the pine siskin travels as far south as southern Florida and the Gulf coast. It shares the redpoll's tameness and in addition has a bellicose nature that is surprising for such a small bird. Pine siskins are only 4¼ inches in length.

A flock of pine siskins at a North Carolina feeding station took to pursuing house sparrows whenever any made an appearance. The hostess to this siskin flock reported without misgivings that the house sparrows became so thoroughly intimidated that they ceased coming altogether. They did not reappear until several days after the last pine siskins had departed in the spring. Part of the reason for the pine siskin's success is a threat display that is similar to the performances of the white-breasted nuthatch. The tail is spread and at the same time the wings are elevated revealing conspicuous yellow patches in the wing linings. The bird that is being confronted is gaped at with a wide-open bill. The effect is so startling that even much larger birds sometimes give ground. Other tactics include aerial pursuit of other birds coming to feeders.

When pine siskins arrive at feeding stations along with evening grosbeaks, there is little friction. The pine siskin has enough sense to be wary of this much larger relative with its huge bill. Instead of making war, the pine siskin darts in among feeding grosbeaks and seizes whatever particles of food it can. After the grosbeaks depart, the pine siskins go over every sunflower hull in search of small tidbits. The role of the pine siskin is often that of a gleaner.

Pine siskins are sometimes excessively tame birds that land on people's heads and shoulders and allow us to pick them up. The most extraordinary account of this tameness is by a Mr. Davis of Leominster, Massachusetts,* who had been offering food to a flock of siskins and soon found himself besieged by the tiny birds every morning. They got in the habit of entering his bedroom early in the morning through an open window and then to gain his attention would begin tugging his hair and even tweaking his nose with their sharp bills. Needless to say, this was usually enough of a hint to arouse the host into supplying food. This degree of tameness is exceptional. As pine siskins on their southward journeys become exposed to the dangers of civilization, they lose some of their fearlessness.

When a large flock is in attendance at feeders, their swarming tactics remind us of bees. As with other northern finches, the tastes of this bird sometimes run to salt, ashes, charcoal, and other similar substances. Louise de Kiriline Lawrence reported pine siskins with such depraved tastes that they did not disdain ash-dusted snow mixed with slop water. At the feeding station foods taken include suet, suet mixtures, sunflower, canary seed, millet, thistle, scratch feed, rolled oats, peanut hearts, and nutmeats, including those of pecan, hickory, black walnut, and butternut. Since the advent of thistle seeds, pine siskins have become so attached to this fare that they will come to thistle feeders in preference to any others. Therefore, they are most at home on Droll Yankees containing thistle or on thistle-bag feeders. Also

---

*In Forbush's *Birds of Massachusetts and Other New England States*, Boston, Massachusetts Department of Agriculture, 1925.

138

*Birds
That
Visit
Feeding
Stations*

they come readily to any thistle that has spilled over onto the ground. Other feeders patronized at times include trays on posts and trays at first- and second-story windows as well as hanging log feeders.

AMERICAN GOLDFINCH

Easy to identify and a familiar bird nearly everywhere, this small finch is one that gives us less trouble than most. Probably our only question will be why this goldfinch passes up some feeding stations and comes to others. Some of my most successful feeding stations have never been visited by a goldfinch; other feeding stations that I have maintained only briefly have been well attended by this bright little finch. Others report similar successes and failures with this bird. Its main requirement from us is water, not food. An unusually competent bird, the American goldfinch seems to have no trouble finding adequate supplies of natural food.

When this goldfinch does find our feeders, it comes enthusiastically and often in large numbers. This is particularly true during invasion years when the goldfinch, like its northern cousins, appears in tremendous flocks. There are occasions when as many as several hundred may crowd onto our feeders. Strictly speaking, the American goldfinch is not one of the northern finches. The flocks we see in winter may be derived from birds that have bred locally, or they may have come from more distant sources. The breeding range of the American goldfinch is from southern Canada to deep within southern portions of this country. During the winter, the goldfinch is very much of a wanderer and not unexpected anywhere from Nova Scotia and southern Ontario to Florida.

Once at the feeder, goldfinches remind us very much of pine siskins and redpolls. They swarm all over everything and are not the least deterred by the presence of other, much larger birds. If there is an adjective that describes the deplorable manners of this bird, it is "impudent." Some goldfinches have a habit of snatching partially opened sunflower seeds from the beaks of larger birds. This routine does not sit well with the evening grosbeaks and purple finches that are frequently the victims. But there is little that these larger birds can do about it; the thief is away in an instant. There are also occasional goldfinches that have it in for every other bird at the feeder.

Goldfinches do much of their feeding among hulls and broken seeds left by
other birds. Tidbits are gleaned from feeding trays and on the ground below. Goldfinches take delight in hanging feeders. They are as accomplished as chickadees in
clinging to any vertical surface that provides a toehold. A new feeder, called the
Fadco Anti–House Finch feeder, caters to the goldfinch's ability to hang by its feet
when it feeds. The feeding vents are below the perches instead of above them.
Goldfinches, as well as pine siskins and redpolls, are able to use this feeder but rarely
house finches. It is a bizarre sight to see birds hanging by their feet with heads
downward as they feed. The feeder comes in two models: one for thistle seeds and
the other for sunflower seeds. As with the pine siskin, the goldfinch has a marked
preference for feeders with thistle and a tendency to come to the ground for this food.
Goldfinches also patronize bird tables, window trays, trays on posts, and occasionally
hummingbird feeders. Like the evening grosbeak, goldfinches do most of their feeding
when with us early in the day.

Food is as important as feeders in attracting goldfinches. One must remember
that the goldfinch is highly competent in finding a wide range of natural foods. Many
of the small seeds that ripen in our lawns, flower beds, and gardens are to the
goldfinch's liking. Among the seeds that are in special favor are those of evening
primrose, hollyhock, mullein, thistle, dandelion, zinnia, cosmos, coreopsis, bache-
lor's button, lettuce, and Swiss chard. Green foods, such as beet leaves, are sometimes
consumed. If we are to wean goldfinches away from the natural bounty that is all
around us, we need to pay particular attention to the menu we offer. The thistle
seeds that are now being imported from Ethiopia in large quantities as a bird food
are one of the best foods to use in tempting goldfinches. Besides thistle, try other
well-liked foods such as sunflower, suet, suet mixtures, peanut butter, scratch feed,
sorghum, millet, canary seed, and cracked nutmeats. And do not overlook water.
This is always one of the most important lures with which to entice goldfinches,
birds that are especially attracted to water for drinking and bathing.

RED CROSSBILL

It is a rare treat to see either red or white-winged crossbills at a feeder, or, for that
matter, anywhere in our neighborhood. The northern coniferous forest is the home

140

*Birds
That
Visit
Feeding
Stations*

of the crossbills. Occasional appearances southward are to be associated with the failure of the cone crops on which these birds depend.

Of the two crossbills, the red journeys the farthest south during the occasional invasion years that see other northern finches on the move and appearing far south of their normal winter ranges. The red crossbill is sometimes seen in winter in the Carolinas and other southern states. During a recent winter, a flock of red crossbills was present from early December until mid-March at a feeding station at Gadsden, Alabama.

In keeping with the strange tastes of northern finches, crossbills are attracted to such seemingly unappetizing fare as soapy dishwater thrown out on the snow, spots of dog urine in the snow, waste tea leaves, ashes, charcoal, dry earth, bits of mortar, and salt. Some of these substances are needed as grit, which is so necessary among birds whose diets are composed largely of vegetable matter. The vegetarian crossbills, with their scissors-like bills, are specialists in extracting seeds from green or dry cones of conifers, and this often brings them into contact with sticky, resinous material. A need for something to counteract the resin may be part of the explanation for the crossbills' craving for the unpalatable substances that have been mentioned.

Our best luck with crossbills is often a result of something which they have found and which we would never think of offering. Ernest H. Baynes, after observing crossbills of both species returning again and again to a spot in his garden, used a magnifying glass to see if he could discover what it was that was attracting them. The answer was a clay soil on which salt had been sprinkled in order to kill weeds. Red crossbills, however, do sometimes join other birds at feeders. They feed on the ground or use bird tables and window shelves.

Once in the habit of visiting us for food, they show themselves to be as attentive and persistent as any of our visitors. Red crossbills at an Ontario feeder were observed gorging themselves on sunflower seeds, and in some cases single individuals ate the seeds steadily for an hour or longer. Besides sunflower, which is the mainstay of crossbills at feeders, they will take hemp, some nutmeats including almond, and dry, uncooked farina or cornmeal. Food is taken at bird tables, trays on posts, window trays, and the ground. Although information is lacking on this point, crossbills would probably come to hanging feeders for favorite foods.

More unexpected than the red crossbill, this far-northern bird rarely does us the favor of appearing at our feeding stations. When it does appear, it can easily be recognized because of white wing bars and its strange overlapping crossed mandibles. Although we regard this crossbill as being aloof, it is not because of the bird's shyness but probably because of its unawareness of our foods that we are so infrequently visited. The white-winged crossbill has the same tameness that is seen in other northern finches. Donald J. Lennox of Whitefield, New Hampshire, tells of the tameness of a small flock that arrived with chickadees and other finches after a December snowstorm. The crossbills began taking food from his hand only the second day after their arrival. Soon they showed what seemed to their host to be remarkable intelligence. Along with pine siskins, they associated the opening of a certain door with food. When Mr. Lennox appeared at this door, both the siskins and crossbills would be waiting. Both species would instantly fly down, as the door was opened, and alight on the food container in Mr. Lennox's hand or on his fingers and begin eating. The crossbills would also appear outside a certain window early in the morning and begin calling for food.

Like the red crossbill, this crossbill is not particular about feeders and shows a special preference for sunflower. It is known to come to bird tables and probably has the same feeding station preferences as the red crossbill. Foods taken at feeding stations include sunflower, hemp, suet, pieces of meat, and doughnuts.

The tastes of the white-winged crossbill vary from sampling soapy dishwater to extracting seeds from hemlock cones.

During the summer, towhees are little-seen birds that keep to dense cover. We would have small inkling of their presence if it were not for call notes that are variously described as sounding like "towhee," "chewink," and "joree." All are common names that have been applied to this secretive bird. During the fall, towhees become more visible and we sometimes see small flocks in the open but always near dense cover. Most towhees pass the winter in states lying south of Pennsylvania and Ohio. The few that remain in more northern states eke out an existence with the help of wild fruits and berries and feeding stations.

Towhees may appear at feeding stations at any season. If we find ourselves with a pair or two in early summer, chances are that we will soon be hosts to a small flock. When young join their parents at feeders, it is a tumultuous scene with each bird bent upon having the upper hand. Usually there is a cantankerous male that sends the whole bevy scurrying back to the bushes. Almost every other feeding station visitor seems to outrank the lowly towhees, and many times a brown thrasher or cardinal seems to go out of its way to give chase to the nervous towhees. Lacking a will to hold their own, the towhees retire to the nearest dense shrubbery at the least sign of trouble.

In winter look for towhees near the ground, especially below evergreens and near brush piles. Almost always the birds will be scratching in leaves. Towhees are such energetic scratchers that they send the leaves flying wherever they busy them-

*The rufous-sided towhee
characteristically feeds
on the ground.*

selves. Birds scratch by making two hops forward and a long sweep backward. Even at a feeder, towhees continue their active scratching.

So long as there is ample food on the ground, this is where towhees feed. Lacking such supplies, birds will sometimes visit bird tables, trays on posts, and window trays. When dining upon sunflower, they have a way of sending seeds off in every direction. In attempting to open the seeds, they may use a different technique from other members of the sparrow and finch family that characteristically hold a sunflower seed flat against the cutting edges of both mandibles and then, by means of chewing motions and pressure, break open the hard outer husk. Towhees, on the other hand, sometimes hold a seed, not flat, but sideways between the mandibles. When pressure is applied, either the entire seed shoots off into space or the hull breaks apart and the bird is left with the kernel. When the former happens, a bird will generally leave the feeder to search for the missing seed. This kind of frugality may be exhibited even when there is an abundant supply of seeds at the feeder.

Besides sunflower seeds, towhees consume suet, suet mixtures, scratch feed, barley, millet, canary seed, thistle, melon seeds, nutmeats, grapes, rolled oats, and white bread.

DARK-EYED JUNCO

During the colder months, juncos, or "snowbirds," are found throughout much of North America, but true to their hardy natures, the greatest number by far stay in more northern states while some remain as far north as southern portions of Canada. Recently the slate-colored junco, so familiar to those in the East, has been lumped with several western juncos to create the single species known as the dark-eyed junco.

Driving winds and swirling snow do not daunt this plucky bird. The coldest winter days see the junco as lively as ever and with a *joie de vivre* that bolsters our sagging spirits. It is always reassuring to look out on such days and see juncos blithely hopping about near our doorsteps and awaiting the first handout of the day. Like the chickadee, the junco is a symbol of the dauntlessness of birds at feeding stations during severe winter weather.

Well deserving the name "snowbird," the junco pays its calls most often during bad weather. Junco attendance at feeders usually does not begin in earnest until after

144

*Birds
That
Visit
Feeding
Stations*

the first snowfall of the season. Juncos also have a habit of showing up during hard rain showers. During good weather they usually desert our yards for roadsides, open fields, and woodland borders. Here their likely purpose is finding food in the form of weed seeds.

How is it that juncos return so quickly to our premises when the barometer falls? The answer is that birds that have visited our feeders during previous winters lead the way. In banding juncos I always discover that there are a few old-timers in each flock. Such birds must retain a canny memory of exactly where food can be found during an emergency. So long as natural foods are plentiful and the weather is cooperative, junco flocks roam the countryside; a hint of bad weather and the birds are back in yards with feeding stations.

Even when feeders and food supplies are buried under snow, we need not be too concerned about the juncos. They are resourceful, adaptive birds that usually manage very nicely under trying conditions. One of the junco's survival tactics is to burrow into the snow to reach food that has been covered over. If the snow is soft, juncos simply push their way through. Redpolls also have this habit. Not only is tunneling a way to reach food, but once under the snow, birds find protection from the wind and cold.

One evening when living in Massachusetts, I sallied forth with a flashlight to see if I could find out where the juncos that were visiting my feeders were spending the night. Once again, I found the junco to be a resourceful bird. Some were in the densest branches of a blue spruce, others in a hemlock, and still others in a red cedar.

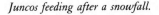

Juncos feeding after a snowfall.

Besides these nearby roosting sites, there were evergreens at a farmhouse about a quarter of a mile away that held some of the juncos that visited my feeders. Properly speaking, these were my neighbor's juncos. Yet each morning these birds traversed much the same route through a wooded area to reach my feeding stations. Sometimes other birds, such as chickadees and tree sparrows, used this same route. There was always much coming and going by birds along this pathway. Toward dusk some of the juncos at my feeders would slip away and disappear along this route toward the farmhouse.

Juncos are highly inquisitive and will attempt to feed from every kind of feeder, including small hanging ones. Not even hanging log feeders are too difficult for them. With much fluttering of wings, they can cling long enough to obtain a few mouthfuls of mixtures containing peanut butter. Juncos perform difficult feats after watching other birds. Although not physically equipped for clinging or balancing, they do surprisingly well and even master feeders intended only for such acrobats as chickadees and titmice. They are most at home on the ground and only a little less so at bird tables, trays on posts, and window trays. Juncos are equally versatile in what they eat. Foods that are well received include sunflower, suet, suet mixtures, scratch feed, sorghum, millet, canary seed, rape, peanut hearts, pecan meats, doughnuts, cornbread, and white bread.

TREE SPARROW

Many give up when it comes to identifying the sparrows. The tree sparrow, however, is not particularly hard to recognize. It can be recognized by white wing bars, a reddish cap, and a dark spot in the middle of an unstreaked breast. Moreover, the tree sparrow is *the* common sparrow that comes down from the north to occupy territory that has been vacated by other sparrows that have gone still farther south. We find this sparrow in winter from southern Canada to South Carolina and Arkansas. Although other sparrows share much of this region in winter, the tree sparrow is dominant at the northern edge. It is a cold-weather sparrow that seems to rejoice in the harshness of northern winters.

So far as habits are concerned, the tree sparrow has much in common with the junco. It is also a bad-weather bird and makes its appearances at feeding stations

146

*Birds
That
Visit
Feeding
Stations*

mainly on cold, windy days, when snow covers the ground; when the weather ameliorates, it is off to overgrown fields and woodland borders. Here it pursues other activities besides food finding.

During a normal winter day, according to Bent's account of this species in his *Life Histories*, foraging groups of tree sparrows spend a maximum of six to ten minutes at a time in feeding activity. This is followed by a twelve- to twenty-minute period of either perching, preening, bathing, or social activity that may carry the group into another foraging area. Activities such as these are followed by another session of feeding. In sunny, spring-like weather, tree sparrows are sometimes seen playing "a gay game of tag through the shrubbery." On cold, windy days, birds seem to spend more time doing nothing. On such days, according to the Bent account, birds may stay perched in a sheltered place for twenty or thirty minutes "with neck drawn in . . . and contour feathers fluffed to twice normal size."

Although described as gentle and unsuspicious, tree sparrows are not without a certain unruliness. This is seen in occasional boisterous individuals that never give up in vain attempts to chase every other bird from the feeders. When two such individuals meet, we are treated to an engagement reminiscent of a cockfight. After eyeing each other for a few moments, the two birds will get down to a sparring exhibition. The climax is a bill-to-bill performance in which the birds go straight up in the air and then tumble to the ground. Not until the birds are utterly exhausted or one bird is victor is the fight over with.

Banding reveals that tree sparrows often return to exactly the same location

*Tree sparrows are
undaunted
by bad weather.*

each winter. In this respect, they are like juncos and white-throated sparrows. Writing of the winter flocks of this species that she studied at Ithaca, New York, A. Marguerite Baumgartner* states: ". . . flocks appeared to be loosely defined units of varying numbers and individuals, with a fairly definite flock territory, from which, however, individuals strayed at will. Flocks inhabiting open country ranged more widely than those in denser cover such as marshes. In severe weather, flocks split into smaller groups and wandered more widely."

When feeding, tree sparrows continuously flit their tails and, no matter how much food is available, persist in vigorous scratching. They seem to be about equally at home feeding on the ground and at elevated feeders. Tree sparrows have the same inquisitive nature as juncos and this trait brings them to every kind of feeder that has suitable perching space. These sparrows commonly visit bird tables, trays on posts, window trays, hanging feeders and logs that have perches, and feeding places on the ground. Certain birds show the same ability that juncos have of mastering hanging log feeders. Tree sparrows also show some ability at opening sunflower seeds. Although small seeds make up by far the largest portion of the feeding station diet, these birds occasionally partake of suet, suet mixtures, and peanut butter. The main feeding station foods accepted, besides sunflower, are millet, canary seed, scratch feed, rape, and white bread.

CHIPPING SPARROW

We could not ask for a tamer, more companionable bird than this one. Over much of North America the chipping sparrow is a summer resident; from Virginia and Tennessee southward it is a winter resident as well. In more northern states the chippie's appearance in summer is all the more appreciated because of the near absence of other sparrows in our yards at this season. The chippie's tameness is a natural trait that does not have to be fostered by food.

In the fall the chippies that have almost been under our feet all summer begin moving southward. Our disappointment over their departure is sometimes lessened by the occasional ones we see all winter. A few chipping sparrows do not join in the fall migration to the southern states and are found in winter all the way north to the

*In Bent's *Life Histories of North American Birds*, 26 volumes, New York, Dover Publications, 1919–68.

148

*Birds
That
Visit
Feeding
Stations*

Great Lakes and southern New England. As might be expected, those that stay behind are much more responsive to feeding stations than summer residents. Those that winter in the South band together in flocks which roam the countryside. The chipping sparrow is a visitor to yards and feeding stations during its winter sojourn in the South.

Whenever we play host to the chipping sparrow, we need to remember that it is a comparatively docile bird and not up to competing with larger, more aggressive guests. Therefore, we should scatter food widely rather than confining it to a few places. This will give the chipping sparrow a much greater opportunity to secure its share. Most feeding by this sparrow is on the ground. But if bird tables and other elevated feeders are not too crowded, the chipping sparrow will use these places as well. Basically a ground-feeder, the chipping sparrow seems out of place when it does occasionally visit bird tables and feeding trays of various kinds. The tastes of the chipping sparrow run chiefly to small seeds and grain as well as almost every kind of bakery product. Foods that appeal include sunflower, scratch feed, canary seed, millet, rape, peanut hearts, pecan meats, cake and cookie crumbs, doughnuts, cracker crumbs, cornbread, and white bread.

FIELD SPARROW

Those who know this small sparrow, with red cap and plain breast, are impressed by its gentleness. It is one of the few sparrows and finches that always seems to get along well with its own kind and other species as well. It is also tame and friendly so far as people are concerned. These are all qualities that fit the chipping sparrow as well. But unlike the chipping sparrow, the field sparrow does not nest near our homes, rather preferring overgrown fields and pastures. For this reason, we are not likely to see this sparrow in our yards during the summer months. During the fall field sparrows gather into flocks and begin moving about the countryside. Sometimes with chipping sparrows, but more often in flocks composed of its own kind, this open-country bird not infrequently finds its way to our yards and feeders. Here, except for minor differences in appearance, it is an exact counterpart of its close relative. Moreover, both sparrows share the same winter range. Field sparrows are somewhat

Great Lakes region and southern New England. In southern states both sparrows are about equally common in winter and equally disposed toward feeding stations. It is a toss-up as to which one we will see most often.

One winter when feeding birds in coastal southern Massachusetts, I was pleasantly surprised to find that I had a flock of twenty field sparrows visiting my feeders. For a while I saw them every day and some days the flock was almost constantly present in the yard. Then came a week of cold, snowy weather when I did not see the birds at all. This was early January and I decided that the sparrows had migrated after all, even though it was far beyond the time when this event normally takes place. I couldn't have been more mistaken. There came a day when the whole flock returned and commenced eating at the customary places. The birds usually fed in a compact flock and did not mingle with other species. Nevertheless, birds boldly came to feeders occupied by larger birds.

My curiosity had been piqued as to where the flock disappeared when not in the immediate vicinity of my yard. The neighborhood was heavily wooded but with occasional residences and some overgrown fields. Searching the nearby countryside, I at first failed to find the flock. I had, however, neglected an overgrown tangle across the street. It was in this patch of briers and tall weeds that I learned that I could usually find the flock when it was not at my feeders. I never did find an explanation for the reason why the flock visited me so faithfully some days and stayed away other days.

Sparrows of several kinds often flock together—here are a fox (left), two field, three chipping, and two white-crowns.

150

*Birds
That
Visit
Feeding
Stations*

The importance of scattering food widely applies equally well to field and chipping sparrows. This is to prevent other birds from crowding out these mild-mannered guests. On the whole, the field sparrow seems a little more competent than the chipping in getting its share. I have sometimes seen field sparrows feeding confidently among mourning doves and blue jays. Field sparrows can be attracted to whatever feeder holds their favored foods. When I supplied finely cracked corn on the ground, this is where they fed. Elevated feeders with sunflower (which is too difficult for this sparrow) were avoided. But when the finely cracked corn was made available at elevated feeders, the field sparrows came to these feeders as readily as they had to the ground. Although very much of a ground-feeder, the field sparrow is more apt to appear at elevated feeders than the chipping sparrow. It often finds its way to bird tables, trays on posts, window trays, and hanging feeders that have suitable perches. Food preferences are quite similar to those of the chipping sparrow and include scratch feed, finely cracked corn, chick feed, sorghum, canary seed, millet, rape, thistle, peanut hearts, pecan meats, cornbread, and white bread.

WHITE-CROWNED SPARROW

This immaculate, boldly marked bird always excites attention and surely deserves the reputation of being the most handsome sparrow to visit feeding stations. Sometimes thought of as a western species, the white-crown has a subarctic breeding range that extends from coast to coast. In the eastern United States, the white-crown is both a spring and fall migrant and a winter visitor. Although far more common in the West, the white-crown is an easterner as well, its breeding range extending all across northern Canada eastward to Labrador. Since about 1950 there has been an expansion of winter range both eastward and northward through Ohio, New York, and southern New England. It is now no longer a great surprise to find the white-crown in winter in this part of the East. This range expansion has been greatly facilitated by the increased number of feeding stations throughout this region. But most white-crowns still spend the winter farther south, and we begin to see this bird more plentifully in border states such as Virginia and Kentucky.

Flocks of white-crowns have a winter territory that is relatively fixed. There is a yearly return by certain individuals to these territories. Observations in the West reveal that within a territory there is a headquarters where birds spend much of their time. I gained an inkling of this in observing white-crowns when they were away from my feeding stations in Virginia. Here the flock had a special place along a hedge-bordered lane where the birds would perch close together in bushes and indulge in little else than preening of feathers.

White-crowns are well-mannered guests, somewhat aloof from the rest of the company, and with a dignified, almost regal bearing. There is almost no fighting or chasing about. One gets the impression that all the white-crown seeks is its meal with as little fuss as possible and freedom from annoyance by other birds. Whatever its reservations may be, the white-crown is a hearty partaker of our fare. The white-crowned sparrow is a ground-feeder that seems out of place at bird tables, trays, or hanging feeders. It comes to elevated feeders probably only when food is in short supply on the ground. There is little in the way of nutmeats, seeds, grain, and bakery products that does not meet with its approval. High on this list are sunflower, scratch feed, millet, canary seed, buckwheat, sorghum, rape, peanut hearts, pecan meats, doughnuts, cornbread, cake crumbs, white bread, and sliced apple.

WHITE-THROATED SPARROW

Except for more northern states, where the whitethroat is present some years and absent others, this is *the most common winter sparrow at feeding stations throughout the East*. Most of us expect our first whitethroats around mid-October. We will have the company of this friendly bird until about mid-May. There is little chance of members of our winter flock wandering off or of new influxes later on. The only big changes are when fall and spring migrants make their appearances. These travelers fill our yards during the few days they are passing through and sometimes they are present in such numbers that they tax the capacities of our feeders and bird baths.

Our home flock of whitethroats is as faithful in attendance as any other birds we can think of. Bird banders call a flock that keeps to a restricted area a "neighborhood group." As banders know from long experience, whitethroats, once they have found a yard, come back year after year; they do this in much the same way that birds return to exactly the same nesting grounds. To be sure, numbers and make-up of the flock change from year to year. Owing to such factors as the short life expectancy

152

*Birds
That
Visit
Feeding
Stations*

of songbirds, we can anticipate a return in the fall of only 20 percent or so of the whitethroats that we had with us the previous season. This is a fairly high rate of return and exceeds that of such other winter visitors as the dark-eyed junco and the tree sparrow. An occasional whitethroat that is able to elude the dangers of predation and the many other hazards that beset small birds may be back in the same yard for five or six consecutive years.

Such constancy deserves a reward. By paying attention to all the many small details of feeding and attracting birds, we make it possible for whitethroats to survive the coldest winter weather. We should remember that whitethroats are adapted primarily to wintering in southern states. Only within the past sixty years has this species taken to wintering in any numbers in more northern states. Like the white-crowned sparrow, the whitethroat has responded to the benefits afforded by man and has steadily ranged farther northward in winter. Unless we do our part, there is a risk in this dependence for our visitors. The most important thing we can do is to keep feeders well supplied without letup during the time that whitethroats are with us.

Whitethroats are model guests. They adapt readily to the presence of other birds at the feeder. They neither give ground in the manner of timid towhees nor do they become overly assertive. Individuals, although loosely part of a flock, come and go pretty much on their own. While some feed, others may be at the bird bath, and still others resting in nearby shrubbery. This is in contrast to the blind obedience to instinct seen in the house sparrow, which causes this regimented species to come and go as though by abrupt commands.

Whitethroats are among the first birds to arrive at our feeders in the morning and always a few are the last or nearly the last birds to leave at dusk. Others come and go through the day without adhering to any special schedule. Along with cardinals and juncos, whitethroats frequently linger on at our feeders until after dark. Sometimes we barely make out their dim shapes with the aid of a flashlight.

Most feeding by whitethroats is on the ground. However, the white-throated sparrow may be tempted to elevated feeders by the presence of favorite foods. This bird is not unexpected at bird tables, trays, suet holders, and some of the less difficult hanging feeders. Small seeds, particularly millet, make up most of the whitethroat's diet at feeding stations. Besides millet, whitethroats take sunflower, suet, scratch

feed, canary seed, thistle, peanut hearts, pecan meats, black walnut meats, doughnuts, cornbread, and white bread.

FOX SPARROW

Hardly have we gotten used to this large, plump sparrow before it is gone. Ordinarily
we do not see the fox sparrow about our homes except during brief spells in the
spring and fall when this species is passing through on migration. Fox sparrows are
essentially birds of wilder districts. They nest amid the stunted spruce barrens of
northern Canada, and in winter those that reach our southern states seek out swampy
woodlands and overgrown fields. During recent years the fox sparrow has shown signs
of becoming more domesticated and some birds now stay well north of the wintering
grounds in the South by making use of feeding stations. Fox sparrows are now not
unheard of in winter as far north as Minnesota, southern Ontario, and New England.

The restless energy of this sparrow is always impressive. If not scratching with
a vigorous leap forward and a sweep backward that sends leaves and dirt flying, the
fox sparrow is half-running, half-flying from one tangle or feeding place to another.
Like the towhee, the fox sparrow is a ground-feeder that is usually found on or close
to the ground. It is also a bird that sticks close to dense cover.

Though a gregarious species that travels in flocks, the fox sparrow is not overly
inhibited by discipline. Members of a flock keep to a limited area but come and go
in much the same manner as whitethroats. The relaxed habits of this bird are in
keeping with a gentleness that is unusual among sparrows. At feeding stations fox
sparrows are wholly absorbed in what they are doing and have no interest in asserting
their rights over other birds.

Fox sparrows feed by alternately scratching and picking up food with rapid jabs
of the bill. Seeds are rolled about between the mandibles until the outside husks fall
away. After light snowfalls the fox sparrow does a service to other birds by scratching
through to bare ground. In this way, seeds and grain that may have fallen from
feeders become available again. Food preferences run to sunflower, suet, suet mixtures,
scratch feed, canary seed, pecan meats, doughnuts, and white bread. Nearly all
feeding by the fox sparrow is on the ground.

Many of us who live in more northern states have the song sparrow's company the year round. Although we lose most of our song sparrows each fall, some always stay behind and these are the birds that become faithful attendants at feeding stations. As far north as Minnesota, southern Ontario, and New England, a fair number of song sparrows brave the cold and snow every winter. They seem as inured to the northern climate as the more common tree sparrow that sometimes throngs to our feeders. Southward, from Tennessee and South Carolina to the Gulf coast, the song sparrow is a winter, not a summer, visitor.

We owe our acquaintanceship with the song sparrow to its habit of frequenting our yards. It is a heavily streaked, brownish bird that otherwise would not command attention. During the fall and winter song sparrows, on the whole, are crotchety among themselves and toward other birds. So fractious are some individuals that milder mannered song sparrows cannot eat at the same feeder with them. We sometimes see several song sparrows waiting patiently in nearby shrubbery until a bully finishes his meal. Song sparrows are so contentious that rarely do we see more than two or three together at a feeder. At some locations I have seen only one song sparrow at a time at the feeders although I knew there were others about. Birds seem somewhat less aggressive during the cold and snowstorms of winter and early spring.

Because of its delightful song that is heard at every season of the year, we are more than inclined to forgive the song sparrow for its few shortcomings. One day in February, when living in Massachusetts, I heard a song sparrow giving voice from the middle of a brush pile. Only after considerable search did I find the singer. The

*Song sparrows
sometimes give voice
to song
in midwinter.*

bird was singing without perceptibly opening its bill. Whatever caused this song, it made me feel more cheerful on that bleak winter day.

Song sparrows are impulsive in their feeding habits. They run out rapidly to wherever we have scattered food on the ground, eat for a short time, and then suddenly dash off before half-finishing. They do not hesitate to come well out into the open and may sometimes feed far out on a lawn or in a driveway. Most of the day, however, is spent in the densest shrubbery, or sometimes in a brush pile. These are havens where the birds can quickly vanish when disturbed.

Seeds are rotated around between the mandibles until any sheath or husk is removed. The song sparrow is a vigorous scratcher and therefore is efficient in uncovering seeds and grain that have become buried in leaves or snow. After a snowfall, it is a common sight to see this sparrow scratching in the fresh snow immediately below the feeders. Experience has taught the bird that these are the likely places to come to uncover sources of food.

Visits to feeders ordinarily begin in early fall and do not cease until the nesting season begins in late spring. Like the cardinal, the song sparrow is an early and late feeder as well as a frequent visitor through the day. The last visit may take place in such dim light that we may not be aware of any birds still present. Although the song sparrow gives the impression of being very much of a ground-feeder, it will surprise us by appearing at times at most elevated feeders. It seems reasonably at home at bird tables, trays on posts, and window trays. Food tastes run chiefly to seeds and grain, while water is one of the main drawing cards. Song sparrows like to drink from and bathe in bird baths all year. Foods taken include sunflower, scratch feed, sorghum, millet, buckwheat, canary seed, rape, thistle, peanut hearts, walnut meats, and white bread.

SNOW BUNTING

Those who live in more northern states should be prepared for occasional visits by flocks of snow buntings. This mostly white-plumaged bird of open country is even more of a hard-weather bird than juncos or tree sparrows. Its visits are timed to coincide with bitter cold and snow. With even a slight amelioration in weather, the snow bunting flocks disappear as quickly as they came.

156

*Birds
That
Visit
Feeding
Stations*

The snow bunting is so much a bird of the open that it rarely visits well-planted yards. Therefore, if we are to play host to this northern visitor, we must take special steps. Donald J. Lennox of Whitefield, New Hampshire, has discovered that the best way to do this is to sprinkle generous amounts of hay chaff along with oat groats on hard-packed snow in the center of the lawn. He states that the buntings quickly find this food and feed upon it as long as the weather is cold and stormy. By sprinkling the food ever closer to the house, he soon has the birds feeding under his windows. In between trips to feeding places, the buntings perch on rooftops and in dead trees. As soon as the weather improves, the birds are off again. However, they remember the feeding places and return with every bad spell of weather as long as the winter lasts.

Flocks of snow buntings sometimes contain other open-country species. The two that join the bunting flocks most frequently are horned larks and Lapland longspurs. The latter are also hard-weather birds that we would not expect near our homes except under the most rigorous winter conditions. Like the snow bunting, these two species will also feed on hay chaff or seeds and grain sprinkled on the snow.

Foods to entice the snow bunting, and also the horned lark and Lapland longspur, include oat groats, hayseed, cracked corn, millet, dog biscuit crumbs, and bread crumbs. It would be highly exceptional to find the snow bunting feeding anywhere but on the ground. Rare appearances can be expected, however, at bird tables and elevated trays.

Snow buntings are bad-weather birds that respond to seeds scattered upon the snow and well out in the open.

FOWL-LIKE BIRDS

Of the fowl-like (or gallinaceous, as they are sometimes called) birds that are found in eastern North America, only two, bobwhite and ring-necked pheasant, are common visitors to feeding stations. Several others, including ruffed grouse, gray partridge, and wild turkey, may appear under exceptionally favorable conditions. Fowl-like birds are usually considered game species, and therefore it is generally thought that during the hunting season they should be far afield eluding the hunter's gun and not accepting the hospitality of our yards. Although we may play host to these birds, we do not necessarily offer them sanctuary. The game birds in this family are highly independent and given to roaming widely through the countryside and outlying suburbs in search of food. Our feeders are only one of many stopping places.

BOBWHITE

This is a familiar bird at more southern feeding stations and sometimes at feeders as far north as southern New England and the Great Lakes. Because of its cheery calls and dashing appearance, the bobwhite is always a desirable addition to the company that frequents our yard. Over much of the year, this bird is gregarious and arrives in flocks, or coveys, numbering around ten to twenty birds. After the bobwhite pairs off in spring, solitary couples may visit us for a while. After the first nesting, birds tend to desert feeders in favor of an insect diet. Nevertheless, birds are now tamer than ever and we may continue to see numbers of them in our yards through the

158

Birds
That
Visit
Feeding
Stations

summer and early fall. Unless frightened away by nearby hunting, the first cool weather of fall may see them back at our feeders again.

Attracting the bobwhite takes more patience and skill than is necessary with most feeding station birds. The bobwhite is relatively intolerant of disturbance and therefore is easily frightened away by frisking dogs, loud noise, or too much movement. We can make this bird feel much more secure by providing proper cover. One way to do this is to leave a portion of the yard (even if only a small corner) in a natural, untouched condition. Also it is a big inducement to this bird if in late summer we leave certain of our vegetable and flower beds in an overgrown state. Not only will the bobwhite and other birds find an extra supply of food in these beds but the rank growth will make excellent cover for the bobwhite.

If two coveys should happen to be present at the feeder at the same time, there is likely to be much squabbling. Rival cocks tend to square off and indulge in the same kind of sparring that we see in roosters. At an Ohio feeder bobwhites took exception to starlings. Whenever any starlings were around, they went out of their way to chase them off. Those of us who are sometimes pestered by having too many starlings at our feeders should perhaps do more to encourage the bobwhite. Except for a few cases like this, however, bobwhites tend to feed peaceably with one another and other birds that may be at the feeder.

Most feeding by bobwhites takes place on the ground below feeders. Rarely will a bird fly up and take its place with smaller birds at a feeding tray. When feeding on the ground, birds often form a circle and feed with heads pointing in. Bobwhites also feed at times in a straight line. They arrive and depart by making short runs for a distance, stopping, and then running again. Rarely does a covey take flight.

Bobwhites eat with rapid pecking motions, and, if not alarmed into premature departure, will consume what appears to us to be huge amounts of food. One must remember that the bobwhite and other of the fowl-like birds store food they eat in a commodious crop that swells ever larger as it is filled. The crop is an enlargement of the gullet where food is held and subjected to preliminary maceration before being passed on to the stomach. The only other common visitors to our feeding stations that have well-developed crops are the doves. They, too, eat a lot of food during the course of a meal.

A bobwhite that met with an accident following a visit to my feeder held no less than 818 items of food in its digestive tract—most of them were in the crop.

Millet, wheat, and buckwheat were the main foods that this bird had been eating.
Thanks to such an excellent capacity to hold food, the bobwhite does not need to eat
frequently. As a result, it does not arrive at our feeders as early as most other birds
and there are long periods when we do not see it at all. At an Ohio feeder visits were
usually around 9:00 a.m. and not again until 4:00 p.m. or thereabouts. Generally
bobwhites take a long midday siesta during which they do little but preen, take dust
baths, or crouch quietly under the protection of brambles and other growth. However,
a covey coming to my feeders in Massachusetts one winter made most frequent
appearances around breakfast time and again around noon. The busiest times were
always on the days preceding a snowfall. In anticipation of difficult times ahead,
birds would spend the day stocking up. This makes good sense in a species such as
this that has an ample crop in which to hold food. When I see bobwhites making
frequent visits to my feeders through the day, I know bad weather is ahead.

At dusk a covey will retire to a protected place and form a circle on the ground,
heads pointing outward and bodies packed close together. If there is an alarm, birds
explode into the air and fly off in every direction. So startling is this performance
that a predator is taken aback and perhaps sufficiently so that the vital fraction of a
second needed to make a kill is lost. Although roosting usually takes place on the
ground, birds may sometimes perch in bushes or trees.

The bobwhite's choice of foods at feeders ranges from nutmeats and sunflower
to millet, wheat, buckwheat, cracked corn, and bread crumbs. This species patronizes
game-bird feeders, open ground, and, rarely, a feeding tray on a post.

RING-NECKED PHEASANT

The male ring-neck can qualify as the largest and one of the most colorful birds we
see at our feeders. Tail included, the male is from 33 to 36 inches long. The handsome
male is sometimes seen at the feeders with an entourage of six or seven hens. These
are his harem. He is usually very solicitous as to their welfare and makes a show of
calling their attention to choice items of food.

The introduced ring-neck is most plentiful in more northern states and does
well in rural districts where there are homesteads, agricultural lands, and wood lots.
There is some tendency on the part of this pheasant to invade out-lying suburbs.

160

*Birds
That
Visit
Feeding
Stations*

Wherever habitat conditions are suitable and the ring-neck is present, there is a good chance of visits to feeding stations. It is a bird to look for at feeders from northern Virginia, West Virginia, Kentucky, and Missouri northward. Like the bobwhite, the ring-neck is seen at feeders through the colder months. Unless scared away by nearby hunting, it is likely to make its first appearance in early fall. Wherever hunting takes place, this bird has an uncanny way of disappearing from sight.

Unless hard-pressed by bad weather, the ring-neck fills its crop early in the day and then spends a long siesta loafing. More feeding takes place before the bird retires. Like other fowl-like birds, the ring-neck devotes much time to dusting. Not only does dusting seem to be a pleasurable pastime but it helps the bird to rid its plumage of lice and other parasites. We may find small depressions in bare ground where ring-necks have frequently dusted and perhaps left behind a few of their feathers. Look for such places in dirt roads and along the bare edges of fields. At night birds roost on the ground or sometimes in trees.

It is an easy matter to supply the food needs of these birds. Simply scatter food on the snow or the bare ground. They are not reluctant to feed in the open quite far from cover. Corn on the cob, shucked whole kernels, wheat, oats, barley, or any of the seeds used in bird feeding go over well. The ring-neck restricts itself entirely to game-bird feeders and food scattered on the ground.

DOVES

The terms "pigeon" and "dove" are used interchangeably, although it is common practice to call larger species "pigeons" and the smaller "doves." One or two species can be counted upon at most eastern feeding stations. In the Rio Grande valley of Texas and in states from the Rockies westward, the number of dove species is greater, and there may sometimes be as many as three or more species together at feeders. Although doves of different kinds get along well together, within a species there is generally much bickering and at times furious fights.

DOMESTIC PIGEON

Many take delight in feeding the domestic pigeon (or rock dove as it is called when in a semi-wild state) in city parks or public squares. Here the bird is perfectly at home and fills a void because of the absence of native birds. On the other hand, the pigeon is seldom welcomed at home feeding stations. In the quieter environment of our yards it seems out of place and its presence leads to needless competition with more desirable native birds. The domestic pigeon acts as though it were aware of our feelings in this matter. It comes warily, if at all, to feeding stations, while thronging about us in the tamest barnyard manner wherever it is fed in public places.

Those who take pleasure in feeding the domestic pigeon should offer it some-

162

*Birds
That
Visit
Feeding
Stations*

thing more than the usual white bread and other bakery products that this bird receives in such quantities. The following is a recommended pigeon feed mixture that contains 14.2 percent protein and 66.9 percent carbohydrates: whole yellow corn, 30 percent; sorghum in the form of kafir or milo, 25 percent; cowpeas or Canada peas, 20 percent; wheat, 20 percent; and hemp 5 percent. Corn is one of the best pigeon foods; other good foods besides the ones mentioned above are bread, popcorn, millet, rape, buckwheat, and rice. Occasionally a domestic pigeon will feed at a suet mixture if there is adequate perching room nearby. One pigeon, feeding at a suet cup in my yard, successfully kept starlings that were competing for this food at bay. The pigeon has the same preference as the mourning dove for food on the ground. When hard-pressed it will come to bird tables and trays.

MOURNING DOVE

The confiding ways and soft cooings of doves suggest a peaceful nature that is in marked contrast to the real temperament of the bird. Mourning doves, like most other species of doves, indulge in furious battles during the mating season and are inclined toward irritability at other seasons. The wing is used both to deliver blows and to fend off the blows of an adversary. In spite of a quarrelsome nature, mourning doves are highly gregarious and are found in flocks at all seasons except the early part of the breeding season.

Mourning doves have responded so enthusiastically to feeding stations that there is some objection, as noted in Chapter 6, to their numbers and appetites. Although they are migrants, mourning doves that have flown south are usually replaced by doves from still farther north. There has been a tendency among mourning doves for the past seventy years to winter ever farther northward. In winter the mourning dove is now found as far west as the Great Lakes region and as far north as the middle portions of New England. A flock of twenty or so birds spent the hardest part of a northern winter in the vicinity of a feeder in southern Vermont. But they departed when the weather ameliorated in late February.

The most impressive thing about the mourning dove at feeding stations is its appetite. After arriving with a flourish of wing beats, a dove will settle down to prolonged feeding. Food is picked up with rapid jabs of the bill, and birds go over and over the same ground as they make sure they have found every last kernel of seed or grain. The longer a bird eats the more torpid it becomes. When first starting to eat, birds move about quite briskly. After a time, food is taken from a squatting position; then, when the bird can hold no more, it may sit quietly in one place and allow the digestive processes to catch up. There may be a final session of eating before the bird flies away. Although the ground is the favored eating place, birds are not hesitant about coming to raised feeders. They have a surprising ability to balance themselves on insecure perches. Before coming to a feeding station in one yard, doves would alight upon a sagging clothesline and wait there until ample room was available at feeding places. Even small hanging feeders of certain kinds are not too difficult for this surprisingly acrobatic bird.

After a long session of eating, mourning doves may join others of their kind for a quiet period of perching motionlessly in tops of dead trees or other exposed sites. In an instant the flock will take wing and perhaps be off to a favorite watering place. The mourning dove is a thirsty bird and may fly many miles to a source of water. Like other doves, other close relatives, and some Australian finches, mourning doves drink without tilting the head back after each swallow. Water is drawn in while the head is in a downward position.

Another important occupation is finding grit. Birds that are seen busily searching driveways and edges of highways are, as likely as not, picking up small pebbles and cinders that will be used in grinding food. Like other birds that consume large amounts of soft vegetable food, the mourning dove requires several times the amount of grit that most birds do. The daily grit consumption is somewhere between fifty and one hundred small, hard objects. Mourning doves also have a craving for salt although not to the extent that is seen in northern finches.

The mourning dove is a complete vegetarian. It has tastes that fit in well with offerings of seeds, grain, and nutmeats. Foods that are well received include wheat, corn, sunflower, buckwheat, sorghum, millet, canary seed, thistle, hemp, rape, cracked pecans, and peanut hearts. As long as there is food on the ground, this is usually where the mourning dove feeds. Lacking sources on the ground, this dove will come to bird tables, trays on posts, and whatever hanging feeders it can manage.

Much smaller than the two species mentioned and confined in our region to the southern states, this dove is a pleasing addition to the feeding station company. It reminds one of an animated toy animal the way it wanders on its erratic course, tail cocked in the air, making rapid jabs with its bill whenever it comes upon food. If one ground dove gets in the way of another, or if a bird of another species competes too vigorously with it for food, one or both wings are raised like warning signals. When the wing is raised, a prominent chestnut patch on the underside is suddenly revealed. Whether other birds are supposed to be intimidated by the raising of the wings or the chestnut on the underside is hard to say.

The ground dove also has the dove-like ability to eat for long periods without pause. It too has a capacious crop. A ground dove that met with an accident near my Florida feeder had eaten no less than 697 food items at the feeder. Food is eaten on the ground, and birds tend to mill about rather than confine their eating to one place. For ground doves one should scatter food well out in the open and not near shrubbery where a cat could hide. Ground doves are slow in making an escape and therefore are easy victims for any mammal that may lie in wait for them.

Ground doves will readily accept buckwheat, scratch feed, sorghum, millet, canary seed, rape, and pecan meats—practically the same menu that appeals to domestic pigeons and mourning doves. True to its name, this dove feeds mainly on the ground. Occasionally, it comes to bird tables or trays on posts.

HUMMINGBIRDS thirteen

With rules of its own and its own specialized equipment, hummingbird feeding is a separate department of bird feeding. Those of us who live east of the Mississippi will count ourselves lucky if we succeed in attracting the ruby-throated hummingbird, the one common species found in the East. However, the statement so often found in bird books that the ruby-throated is the only hummingbird found east of the Mississippi is not precisely correct. Mrs. W. W. Tennant, on the east bank of the Mississippi at Baton Rouge, Louisiana, disproves this statement by feeding not only the ruby-throat, but, from time to time, one to three western species at her feeders. Western hummingbirds turn up occasionally almost anywhere in the East. But to find hummingbirds in the variety and numbers we might wish for, we would have to visit the tropical lands to the south or look for hummingbirds in the western parts of this country. Hummingbird feeding programs in our West sometimes attract as many as five or six species and hundreds of individuals. At least two species are presently found in winter in gardens of southern California. Although there are problems with hummingbird feeding, the results are generally very rewarding.

HOW TO GET STARTED

The first and most difficult problem in hummingbird feeding is getting birds to notice and use your feeder. Once a hummingbird has caught on, it will show the way and you should soon have others. To build up a successful feeding program,

166

*Birds
That
Visit
Feeding
Stations*

however, may take several years. Start feeding in most eastern states in May. This is the month when ruby-throated hummingbirds arrive from their sojourn in the tropics. On returning to our yards, they immediately begin searching for food. To put off our feeding program until later means less likelihood of success. Birds will have either moved on or settled down to other sources of food. On the other hand, once they have found you, hummingbirds will continue to use your feeders daily until the time of fall departure. When back again in the spring, birds that have known your feeders return to them immediately. If the feeders are not up in time, prior customers will hover about the exact locations where they had been accustomed to coming for food.

Once a few have led the way, other hummingbirds will catch on and the feeders will gradually build up a larger and larger clientele. The first year that hummingbirds came to a feeder in a yard in New Hampshire there were four; the next year the number had increased to eight, and the following year to twelve. This kind of progression in numbers is typical when feeding hummingbirds. Presence of food lures more and more birds and many stay to nest. Some successful programs in the East have led to the establishment of breeding populations containing dozens of birds.

Very often the first requirement for attracting hummingbirds is not the special feeders that have been designed for these birds but flowers. Plant certain flowers that will bloom early, others that will come into flower later on, and so on through the flowering season. Not only are flowers important in bringing hummingbirds to yards but without them the birds would not obtain a balanced diet. Most studies of hummingbird feeding habits show that birds obtain sizable numbers of small insects from the flowers that they visit for nectar. These insects are a highly important part of the diet. Among the flowers that are useful sources of food to ruby-throated hummingbirds are trumpet creeper, jewelweed, sage, bee balm, fuchsia, gladiolus, columbine, nasturtium, petunia, penstemon, larkspur, hollyhock, zinnia, and morning glory.

In order to get the attention of hummingbirds, feeders should be out in the open where birds can see them. A good place to try is a garden bed where birds are visiting flowers for nectar and other food. Once birds start coming to a feeder, you can move it to a more convenient location, say, to a spot in full view of the window where you do most of your observing.

Feeders that are sold commercially are nearly always a bright color that will attract the hummingbird's attention; also many include artificial flowers in the design, another way to lure hummingbirds. Although hummingbirds respond especially well to red, they are drawn to orange, yellow, and still other colors. If you are using a feeding vial that is not already colored, you can achieve the proper effect by wrapping the feeder with colored ribbon or colored crepe paper. The red paper poppies seen on Memorial Day are handy objects to attach to a feeder and will frequently get the attention of hummingbirds. Another, and sometimes better, lure is a flower of the kind that hummingbirds are coming to. Insert the flower in the feeder opening and let some of the syrup seep around the petals. Once birds get a taste of the solution you are using, this is usually all that is necessary. They will keep coming back for more.

PROPER FORMULA

The correct formula to use in feeding hummingbirds has been the subject of much controversy. For many years a one part sugar to two parts water solution was accepted as the standard mixture for feeding hummingbirds in the wild. About ten years ago a switch to honey was recommended because of the greater nutritional properties of honey versus sugar. By the time honey had come into popular usage, it was discovered

A ruby-throated hummingbird at a trumpet vine.

168

*Birds
That
Visit
Feeding
Stations*

that occasionally hummingbirds that had been using honey were succumbing to a fatal fungus disease that affected their tongues. Dr. Augusto Ruschi, the well-known Brazilian authority on hummingbirds, was the one who discovered the cause of this disease. Fermented, moldy honey-water mixtures are the source of the fungus disease described by Dr. Ruschi. Honey is therefore far too risky to use in feeding hummingbirds.

The proper formula for feeding hummingbirds in the wild is one part white granulated sugar to four parts water. A higher ratio of sugar to water, it is thought, could be damaging to the hummingbird's liver. The water should be boiled first in order to kill bacteria and thus reduce the possibility of fermentation. Add the sugar after the water has reached a lukewarm temperature. Stir and refrigerate until needed to fill feeders. Apply fresh solution only to vials that are empty and that have been cleaned.

If the solution is not changed or used up by hummingbirds in a few days, it is likely to go bad. The first clue we have to an aging solution is black specks in the liquid and dark mold beginning to form on the inside surface of the glass or plastic reservoir that holds the solution. To correct the problem, empty the feeder, rinse with warm water, and refill with fresh solution. If, after rinsing, mold still persists, try using a rinse to which vinegar and uncooked grains of rice have been added. Shake vigorously and empty. In stubborn cases use a small stiff brush with a flexible wire handle to get at any remaining mold deposits.

*A ruby-throat
at a sugar-water vial.*

The wild hummingbird receives its protein from small insects, many of which live in the flowers that hummingbirds visit for nectar, and could not survive on our artificial diets. We provide some of the energy that helps keep this animated mite of bird going. To attempt to do more than this is unwise and unnecessary. I would leave fortified or balanced diets that contain protein supplements and artificial coloring to zoo keepers and stick to simple sugar-water formulas. Alfred G. Martin in *Hand-taming Wild Birds at the Feeder* writes: "I have been feeding sugar to hummingbirds for fifty years and have kept them under close observation. I have never seen one leave a feeder without going directly to flowers to feed on nectar and insects. There seems to be no ill effects from sugar."

FEEDERS AND THEIR MAINTENANCE

It has truthfully been said that the kind of feeder used is not nearly so important to the hummingbirds as it is to the person who is feeding them. A usable feeder can be made from a test tube, glass, pyrex, or plastic vial. Simply wire to a stake in the ground and keep the container in a tilted upright position. Over the years many improvements, chiefly for the sake of our convenience, have been made in humming-bird feeders. Many feeders are based upon the vacuum principle which allows liquid to remain at a constant level in a feeding cup or tube that is supplied by an inverted storage container. Certain others are better designed to prevent leakage or drip (a problem that crops up in vacuum-type feeders). The beginner should test out a number of feeders and then decide for himself which is best for his needs and those of his customers.

If feeders are emptied and fresh solution added every three or four days in hot weather and every week in cooler weather, chances are that intensive cleaning procedures will not be needed. Keep feeders in partial shade in hot weather. Like any other bird feeder, hummingbird feeders should be in locations easily seen from the window. Safest from the standpoint of window strikes is a location at the window. Avoid having red flowers or any bright red object clearly in view inside the house. The hummingbird's attraction to red may cause it to fly into the window in an effort to reach a red object inside.

170

*Birds
That
Visit
Feeding
Stations*

Hummingbirds are fussy and will not come to feeders that have been neglected; they are quickly discouraged when they find the feeders empty.

PROBLEMS WITH OTHER BIRDS

One of the most convincing testimonials to the adaptability of birds is the fact that at least sixty-eight species other than hummingbirds have learned how to use hummingbird feeders. Whether hovering before the feeders on rapidly beating wings or making use of perches, birds of many kinds—including seven species of woodpeckers, six titmice, four nuthatches, three mimic thrushes, sixteen warblers, six orioles, four tanagers, and sixteen sparrows and finches—have succumbed to the sweet taste of sugar. This is not an overly serious problem as we are apt to enjoy these visitors almost as much as the hummingbirds.

If other birds do pose a problem, a workable solution is to set aside special, more accessible sugar-water feeders for them and use more restrictive feeders (with small openings and no perches) for the hummingbirds.

PROBLEMS WITH INSECTS

Insect competition is one of the most vexing problems in hummingbird feeding. Bees, wasps, and ants are sometimes attracted by the sweet syrup in such numbers that they interfere with the hummingbirds. As a first step, try moving the feeder to a new location, which often solves the ant problem. But other steps may be needed. Woodsworld, a California manufacturer of hummingbird feeders, in its brochures on feeding, provides good advice on dealing with this problem. The company recommends spraying the outside of feeders frequently with a garden hose to remove traces of sticky syrup that will attract insects. It is best to locate feeders in semi-shade, they say, as bees and wasps are more likely to appear when feeders are in bright sun. Finally, an effective way, according to Woodsworld, to keep insects from settling upon the feeder or crawling upon wires or other supports is to coat these surfaces with salad oil. Where insects present serious problems, salad oil becomes almost as important in a hummingbird feeding program as sugar-water. Other good advice offered by Woodsworld is "Under no circumstances should a feeder or any place that hummers perch or feed be sprayed with insect spray as hummingbirds, like insects, are subject to minute residues of any poisonous substance."

EFFECT UPON MIGRATION

Hummingbirds that nest locally can be expected to use feeders all summer and their progeny will join them at the repast. Migrating hummingbirds may join the local birds in late summer and this will temporarily swell the numbers coming to feeders. There is no evidence that presence of syrup at hummingbird feeders acts to retard hummingbird migration southward. The small ruby-throat starts on its way in late summer regardless of the state of the food supply. In spite of its small size, this dauntless bird makes a long nonstop flight across the Gulf of Mexico and onward into Central America. In California and northward into British Columbia, Anna's hummingbird is a semi-permanent resident. To stop feeding at the end of summer would impose a serious hardship upon this bird. In southern California, besides wintering Anna's, there are small numbers of Costa's and Allen's hummingbirds that spend the winter. In southern Arizona and New Mexico, as well as along the Gulf coasts of Louisiana and Texas, even more species of hummingbirds spend the winter. In many cases, these birds, after migrating part way, have lost the urge to continue and are obliged to stay wherever they find themselves. Living upon insects, nectar from late blooming flowers, and, importantly, syrup offered at hummingbird feeders, they are often able to survive the winter quite nicely. Their presence calls for renewed attention to offering food at hummingbird feeders.

BASIC RULES IN ATTRACTING HUMMINGBIRDS

1. Plant favorite hummingbird flowers.
2. Start feeding as soon as hummingbirds return in the spring.
3. Gain attention by making feeders conspicuous.

172

*Birds
That
Visit
Feeding
Stations*

4. When first attracting, you may use a solution that is one part sugar by volume to two parts water; be sure to switch soon to a weaker, safer mixture of one part sugar to four parts water.

5. Boil the water used in the solution in order to kill bacteria.

6. Do not use honey.

7. It is generally unwise to experiment with fortified foods.

8. Test several feeders and settle for the one or ones that suit you and your hummingbirds.

9. Brushing salad oil onto exposed parts of feeders and supports is one of the best ways to reduce insect competition.

10. If birds other than hummingbirds begin coming to sugar-water feeders in undue numbers, discourage them with perchless feeders; at the same time, if you like, reserve a few feeders with perches for these visitors.

11. Keep feeding in the fall as long as any hummingbirds are present.

RUBY-THROATED HUMMINGBIRD

This small hummingbird, which has a breeding range from Alberta and the eastern edge of the Great Plains eastward to the Atlantic coast, is neither the smallest, plainest, nor most colorful of the hummingbirds. Rather it is a typical representative of the New World family of hummingbirds and shows all the typical traits of the family. The brightly colored male often tries to dominate feeders. Certain individual males are highly belligerent and resent the presence of other hummingbirds and of other species as well. Although much of the interplay between birds at feeders is sheer exuberance, there are cases when a male whose breeding territory includes the area around a feeder becomes overly aggressive in his attacks upon other birds. When this occurs, try moving the feeder to a new location. Once the feeder is outside the male's territory, the attacks will subside.

The ruby-throat, like most other hummingbirds, is fearless in the presence of man. Birds readily alight upon a hand or finger that holds a feeding vial. Unlike songbirds that have been hand tamed, the ruby-throat does not distinguish between old friends and strangers. Hummingbirds will come to anyone who supplies food. There are many recorded instances of birds probing or investigating bright objects we are wearing. These may be an earring, a hair ribbon, a bright handkerchief, or a red dot on a tie. It has been supposed that one reason hummingbirds feel so secure in our presence is that they have almost unlimited self-confidence. Quick flight and instant maneuverability permit them to dash away at the least suggestion of danger.

The busiest time for hummingbirds at feeders is the early part of the morning and again in late afternoon. Although visits may take place all through the day, the early and late visits reflect the great need these birds have for an energy-giving lift before and after nightfall. Once having caught up on food requirements, a humming-bird indulges in idle loafing and activities such as aerial acrobatics, bathing, and preening of feathers. It will be noticed that the same hummingbird will return again and again to an exposed perch. Perches are leafless twigs or even clotheslines or TV antennas. Birds may remain motionless upon a favorite perch for many minutes. Hummingbirds bathe by ruffling their feathers amid leaves that are wet from the dew or rain; also they fly through the sprinkle of a hose or the water-drip that is falling into a bird bath. They never descend to a puddle or bird bath to bathe.

The ruby-throated hummingbird is with us scarcely more than three months. The sexes migrate separately, the males returning a few days ahead of the females in spring. In more northern states we look for the return of hummingbirds around the middle to end of May. In the fall adult males start south a month before the females and immature birds. Many birds have departed by the end of August. But the exodus has not been completed until late September or early October.

The best policy in regard to hummingbirds is to grow plenty of the flowers that are well liked for nectar and the insects they contain and supplement this most essential part of the diet with a sugar-water solution that rarely should be stronger than one part sugar to four parts water. The only feeding stations used by humming-birds are special hummingbird feeders.

fourteen

WOODPECKERS

Precise, methodical birds, and yet exhibiting many personality traits, the woodpeckers hold a special fascination for many of us. My interest in woodpeckers goes back fifty years, and I still find them as enjoyable as any of the birds that visit my feeders. Like the chickadees, they lend courage and cheerfulness to the winter landscape.

Nineteen of the twenty-two species found north of Mexico accept feeding station fare. Woodpeckers are apt to wait longer than other birds before they will accept a new feeding station. Once on to our food, they are among the most faithful of visitors. Several species visit our feeders the year round. Those that come through the summer bring us added pleasure by escorting their young to the feeders.

NORTHERN FLICKER

Not all woodpeckers live up to the family's reputation of being hard-working birds that are forever pounding upon wood. The northern flicker has the fewest woodpecker-like attributes of any North American species. Much of its time is spent on the ground, where it hops about and probes anthills with its long tongue. We sometimes hear it beating a tattoo with its bill upon the gutter or gables of the house. Its nest hole is usually in a rotten tree trunk, but sometimes it drills a hole below the eaves in a house or barn. In summer this bird's diet is composed chiefly of ants and beetles. In winter the diet is a mixture of insects, fruits, and berries.

Now and then flickers drop in warily at our feeders to sample suet and a few other foods. That we see flickers much less often at our feeders than other common woodpeckers is partly explained by the flicker's wariness and partly by our failure to install suitable feeders. The flicker is most at home on a hanging log feeder or suet holder fastened to a tree trunk; occasionally one will come to trays or hanging feeders. Even though more of a ground feeder than the red-bellied woodpecker, the flicker rarely joins the throng of birds that may be feeding below feeders. This reluctance is an indicator of this bird's lack of confidence when it gets close to our dwellings.

In a southern yard with several hanging log feeders suspended from tree limbs, I once watched three flickers taking a leisurely meal. There was no bickering among these birds or between them and other woodpeckers visiting the log feeders. The flicker does not live up to its rather formidable appearance. It is mild and unobtrusive. Even the smallest birds can eat next to it without fear of reprisal.

Unlike many woodpeckers, the flicker is a gregarious bird. It is found in small flocks with others of its kind at every season except the nesting season. A pronounced migration in the fall takes a large share of the more northern population into the sunnier climate of our South. Still a few choose to remain behind. It is not unusual to find this bird braving the snow and cold of New England and the northern Great Lakes. Many of these birds attempt to get through the winter without the advantages of feeding stations.

Suet and fat mixtures are the best foods for attracting the common flicker. Birds sometimes sample other foods as well, and they show a liking for scratch feed, meat scraps, cracked walnuts and pecans, halved oranges and apples, and white bread.

PILEATED WOODPECKER

Once regarded as a declining species, the pileated woodpecker has recovered from a low point reached during the early years of the twentieth century and now is once again seen throughout many wooded parts of North America. A permanent resident, the pileated does little extensive wandering and does not have an instinct to migrate southward in fall. With its powerful bill and ability to chisel through many inches of wood to get at the tunnels of boring insects, the pileated woodpecker is self-

Flickers are hard to entice but will occasionally come to hanging log feeders.

176

*Birds
That
Visit
Feeding
Stations*

sufficient and more than equal to the cold of our northern winters. In addition to its insect diet, the pileated takes a wide variety of fruits and berries.

About fifty years ago the pileated began to appear at feeding stations. Those who had the good fortune to have this spectacular bird at their feeders could hardly believe their eyes. With its flaming crimson crest, large size, and ferocious look, the pileated is a bird that inspires wonder, if not awe. On its part, the pileated did not seem sure of its new surroundings and was inclined to be furtive. As birds got used to feeding upon such unaccustomed foods as suet, their wariness gradually wore off. The experience of John Alexander Hardy of Salisbury, Connecticut, with the arrival of the pileated woodpecker at his feeders seems typical.* On first appearing in April, a pileated would warily visit a suet holder 30 feet from the Hardys' kitchen window. If anyone made the slightest movement or noise, the bird would hastily fly away. By May the bird was much tamer and was joined by its mate. The second bird was also shy and had to go through a taming process. In time, both birds would come confidently to the feeder even when people were eating out-of-doors only 50 feet away. One of the giant woodpeckers always approached the feeder from the right, the other always from the left. Feeding times were also precise. At first the birds came about six in the morning and again about seven in the evening. In early July two offspring appeared with the parents. Not long after this event, the feeding hours had changed to approximately an hour later. The morning feeding period gradually advanced each day until it coincided with the lunch hour of the human occupants.

Although the pileated is seen at feeders more often these days, it is still an exciting event to have a woodpecker come so close to us. We cater to its tastes chiefly with suet; other foods to try include cracked corn, kernels of nutmeats, meat rind, and hamburger. The pileated comes to small hanging feeders that can accommodate its weight and large size but is most at home at trays or suet holders fastened to tree trunks.

RED-BELLIED WOODPECKER

This is *the* woodpecker that is best known at feeding stations in the South. It is also one of the southern birds that has made spectacular advances northward during the

*Letter in *Audubon Magazine*, January–February 1958.

past one hundred years. Although rarely seen north of our southern states in Audubon's day, the red-bellied is now well established in many of our northern states and in southern Ontario. A few hardy pioneers that wander northward in the fall lead the way. Whenever such birds survive the winter, it is a good sign that a nesting pair will soon be seen.

It is always a surprise that this dominantly southern woodpecker is almost as much of a food storer as blue jays and nuthatches. Even in Florida the red-bellied expends much time and energy in the gathering and storing of food. Sunflower seed, cracked corn, and other feeding station foods are stored along with acorns. Birds take these foods to numerous hiding places before finally settling upon a safe site. The red-bellied is aware that other birds and mammals are ready to pilfer its stores. It seems doubtful, however, that the red-bellied ever makes much use of hidden food. In the South especially food storing is largely a game that may serve its purpose as an outlet for surplus energy.

The red-bellied is one of the most omnivorous of our woodpeckers. In seeking a wide assortment of foods, it comes to picnic tables for scraps and even descends to the asphalt of parking lots if it should spy a piece of bread. In Florida it is sometimes found seeking over-ripe fruit in citrus groves. Like the flicker, the red-bellied rarely indulges in heavy drilling to get at insects; it does most of its foraging on the surface of trunks and branches and in the South explores hanging festoons of Spanish moss.

There is little at the feeding station that escapes the eye of this inquisitive woodpecker. On the ground one minute to pick up pieces of cracked corn, it is next seen at a suet holder or window tray. The red-bellied rarely gives way to other birds. It stubbornly tries to hold its ground against brown thrasher, mockingbird, or starling. On the other hand, it seems perfectly willing to share the feeders with less contentious guests. When it departs, it usually carries away a beakful of food. Sometimes the food is stored, sometimes taken to a special spot to be pounded apart and eaten. A red-bellied at my feeder always carried sunflower seed to the same crotch in a tree where the seed could be opened to better advantage.

The red-bellied seems content with almost anything we have to offer. Among its favorite foods are suet, suet mixtures, cheese, raisins, cracked pecans, cracked corn, peanut hearts, sunflower, canary seed, and halved apple or orange. With no strong preference as to feeders, the red-bellied takes food at bird tables, trays on posts, window trays, suet holders, hanging feeders, logs, and hummingbird feeders. In addition, it takes a sizable share of its food from the ground.

RED-HEADED WOODPECKER

This woodpecker cannot safely be pinned down by any of the adjectives we apply to other woodpeckers. It is noisy, gay, mischievous, irascible. At the same time, it shows little of the methodical precision of other woodpeckers.

At one time the red-head was well known in the East. It was *the* woodpecker that most people thought of when any mention was made of birds of this family. There seems to be no precise information as to when the red-head disappeared from large areas of the East. Its departure anteceded the motor vehicle and starling—two of the reasons given for the difficulty the bird seems to be in at present. The red-head, as it swoops low over roads and highways, is often a target of onrushing vehicles. The starling preempts the nesting sites of this bird and other hole nesters. But even without these hazards, about one hundred years ago the red-head seems to have become rare in portions of its eastern range.

During this century the red-head has remained fairly common in parts of the South and Midwest; it has expanded its range westward and in recent years has occupied new territory within sight of the Rockies. As if this picture were not complicated enough, the red-head sometimes returns in some numbers to parts of the East where it has not been seen for many years.

The movements of this bird are dictated largely by the success or failure of the mast crop. If acorns and beechnuts are plentiful, the bird stays where it is. On the other hand, if food of this kind is scarce, flocks of red-heads may launch forth on massive flights that will take them into a completely different part of the country. Sometimes the birds do not return in spring from such flights.

Through the winter birds live on mast of various kinds, and like the red-bellied woodpecker, devote a great deal of time and energy to food storing. Probably very little of the stored food is ever used. With the return of insect life in spring, birds use fence posts and tops of dead trees as vantage points from which to sally forth after flying insects. These birds will live chiefly upon insects until the following fall.

It is during the colder months that we have our best opportunity of luring this bird to our feeding stations. One of our most colorful visitors and a friendly bird, we count ourselves lucky to have its patronage. Red-heads, however, are intolerant toward most other visitors at the feeder and will sometimes try to clear the feeding tray before accepting food themselves. Although we may find ourselves with a pair or two, this is no assurance that we can count upon the continued presence of this bird. In keeping with a restless nature, our red-headed visitors may suddenly leave us and not return. Those that do stay are not hard to please. These birds take food mostly from bird tables and trays; they also utilize suet holders, logs, and the ground. They enjoy sunflower, cracked corn, raisins, bread, and nutmeats.

YELLOW-BELLIED SAPSUCKER

Aberrant woodpeckers, with habits that make them unpopular, the sapsuckers are strange guests that appear in fall and winter. We are not always sure how warmly to welcome these birds. Many of us are aware of the neat rows of small holes the sapsucker makes in nearly every kind of tree, shrub, and woody vine. Choice ornamentals seem to be selected above everything else. While the damage is seldom serious, the small holes do not enhance the appearance of plants that receive this bird's attention.

Sapsuckers obtain sap and a layer of soft inner bark known as cambium at these drillings. Anyone keeping a close watch upon a sapsucker will see that it follows a route that takes it from one feeding site to another. At each site a bird will stop to imbibe and perhaps continue its damaging work. Strangely, many neighboring trees or shrubs of the same species escape this kind of defacement. Sap is a refreshing, often sweetish substance that has a wide appeal to birds and other animals. Although other woodpeckers are suspected of drilling holes for sap, this kind of activity is by and large a monopoly of the sapsucker. There is little that the sapsucker can do to prevent other visitors from helping themselves to liquid that drips from each tiny hole. Bees, wasps, butterflies, squirrels, hummingbirds, other woodpeckers, and almost any bird species that can adapt its feeding methods to tree trunks indulge in these repasts. When a sapsucker works on a maple near my feeding station, many of my guests leave my offerings for the tasty refreshment that awaits them.

The sapsucker does not live exclusively upon sap and cambium. It supplements this diet with fruits, berries, and insects. The few sapsuckers that remain as far north

180

Birds
That
Visit
Feeding
Stations

as the Great Lakes and New England in winter are very much dependent upon feeding stations. As far south as northern Virginia, wintering sapsuckers do not seem overly dependent upon the fare at my feeding stations. There are many days when these birds do not appear at all.

Although some of its habits do not please us, we usually extend a welcome to this strange woodpecker. Among the foods that it will accept at feeding stations are suet, suet mixtures, doughnuts, grape jelly, and sugar-water for hummingbirds. The yellow-bellied sapsucker prefers tree-trunk feeders in the form of small trays and suet holders; it also comes to bird tables, hanging logs, and hummingbird feeders.

HAIRY WOODPECKER

Many of those who feed birds do not distinguish between hairy and downy woodpeckers. They look so much alike, have such similar habits, and are such good patrons of our feeding stations that the small differences between the two birds are apt to be overlooked. But as we get to know these two woodpeckers better, we begin to realize that there are significant differences. The hairy is considerably larger and has a proportionately much larger and heavier bill. Its call note is similar to that of the downy but sharper and louder. There are also differences in behavior. The hairy is not as tame as the downy and is likely to fly away if we approach the window where one is feeding outside. An exception is the larger race that is found in the boreal forests of the North. This bird is quite tame and will allow a close approach.

Then, too, the hairy is more solitary in its habits. When we find it in the woods, it is usually alone or with a mate. The downy, on the other hand, while objecting to close association with others of its kind, frequently joins other small woodland birds and travels with them as they search the trees for insects and other food.

Two species that are closely related and occupy much the same range are called sympatric. The hairy and downy furnish good examples of sympatric species that visit feeding stations. In

*A hairy woodpecker safely partakes of suet cakes
and sunflower seeds at a nonmetal holder.*

defense of territory and relations with other birds at feeding stations, the downy and hairy totally ignore each other and seldom engage in disputes with other birds. But should an outside hairy or downy invade the territory of another hairy or downy, there are sure to be disputes. Usually the pair holding a territory win out over the invaders.

Many times there is some overlapping of territory so that we may have several pairs of downies or hairies coming to a feeding station during a day. Through banding, I learned that as many as ten downies and four hairies came to my feeding stations during the course of a day. A severe snowstorm may bring every individual of both species to the feeders at one time. Under such conditions, territorial rights are seldom observed and the small woodpeckers tend to feed together without friction. Almost everywhere in the East the hairy is considerably less common than the downy.

Although regarded as permanent residents, both downy and hairy woodpeckers do some wandering during the colder months. There is often a marked movement southward by birds from more northern portions of the ranges of the two species. It is likely that a fair share of the hairy and downy woodpeckers we see at our feeders in winter are birds from farther north.

The hairy, though eating most of its food at the feeding station, takes some foods, especially sunflower seeds, to places where it is easier to break open the outside hulls. A bird at my feeder was in the habit of taking sunflower seeds to the gnarled roots at the base of a tree. A seed would be inserted in a crevice and then pounded open by blows of the bill. The technique was very similar to that used by nuthatches.

So long as a favorite food or two are present at the feeder, the hairy comes to these and rarely samples anything else. Nevertheless, birds do accept a number of other foods. Besides the favored suet, fat mixtures, and sunflower, they take such foods as meat scraps, cracked pecans, meats of the black walnut, peanut butter, cheese, apple, and banana. The hairy woodpecker shows a preference for suet holders and hanging logs and sometimes eats at bird tables, trays, and hummingbird feeders.

DOWNY WOODPECKER

To many this is the favorite of all feeding station guests. Only the black-capped chickadee seems to excel it in friendliness and dependability. We look for both species

182

Birds
That
Visit
Feeding
Stations

with the first cool weather of the fall. The two will be with us through the winter and sometimes on through the summer. But it is in winter that visits by these cheerful birds are most welcomed.

The downy seems to delight in the kind of wintry weather that keeps us indoors and works hardships upon many of our other guests. Even during the driving snow of blizzards, it goes about its business much as usual. It clings to a feeding log eating for a long time and then perhaps hops onto a windowsill feeder to sample a doughnut. Although keeping out of the wind to some extent, it seems little daunted by cold, blustery weather. One of the few concessions that the downy makes to bad weather is to spend longer hours in its roosting hole.

There are times during and after snowstorms when my feeders are overrun by starlings. Most of my visitors are hard-pressed on these occasions to get enough food. Not the downy. It ignores the noisy, fractious starlings and somehow slips by them to reach its favorite foods. On the other hand, somewhat larger woodpeckers, like the hairy and red-bellied, show their resentment by gaping at the starlings with half-opened beaks. This show of defiance only antagonizes the starlings. A woodpecker or bird of another species that tries to brave the starling horde is likely to receive rough treatment.

The downy, in keeping with its adaptable nature, finds many of our foods to its liking. It hops awkwardly about feeding trays and sometimes drops down to the ground to pick up food. Now and then a bird will tackle a dog bone that has been left on the lawn. Nutmeats, including coconut, are well favored by this woodpecker, and so are fats, doughnuts, cornbread, and American cheese. Grain and a few seeds are taken, including sunflower and cracked corn. Versatile in regard to feeders, the downy may be seen at bird tables, trays, suet holders, small hanging feeders, and hanging logs; rarely does it come to the ground or to hummingbird feeders.

Admired for their beauty and intelligence, the jays, nevertheless, are not overly popular with those who feed birds. There is always the lurking suspicion that a jay is up to some mischief. Usually we are not far wrong in this assumption. One of the most resourceful of birds is the Canada, or gray, jay of the north woods. Not far behind in this attribute is the blue jay, which is found throughout the East, and much the same can be said of the several jays found from the Great Plains and Rockies to the Pacific coast. All of the jays have a liking for our feeding station offerings. Much of this food is carried away to be stored.

GRAY JAY

As soon as smoke spirals upward from a campfire anywhere in the north woods of our northern states or Canada, there is a chance of a visit by this jay. Two or three birds may come gliding out of the forest, where they have been watching the campers intently. They know how to time their arrival so as to take best advantage of the habit that has given them the name "camp robber." As soon as food appears, the birds silently arrive and go about their business. Food is sometimes seized from a frying pan or taken from an eating utensil. Boldness of this kind is not without its reward. Most campers and backwoodsmen toss out a few scraps for the birds. Gray jays will fly off with almost anything. They have been known to take such objects as matches, tobacco plugs, and soap. So far as food is concerned, they seem to like

184

Birds
That
Visit
Feeding
Stations

nothing better than baked beans or bacon. We do not object too strenuously to their small depredations and the fact that they sometimes enter tents and cabins without invitation. There is a rule of hospitality in the north woods that requires the sharing of necessities with others, whether fellowmen or wild creatures.

In towns and settlements where the gray jay sometimes appears in winter, there is also a spirit of giving. Although a few of these birds may accept the hospitality of our feeding stations, there is no mass movement to the places where we live. Only on very rare occasions do birds appear very far southward in winter. It is an event indeed when a gray jay appears at a feeder in New Jersey, Pennsylvania, or states immediately south of the Great Lakes. For the most part the gray jay is content to brave the bitterest winters in the seclusion of the great northern forest where it lives.

Almost any leftovers or table scraps will go a long way toward appeasing this bird's appetite. Among foods taken from the feeding station menu are suet, fat mixtures, oatmeal (cooked), bread, crackers, banana, and grapes. The gray jay is not well versed as to feeding stations and seizes food wherever it can find it.

BLUE JAY

An observer in 1901 spoke of blue jays being very numerous in Minneapolis and reported that "their loud screams" were almost as familiar as "the incessant chatter

The gray jay removes food, soap, and tobacco and then stores the loot in crevices in trees.

of English sparrows." Although one of the more common, better known birds at the turn of the century, the blue jay at that time was not nearly as tame and confiding as it is today. Only gradually has the blue jay lost a deep-seated suspicion of man. Somehow blue jays in the South lost their suspicion sooner than those in the North. At the present time, the blue jay watches us closely and tends to avoid familiarity. Nevertheless, the blue jay is one of the first birds to visit feeding stations in northern states, and everywhere it enters our yards freely and makes use of whatever we have to offer.

Blue jays are usually present the year round. Although given to wandering and to pronounced migrations southward some years, the places of birds that leave are frequently taken by others that have moved in from somewhere else. We seldom gain an accurate picture of the blue jay population by watching our feeders. There are times when birds come in a steady procession all day and other times when weeks go by with few if any of these gaudy blue birds at the feeders.

We are often left with the impression that the blue jay is an eager enthusiast that turns wholeheartedly to first one source of food and then another. The blue jay

A blue jay removing food while chipping sparrows wait; the jay will usually bury it later.

does seem to be easily diverted. Long absences can often be explained by a return to acorns or other natural foods. Sometimes the jays have found something more to their liking at a neighbor's feeder. If we should miss our mischievous visitors, we can always console ourselves with the fact that sooner or later our guests will be back with us again.

There is a common misconception that blue jays go out of their way to chase other birds from feeders. This is not strictly true. Ever up to some mischief, blue jays sometimes imitate the calls of a hawk or sound the characteristic jay alarm notes prior to their appearance at a feeder. These tactics are designed to send other birds away in a panic. Although the ruse may work a few times, other birds quickly catch on and, in spite of the clamor, keep right on eating. If anything, blue jays are rather gentlemanly in their table manners. Sometimes, when eating at a small feeder, birds will wait their turn—while one is at the feeder, others wait patiently nearby. Once at the feeder jays go about their business quickly and politely, for the most part ignoring other birds. If challenged, the blue jay is a formidable antagonist and will not put up with any nonsense.

*A blue jay's warning notes
often save the lives of small birds.*

Problems connected with blue jays taking away food and depredating nests have been discussed in Chapter 6. The fact that so many of our sunflower seeds and other foods are buried by this jay, and probably few ever retrieved, is not to our liking. To a large degree, the blue jay redeems itself by the prompt warning it gives other birds whenever there is any sign of danger. The blue jay's warning notes are understood and usually heeded. Many a cat or small bird-hawk has been cheated out of a meal by these timely warnings.

Blue jays have omnivorous tastes and will accept almost anything we offer at the feeder. But if there is one food that has special appeal, birds will generally take this food in preference to everything else. After a time, there may be another food that catches the blue jay's fancy and which will take first priority. Blue jays have a special fondness for sunflower, peanuts, peanut hearts, cracked pecan meats, and other nutmeats. Among the other foods that may hold them for a while are wheat, cracked corn, sorghum, millet, buckwheat, raisins, apple, white bread, cornbread, and crackers. Although blue jays come to most feeders, including bird tables, trays, suet holders, hanging feeders, and sometimes hummingbird feeders, they are most at home on the ground.

sixteen	# CROWS

Although in the same family with the jays and having many of their mannerisms, the crows seem to have far less appeal to most of us. Part of this is the melancholy black attire that is so characteristic of the crows. Also we tend to resent the way this bird flies off as soon as it sees us. The crow has not forgotten the bitter persecution it has received at the hands of man. The common crow is the only member of the family in the East that visits feeding stations. The smaller fish crow, which is found chiefly in the South and along rivers and the seacoast, has not yet shown any signs of responding to our offerings.

COMMON CROW

Taking great pains to find out how welcome they may be before settling down to a feeding routine, crows at first visit us ever so warily and sometimes only in the early morning hours. Then, as visits are extended to more convenient times, birds come only a few at a time and always under the watchful eyes of a sentry or two. Gradually more confidence is gained and birds come at any hour and without taking elaborate precautions. At my Virginia feeders birds eventually became so relaxed that none would fly away when I would tap upon a windowpane.

Most feeding takes place on the ground. However, at my Virginia home crows had a way of reaching suet mixtures in cans fastened to tree trunks. Cans were frequently dislodged, and I sometimes found them on the ground far from the place of attachment. Birds walk about as they pick up food that has been scattered on the ground. If sentries have been posted in nearby trees, feeding birds eat without haste and show no sign of nervousness. As soon as an alarm is sounded, the diners quickly take flight and are gone before we know it. Bread, suet, and suet mixtures are favorite foods with the crow, and grain is also relished. Too wary, as a rule, to accept food at feeders, the crow usually restricts its feeding almost entirely to the ground.

seventeen

CHICKADEES AND TITMICE

We are fortunate in North America in having a goodly representation of the tits, or titmice, that are such favorites in England and elsewhere in the Old World. Nearly all are tame, adaptable birds that respond readily to foods offered at feeding stations. With only a little patience most chickadees and titmice can be taught to take food from the hand or even the lips. No feeding device is too intricate for them. Some individuals even learn to get in and out of banding traps with falling doors. They do this by avoiding the treadle that triggers the door mechanism. Our chickadees and titmice are undaunted by squirrels and larger birds at feeders. The coldest, bleakest winter days find them cheerful and full of life. When more food is needed at the feeding station, they may remind us by vocal complaints or by tapping with their bills upon windowpanes.

Because of our propensity for being inconsistent with common names of birds, we have called some of our species "chickadees" and others "titmice." All, however, belong to the genus *Parus* and are close relatives. We can see the close relationship both in appearance and in behavior patterns. Our four eastern species are the black-capped, Carolina, and boreal chickadees and the tufted titmouse.

NUMBERS AT FEEDERS

In the case of non-flocking species, such as brown creeper, mockingbird, or hermit thrush, we can usually arrive at a reasonably close estimate as to numbers using our feeders by watching to see how many individuals are on or near the feeders at one time. On the other hand, we are likely to underestimate the numbers of gregarious or flocking species and also those of birds like the downy woodpecker and white-breasted nuthatch that establish territories and try to keep out others of their kind.

The titmice, which travel in small flocks, furnish a good example of how difficult it is to estimate numbers. We never see many at a time and generally conclude that we have few more than we see at one time at the feeder and immediate vicinity. The weakness in this method of estimating numbers lies in the fact that even during the course of a morning we may have played host to three or four small flocks of tufted titmice or chickadees. When one flock leaves to resume a search for natural foods, another flock may soon arrive to take its place. Each flock that passes through may come back several times during the day for additional meals.

The only way to reach an approximate estimate of numbers is through bird banding. Although primarily a technique for determining the migration patterns of birds, banding is useful in solving many other questions. So far as numbers using feeders are concerned, we gain an estimate by banding as many individuals as we can.

One winter, when living in Massachusetts and playing host to birds at a very popular, long-established feeding station, I banded eighty-nine black-capped chickadees and captured another twenty-nine that I had banded during the previous year or that had been banded by other bird banders living nearby. To capture the birds in order to place a numbered aluminum band on either the right or left leg, I used traps baited with the same kind of food the chickadees were eating at my feeding stations. While some of the chickadees that I captured were undoubtedly chance visitors that happened to be passing my way on the migrations that this species sometimes undertakes, most were old standbys and this was apparent from the fact that I captured the same individuals over and over. By the time the

*Bird banding can tell us more about the birds
that come to our feeders.*

192

*Birds
That
Visit
Feeding
Stations*

winter was over I knew that at least one hundred and eighteen chickadees had visited my feeders, and it was safe to assume that another twenty or thirty had also used them but had failed to enter my banding traps. So the total number using my feeders that winter may have been as high as one hundred and fifty. Although I never saw more than ten at one time in the neighborhood of my feeders, the total number coming daily, as ascertained through banding, was approximately a hundred. In this instance and in sampling numbers of other species through banding, I have discovered more than once that the total number of individuals using the feeders is likely to be ten or more times the number that is seen at one time on or near the feeders.

ACTIVITY AWAY FROM FEEDERS

It often seems as though the titmice (including chickadees) spend nearly all their time feeding. This is the impression we get when we watch them outside our windows. But to judge this matter fairly we must take into consideration the fact that we have lured our visitors with food and therefore it is only to be expected that feeding activity will be all-important with them. Once out of sight will these same birds still be looking for food or will other activities begin to assume more importance?

Thanks to the tireless efforts of a British observer, we have for comparison observations made on the daily habits of six species of European tits near Oxford, England. These species, along with treecreepers (brown creepers) and goldcrests, were followed and watched for over a year by the ornithologist John Gibb.* During the course of Gibb's study some twelve thousand observations were recorded—each represented an activity that a bird was engaged in when it was first seen by an observer.

Although many of the titmice were apparently visiting bird feeders outside the wooded study area, there was nothing in the results to indicate a lessening or slowing down in feeding activity once birds were off on their own. In fact, feeding was by far the most frequently recorded activity. During the month of December, for example, observations indicating feeding activity ranged from 96 percent for coal tit to 81 percent for blue tit. Time spent feeding varied little with the seasons, but all species under observation fed more intensively in midwinter and again during the nesting

*"Feeding Ecology of Tits, With Notes on Treecreeper and Goldcrest," *Ibis*, 96:513–43, 1954.

season. Extra feeding effort in winter was associated with such factors as shortened daylight hours and less abundant food supplies. Demands of the young called for renewed efforts during the nesting season.

This study, as well as others by the British, reveals that smaller birds, as a rule, put in more time feeding than do larger ones. Sometimes, however, the smaller bird begins its daily feeding later in the morning than the larger bird and ceases feeding earlier in the afternoon. The coal tit, which weighs less than any of the others, was active for about forty minutes less each day than any of the other species. Gibb suggests that this species may not have to feed as long because it has recourse to food that it stored away during the fall months. Marsh tits may also manage a somewhat shorter day because of food storing.

We see similar relationships between size and time devoted to feeding among the birds coming to American feeders. The three chickadees along with the brown creeper and kinglets are among the smallest visitors seen at our feeders. They are also the busiest birds we will find when it comes to feeding activity. From shortly after sunrise to near dusk these small birds keep up a steady pace of activity that is largely related to food.

INGENUITY

The European titmice are noted for their ingenuity and cleverness. About seventy years ago the European tits learned to open milk bottles placed on doorsteps by removing the caps. They would then consume some of the milk or cream at the top of the bottle. Several birds in other families also learned this trick. Probably the most ingenious feat credited to European titmice is that of string pulling. The bird, perched on a branch to which a string with food dangling at the end is tied, uses its bill to pull the string upward. Each loop of slack string is clamped under the bird's foot and held in place until the entire string with the food has been hauled up to within reach. This trick is less frequently performed by other European birds, including the jay and greenfinch. Birds have looped as much as two feet of string in order to obtain a peanut or some other tidbit.

When I exposed birds at my feeders to small pieces of suet attached to strings, the only two that responded were representatives of the titmouse family. Both Carolina

194

Birds
That
Visit
Feeding
Stations

chickadees and tufted titmice obtained the food, but not in the clever way utilized by their European cousins. Instead of pulling the food upward to a perch, my birds would fly to the food, cling to it, and commence eating, hanging on with their feet.

Although string pulling has occasionally been observed in North American birds, we seldom demand that they perform such feats in order to obtain food. On the other hand, in our efforts to thwart squirrels, starlings, and house sparrows, we have devised feeders that require great ingenuity on the part of all users. One type of feeder emits sunflower or other seeds one at a time only so long as a bird has its weight on a perch that acts as a treadle. The designer was evidently under the impression that each bird coming to the feeder would take its one seed and fly off. However, the two species clever enough to use this feeder—black-capped chickadee and purple finch—quickly learned to stay on the perch and eat each seed as it appeared. So while one bird was having its fill, all the others would be queued up for frustratingly long waits. That chickadees could learn this trick is quite remarkable, since their normal feeding procedure is to pick up a single seed and immediately fly away with it.

BLACK-CAPPED CHICKADEES

Generally regarded as the most friendly of feeding station birds, this chickadee is *the* favorite of thousands who feed birds. The warm greeting it gives us as it repeats "chick-a-dee-dee-dee" and the way it so often alights upon our persons is reason enough to take delight in this bird. Few feeding stations in more northern states are without the black-capped. From southern Pennsylvania, Ohio, and Missouri southward, the black-capped is replaced by the very similar but slightly smaller Carolina chickadee.

The harder a feeder is to negotiate, the better it is liked by the black-capped chickadee. Although it can use every kind of hanging feeder, this chickadee does very well at bird tables, trays on posts and at windows, suet holders, and hummingbird feeders. This bird also sometimes comes to the ground.

We may notice that activity at our feeders picks up as soon as the chickadees arrive. Their sudden appearances may lead to an almost frantic burst of activity which sees a pickup in the attendance of other birds and the rapid disappearance of food offerings. Then, almost as suddenly as it began, the activity will cease and there will be a lull until the next group of chickadees arrives. Why this chickadee-related activity?

The explanation will readily become apparent if you search the winter woods in your vicinity. For the first twenty minutes or so, as you walk along a woodland trail, you may not see a bird anywhere or hear a call note. Then, all of a sudden, there will be three or four birds and soon you are in the midst of a whole flock. Moving in the same direction, the birds will pass you in twos and threes and almost always with chickadees in the lead. Before the flock has passed, you may have noted five or six species. Winter flocks such as these may sometimes contain downy woodpeckers, tufted titmice, white-breasted nuthatches, a brown creeper or two, as well as ruby-crowned kinglets and perhaps several warblers. Although some of the followers join the flock for only a brief period, others are more persistent and may appear at feeders along with the chickadees, which are the real leaders. The arrival of one of these mixed flocks is one of the main reasons for the sudden bursts of activity that we notice at our feeders.

The motivation for such mixed gatherings seems to lie largely in food. Some members are keener-eyed than the rest and find food where other birds would

A chickadee pounding open a sunflower seed.

196

*Birds
That
Visit
Feeding
Stations*

fail. The chickadees excel in ability to spot food. Woodpeckers are helpful in exposing insects that lie buried in rotten wood. Other members, such as blue jays, are more alert to danger than the others and are the first to give alarm calls. Protection, therefore, is another reason that birds band together in mixed parties. In addition, there may be an element of companionship that contributes to this phenomenon.

At the feeder the chickadees' actions and feeding methods almost always follow the same pattern. Birds usually remain at the feeder only long enough to seize an item of food, which is immediately carried away to be eaten elsewhere. Once away from the feeder, a chickadee will place the food, no matter what it is, between its toes and begin hammering at it with its small, sharp bill. Outer husks, such as the hull of the sunflower, are expertly broken apart and the meat inside is then consumed one small piece at a time.

Rarely do two chickadees ever meet at the feeder. The timing of arrivals and departures is so perfect that these birds almost never interfere with each other or with other birds at the feeder. With chickadees there is no problem of etiquette or need for a peck-right relationship in which some birds have higher priorities than others. All such matters are resolved by seizing food as quickly as possible and then making off with it.

If there is anything that chickadees prefer above other foods, it is sunflower seeds. Normally seeds are taken one at a time to a nearby perch; there the contents are eaten after the hull has been split apart. The chickadee is such an expert at performing this operation that it is only a matter of a few seconds before the bird is back for another seed. An occasional chickadee learns to carry off two sunflower seeds at a time. This was true of a hand-tamed bird at my feeder that always flew away with two seeds firmly held in its bill. Some individuals are very fussy about the seeds they take and may pick up and drop four or five before accepting one. To my eye at least there rarely seems to be anything wrong with the seeds that are rejected.

Among the other foods at our feeders that have appeal to the sometimes finicky chickadee are suet, suet mixtures, peanut hearts, finely cracked meats of walnut, butternut, and pecan, doughnuts, and pie crust. Since chickadees sometimes choke on it, peanut butter should not be offered unless well mixed with cornmeal, flour, or other ingredients that reduce the stickiness.

Most writers make little distinction between the Carolina and black-capped chickadees. They point out that the more southerly ranging Carolina chickadee is smaller, lacks the white in the wing, and is not as tame. I would add to these characteristics the fact that the Carolina is not nearly as forward or domineering as the black-capped. In the South, where the Carolina chickadee usually shares the feeder with the tufted titmouse, it is usually the titmouse that is the first with everything. This is not to say that the Carolina chickadee is not quick-witted and intelligent. Rather, it is simply overshadowed at times by its larger relative, the black-capped.

The Carolina chickadee has virtually all the mannerisms of the black-capped, and when the two are together at the feeder, it is hard to tell the two species apart. During the occasional winters when large numbers of black-capped chickadees move into the more northerly of southern states, the two species frequently intermingle at feeders. Whenever these meetings take place, there is little or no sign of friction between the two. Like the black-capped, the Carolina chickadee shows a strong preference for sunflower, suet, suet mixtures, and finely cracked nutmeats. It also shows the same versatility in mastering feeders as its black-capped relative. The Carolina chickadee takes special delight in the small hanging ones.

BOREAL CHICKADEE

This small, hardy bird is as much at home in the north woods wilderness, where it lives, as the gray jay. Although not as forward as the gray jay in coming about campsites, this small chickadee is highly resourceful and fully equal to the rigors of the northern winter. There are only occasional winters when the boreal chickadee moves southward, and even then it does not come as far south as its close relative, the black-capped chickadee. Appearances as far south as Pennsylvania and other states that border the South are exceptional.

Boreal chickadees are quick to take advantage of feeders and accept the same foods that are taken by Carolina and black-capped chickadees. Feeder preferences are probably similar to those of the preceding two chickadees.

Because of its larger size and uniform coloration, the tufted titmouse seems an altogether different bird from the chickadees, which are such close relatives and which so often appear at the same feeders. A brief period of watching will reveal that the tufted titmouse has all the characteristic ways of the family. Birds arrive one at a time at the feeder to carry off food in typical chickadee fashion. Each food item is taken to a perch where it is placed firmly between the toes and hammered upon with the bill until broken apart. Every feeding device is quickly mastered and any new object placed at the feeder is sure to be investigated. The tufted titmouse will perform remarkable feats to reach food that we have purposely made more inaccessible.

Like the red-bellied woodpecker, cardinal, and several other birds that were once regarded as exclusively southerners, the tufted titmouse has been pushing northward for many years and is now well established in southern Ontario and most of our more northern states from Minnesota eastward. Although the reverse might be expected to be true, the more northerly ranging tufted titmice are less confiding and tend to be slower about coming to feeding stations than those that live farther south.

Watching tufted titmice after they left my Virginia feeders, I discovered that about half their trips were for the purpose of hiding food. Food was either taken to the ground and hidden under leaves or tucked into crevices of rotten stumps and logs. So stealthily does the tufted titmouse go about its food storing that we would not be aware of this activity unless we watched birds very closely whenever they left the feeders with food. Usually food storing is conducted some distance from the house and therefore beyond the range of our vision if we are watching from indoors.

As with the chickadees, sunflower, suet, suet mixtures, and nutmeats are staple foods. If there is any difference in tastes, it is the tufted titmouse's greater receptiveness to bakery products. The titmouse has a special liking for doughnuts, cornbread, white bread, and cookie crumbs. While it has a preference for small hanging feeders and logs, the tufted titmouse will accept bird tables, trays, hummingbird feeders, and food on the ground.

NUTHATCHES

This distinctive group of tree-climbing birds is well represented at eastern feeding stations by the white-breasted nuthatch and, to a lesser extent, the more northerly ranging red-breasted nuthatch. Few feeding stations are visited by the small brown-headed nuthatch of southern pine forests. The droll mannerisms and odd appearance of the nuthatches contribute an element of humor to the feeding station scene. We are sometimes reminded of a circus when we see the performances of titmice and nuthatches. The first are the acrobats and the latter the clowns.

WHITE-BREASTED NUTHATCH

Whenever the chickadee and downy woodpecker appear at feeding stations, there is a good chance of seeing the third member of the triumvirate, which is the white-breasted nuthatch. The three form a congenial company that take turns at suet holders, hanging log feeders, and other elevated feeders.

The white-breasted nuthatch, like the other two, is a daily visitor to feeders through the colder months. Occasionally a pair will continue to come through the summer. Almost always it is the same pair that remain faithful to our food supplies. Like the downy woodpecker, the white-breasted nuthatch is intolerant of trespass by other members of its species. This does not necessarily mean that a pair will have exclusive dominion. Outside birds frequently find their opportunity when the resident pair is away feeding elsewhere. Also territorial claims tend to break down during very harsh weather. During and after winter snowstorms, it is not unusual to find five or six of these nuthatches at a time at our feeders.

Not only is the white-breasted a comical caricature of a bird, with its short legs, abbreviated tail, large head, and overall plumpness, but it acts the part of a clown. On arriving at a tray filled with sunflower seeds, this fussy bird begins arranging things to its own taste. Empty hulls and sometimes perfectly good seeds may be taken to the edge of the tray and dumped over the side. This is a kind of tidying-up process that sometimes precedes serious feeding activity. Now and then, after dropping something over the side, the white-breasted will have second thoughts and attempt to catch the object before it reaches the ground. Failing in this, the white-breasted may drop to the ground to retrieve whatever has fallen.

If the white-breasted should happen to find a squirrel, chipmunk, or bird of another species in command of a tray where it is about to feed, it may go through a strange performance designed to scare off the competitor. While one or both wings are raised straight above the back, the bird will sway back and forth with feathers fluffed out and the long, sharp bill pointed directly at the adversary. The "pendulum act," as it is called, may be conducted on the feeding tray or sometimes while a nuthatch is awaiting its turn on a tree trunk near the feeder. There is no question but that the performance is designed as a means of scaring away other diners. But

*When a mixed flock arrives—
here a downy woodpecker, a white-breasted
nuthatch (feeding), and two black-capped
chickadees—some members usually have
to wait their turn.*

how effective is this act? I cannot recall a single instance of another bird or mammal departing in the face of this bizarre performance.

A period of intensive feeding activity by the white-breasted may be followed by a long absence from the feeder. During periods when feeding is taking place, birds come and go in much the same way as chickadees. Something is always carried away in the bill. This food is either eaten at more leisure somewhere else or stored for possible future use. Large pieces of food, nuts, sunflower seeds, and the like, may be taken to a convenient crevice, such as a cavity in the bark of a tree trunk, and there pounded apart. This "nuthatching," as it is sometimes called, has given the bird its name.

Whenever the white-breasted goes on a food-storing binge, there may be a period of furious activity that will last as long as an hour. Trip after trip is made to the feeder and each time food is hauled away for hastily made caches in nearby trees or sometimes the chinks of the feeder itself. Few birds are more careless when it comes to food storing. The caches of the white-breasted are quickly found by other birds and mammals. Sometimes a cache is robbed even before the white-breasted is back at the feeder for its next load. Away from the feeder, the white-breasted is equally busy with food storing—now it is acorns, beechnuts, and other natural foods.

This nuthatch has much the same food preferences as the titmouse. First in priority are sunflower, suet, suet mixtures, and nutmeats. Halved pumpkin, squash, and cantaloupe seeds are well received, and so are peanuts, peanut hearts, buckwheat, cracked corn, white bread, cornbread, and doughnuts. This nuthatch's ability to master small hanging feeders doesn't seem to keep it from taking food at bird tables, trays on posts, window trays, suet holders, hummingbird feeders, and the ground.

RED-BREASTED NUTHATCH

After getting well acquainted with the white-breasted nuthatch, it is always a surprise to discover a second, smaller nuthatch that differs in many ways from the one that we are so used to. A bird of the northern evergreen forests, the red-breasted nuthatch moves southward in small numbers during some fall seasons; other years these movements are of great magnitude and constitute what are called invasions. Sometimes invasions take birds as far south as northern Florida and Texas.

202

*Birds
That
Visit
Feeding
Stations*

Unlike its white-breasted relative, this nuthatch is gregarious and travels in flocks with others of its kind. It is not unusual to encounter as many as five or ten of these nuthatches at a time at our feeders. The red-breasted nuthatch is almost as aware of artificial food supplies as the white-breasted. Even when on its migrations, it may deign to stop by. Hanging and tree-trunk feeders are to its liking, and it has the same habit as its larger relative of carrying off large quantities of food. An observer in Illinois reported seeing this nuthatch press seeds into the ground in much the same manner that squirrels use in disposing of food. Most of the food carried away by this nuthatch is stored in crevices in trees.

In more northern states the red-breasted is sometimes a fairly constant visitor to feeders through the winter. Invaders that reach more southern states are apt to be quite erratic in their appearances. Not infrequently, natural foods, especially pine seeds, take priority over feeding station fare. Nevertheless, these birds respond well to sunflower, suet, suet mixtures, peanut hearts, nutmeats, melon seeds, and white bread. Feeder preference is the same as that of the white-breasted and includes bird tables, trays, suet holders, hanging feeders, and hummingbird feeders.

*A red-breasted nuthatch
hiding a seed.*

We have only one of the small tree-climbing birds known as creepers in North America. Our single creeper, however, has a wide range extending from Alaska to Newfoundland and reaching well into our more northern states. In winter, the season when this creeper appears at feeding stations, the bird may be found almost anywhere in wooded regions from the far North to Florida and Texas.

BROWN CREEPER

Seldom do we see more than two or three brown creepers at a time in the vicinity of our feeders. Always seemingly busy in searching the bark and crevices of trees, these odd little birds rarely appear to take notice of our feeding station supplies. Yet if we watch one of these birds closely, we will see that a disproportionate amount of time is spent on tree trunks in the immediate vicinity of the feeders. Still closer inspection will show us that the attraction of these tree-trunk sites lies in the small bits of suet and other fatty foods that other birds have brought from nearby feeders. In wiping their bills, storing food, and still other ways, birds leave behind enough food in the bark and crevices of trees to be of interest to the brown creeper, which is primarily a gleaner and seldom overlooks a particle of food so long as it is something suited to its tastes.

Now and then the brown creeper goes directly to the main source of supply. If other birds are about, the brown creeper suddenly realizes its mistake and hastily flies

204

*Birds
That
Visit
Feeding
Stations*

away. Few birds are more timid in the presence of other species and few are more anxious to avoid hostile encounters.

Besides visiting tree trunks near the feeder and suet holders, the brown creeper also avails itself at times of the fallen tidbits of fatty foods that accumulate on the ground below feeders. After descending to the ground at the base of a tree, a brown creeper will hop about on its tiny legs as it picks up tidbits so small that most other birds overlook them. Sometimes these excursions take birds five or six feet from the tree trunk that was used by the creeper in descending to the ground.

The best way to assist the brown creeper in its tireless search for food is to smear a suet mixture into the bark crevices of trees that are visited frequently. Besides suet and fat mixtures, the brown creeper takes finely chopped nutmeats, including peanut hearts. One observer reported that this bird took small pieces of boiled potato. Although tending to avoid feeders if it can, the brown creeper is occasionally seen at suet holders and hanging logs.

A brown creeper finding suet secreted in bark.

WRENS twenty

Four of the six wrens found in the East are familiar birds of yards and gardens. More often heard than seen, the wrens generally scurry about so quickly that we have a hard time getting a good enough look to make an identification. Visits to feeders by wrens are also hurried, and many times we are not sure if the visit was to satisfy the bird's curiosity or really for food. Though the visits may be brief, wrens do accept a variety of feeding station foods and sometimes they become frequent guests.

HOUSE WREN

This wren that we hear all summer and that makes such free use of birdhouses is not a frequent visitor to bird feeders. Chance visits by this wren occur most often in the Deep South, where most house wrens spend the winter.

A house wren that came to a rustic stump feeder in a yard in Georgia always approached the feeder from the same direction. Once at the feeder it would disappear into a hole in the stump and then would emerge at an opening that gave access to a small feeding platform. The other birds at the feeder would often be so startled by the sudden appearance of the wren that they would fly away in alarm.

Foods taken by the house wren include suet, suet mixtures, pecan meats, cornbread, white bread, and cracker crumbs. In keeping with family traits, the house wren investigates every kind of feeder. Food seems to be taken most often at bird tables and small trays.

WINTER WREN

Well named, this tiny wren appears in our yards only after cold weather sets in. Making itself at home in woodpiles, brush heaps, and tangles, the winter wren keeps out of the cold wind and also stays out of sight. Now and then a single bird, or sometimes a pair, will appear at the feeder. Food is eaten hastily, and if there is any disturbance, the winter wren disappears as quickly as it came.

The winter wren's tastes seem to be exactly the same as those of the house wren. Feeder preferences, if any, are not well known. Like the house wren, the winter wren seems to come mainly to bird tables and small trays.

BEWICK'S WREN

All but unknown on the Atlantic coast, the Bewick's wren makes its home in the Mississippi valley and adjacent regions. This wren is present the year round. Feeding stations seem to have only a mild attraction and rarely are visited at any season except the winter. Like other wrens, the Bewick's does a lot of exploring and not infrequently finds its way into sheds and houses. Many times we have to rescue these venturesome explorers. Once inside a house, wrens rarely know how to find their way out again.

Suet, fats, and finely ground nutmeats are standard with this wren when it is at the feeder. The Bewick's wren, like the others, investigates feeders of all kinds but takes food mainly at bird tables and small trays.

CAROLINA WREN

A large reddish-brown wren with a white stripe over the eye is sure to be this common wren of eastern states from the Great Lakes and southern New England southward. With us the year round, the Carolina lets its presence be known through loud whistles and a melodious song that may be heard at any season. This is *the* wren to expect at feeding stations. Not as brief in its visits as the other wrens, the Carolina sometimes settles down for a lengthy meal. It is not deterred by the presence of other birds. The pair that comes to my feeders in Virginia is undaunted by the presence of purple finches and even larger birds. Whenever the competition becomes too great, the Carolina disappears as suddenly as it came.

Sometimes this bird exhibits a mouse-like habit of disappearing into drain pipes and other cavities. Like other wrens, the Carolina frequently finds its way into houses and must be rescued. But the Carolina is largely unseen, and there are days at a time when the only indications of its presence are loud, piercing whistles that come from nearby woodland.

The Carolina wren has a wide range of tastes and seems particularly fond of bits of meat. We can offer it nothing more tempting than pieces of ground raw hamburger. Among the other foods that are well received are suet, fat mixtures, sunflower, peanut hearts, cracked pecan and walnut kernels, American cheese, cornbread, raisins, and banana. As versatile with feeders as with foods, the Carolina comes to window feeders, bird tables, trays, suet holders, small hanging feeders, logs and hummingbird feeders. They also search the ground for fallen tidbits.

The Carolina wren relishes an occasional offering of raw hamburger.

twenty-one

MIMIC THRUSHES

The birds that belong to this family have a common ability to imitate other birds and sounds of various kinds. The mockingbird is the most accomplished mimic of all and also has a thrilling song of its own. The mockingbird, catbird, and brown thrasher are familiar birds of eastern yards and gardens and are found in wilder regions as well. Of the three, the mockingbird is the most adaptable and seems as much at home in city suburbs as in the remotest wilds. The catbird and brown thrasher, on the other hand, require well-planted yards if they are to appear about the habitations of man. Several thrashers of arid parts of the West are little-known birds that do not tend to accept man or his environment.

MOCKINGBIRD

No longer regarded as a typically southern bird, the mockingbird has moved so far northward during the last several decades that we now think of it as a resident over the entire eastern United States and portions of southern Canada as well. The northward movement is still in progress and takes form each fall in the appearance of solitary birds well north of the normal range. Pioneers that are moving northward would be hard put to survive the winter if they did not have access to feeding stations. With sufficient food at hand, mockingbirds are often able to endure winters as far north as northern New England, southern Quebec, and Nova Scotia.

Response to artificial foods varies greatly among individuals and also from place to place. Birds near the northern range limits are likely to be wholly dependent upon feeding stations in winter for their survival. Farther south, where there are abundant supplies of natural fruits and berries, the mockingbird often seems to have a take-it-or-leave-it attitude. There will be spells when the feeding station is well patronized by these birds and other times when they will fall back entirely upon natural foods. The mockingbird rarely visits feeders during the summer.

One of the most striking features concerning the food habits of the mockingbird is the comparatively small amount of time devoted to feeding activity. Much of the day is spent in singing, teasing or harassing other birds and mammals, and simply watching everything that is going on from an elevated perch. This is in sharp contrast to the almost constant feeding activity seen in titmice and other small birds. Less time devoted to feeding is consistent with the mockingbird's larger size and the ease with which it can usually appease its appetite.

The mockingbird goes to great lengths to protect its food supplies. It is not unusual to see a single mockingbird engaging a whole flock of robins or starlings that may be making inroads upon a fruit or berry supply. The most vicious attacks are reserved for an outside mockingbird that has the courage to trespass upon an owner's territory. These battles are not purposeless. Unless a food supply is protected,

*A determined mockingbird
can often fight off
a whole flock of robins.*

210

*Birds
That
Visit
Feeding
Stations*

other birds in a relatively short time will devour the food that would keep one or two mockingbirds going all winter.

Problems that result from overly aggressive mockingbirds have been discussed in Chapter 6. The tumult caused by such individuals is not always detrimental to a feeding station operation. This is particularly true when the aggression is directed chiefly against squirrels, cats, and an occasional marauding snake. At times mockingbirds wage vendettas against house sparrows or starlings. It is unusual for a mockingbird to direct its aggression against the entire feeding station company.

Mockingbirds are bold about coming to window shelves. They are also amenable to hand taming. They tend to avoid difficult hanging feeders and accept food mainly at bird tables, window trays, suet holders, and sometimes hummingbird feeders. So far as foods go, the mockingbird exhibits a wide range of tastes and is especially fond of table scraps. Of commonly used foods, only seeds and grain are refused. Among the many foods that do appeal are raisins, currants, suet, suet mixtures, peanut butter, peanut hearts, nutmeats, doughnuts, cornbread, white bread, sliced apple and orange, halved pear, figs, grapes, and banana.

GRAY CATBIRD

Not so noisy and boisterous as the mockingbird, the gray catbird is altogether an easier bird to play host to. Demure, retiring, and yet spunky, the catbird is such a popular guest that those of us who live in more northern states are sad to see the last one depart in the fall. Catbirds are found in summer from southern Canada to the Gulf states. During the fall all but a very few retire to the warmer parts of the South.

The gray catbird is more apt to come to a windowsill or doorway for food than to the feeding station. Sometimes a catbird becomes tame enough to come running toward a person who offers food. Alfred G. Martin tells of a gray catbird that learned to catch raisins in midair after the bird had gotten in the habit of running toward him for food. The gray catbird also has a way of asking for food when we dine out-of-doors. This is as true in public eating places as it is in our own backyards. One that frequented an outdoor restaurant in Florida went from table to table looking for tidbits or handouts from the customers.

Although not overly responsive to opportunities at feeding stations, the gray catbird does at times become attracted to something on the menu and will make repeated trips through the day for this food. This holds for the gray catbirds that are with us in summer and also for the occasional bird that stays behind in winter. I am always surprised at the gray catbird's ability to reach a feeding device that happens to hold a favored food. Gray catbirds were among the few birds to find their way into the upper shelf of a glassed-in, weatherproof feeder of mine. These birds also show surprising ability at clinging to hanging log feeders. Probably the feeder that most appeals to the gray catbird is an upper-story window shelf. Here there is apt to be less competition from other birds, and therefore the catbird can eat more leisurely.

We cater to the gray catbird with such usual foods as raisins, currants, banana, suet, suet mixtures, peanut butter, peanut hearts, cottage cheese, cornbread, and nutmeats. These birds are also known to eat seeds and grain, but as a rule, only after such foods have been softened through exposure to the weather. The catbird probably has more unorthodox tastes than any of our other visitors. Some of the less conventional foods this bird takes are milk, puffed wheat or cornflakes in milk, butter, mushrooms, boiled potato, and fried fish. The gray catbird will try almost any feeder, but its preference seems to be for second-story window trays. It comes to bird tables, trays on posts, suet holders, hanging feeders, and hummingbird feeders.

BROWN THRASHER

Early in this century brown thrashers were all but unknown at feeding stations. Today the brown thrasher is almost as common as the cardinal. This is a transformation that has come about through a gradual taming process. Although still showing traces of shyness, the brown thrasher has become much more used to human beings and readily accepts our food offerings.

Our best opportunity to become acquainted with the brown thrasher is at feeding stations in the South. Here it is a year-round visitor and present in most yards that have adequate shrubbery and other plantings. In northern states the brown thrasher is much less common and also seems shyer and more reluctant about coming to feeders. On the other hand, the occasional bird that stays behind for the winter becomes wholly dependent upon feeders and also loses its shyness.

The brown thrasher uses its sturdy bill to rake away leaves, break open the

212

*Birds
That
Visit
Feeding
Stations*

husks of seeds, pound apart shells of thin-shelled nuts, or dig holes. One day I found a brown thrasher using its bill to dig a hole in my compost heap. Loose leaves and dirt flew as the thrasher, using its bill like a golf club, swung first to the right and then to the left. Doubtless, the bird was finding an abundant supply of animal food in the rich soil. Furious jabs of the bill directed at sunflower seeds, acorns, and the like often do not break open these foods but send them flying off in every direction. Unlike a number of other birds, the brown thrasher has not learned to hold objects between its toes. However, in pounding upon objects the brown thrasher inadvertently creates small pits or craters in the soil, particularly where the soil is loose or sandy. Sooner or later an object being pounded upon falls into one of these holes. The brown thrasher has now won its battle. The object no longer rolls away but stays in place while it is being pounded upon.

Where brown thrashers do their pounding, the ground becomes pockmarked with small craters. The earth below one of my feeders became dotted with these holes, which in turn became traps for seeds and grain that fell from the feeder. The brown thrasher that had done the digging became aware of the advantage of visiting these holes for the food they held. Was it possible that the bird had purposely dug the holes both as receptacles for food being pounded open and bins for collecting other food? While this much premeditation seems unlikely, we can give credit to the brown thrasher for making good use of its digging prowess.

The winter of 1958 was notable for the many brown thrashers that stayed behind as far north as the New England states and New Brunswick. No less than

*The brown thrasher digs many
small craters in the course
of pounding food open.*

fifteen were reported spending the winter in Maine and thirty-two in Massachusetts. Although some of these birds appear to have perished during severe weather, many were still present at the end of winter. The most important factor in the survival of this bird during northern winters is food. One winter a brown thrasher that was present at a feeding station in Minneapolis survived temperatures as low as 27 degrees below zero. This bird apparently got through the winter nicely on a diet composed chiefly of ground suet.

For some reason the brown thrasher is unpopular with other feeding station visitors. Its presence seems most resented by larger birds—especially mourning doves, red-bellied woodpeckers, and mockingbirds. The brown thrasher reacts violently to the slightest signs of objection. It faces its antagonist and begins to lunge with its long, pointed bill. Few birds are willing to face such an adversary. The brown thrasher reserves the same hostile treatment for any other brown thrasher that dares trespass.

Most feeding takes place on the ground. Brown thrashers sometimes venture quite far out onto an open lawn. So long as there is dense shrubbery to retreat to, the brown thrasher does not seem to object to open terrain. Although most feeding at stations takes place on the ground, these birds occasionally visit bird tables and large feeding trays. They practically never take food at small hanging feeders, but they do sometimes use hummingbird feeders. Scratch feed is all that is needed to attract and hold this bird. Other foods taken include suet, suet mixtures, raisins, sunflower, wheat, millet, cracked corn, nutmeats, doughnuts, cornbread, white bread, and halved orange.

twenty-two

ROBINS AND THRUSHES

The large family to which the thrushes belong (Turdidae) is represented in North America by the robin, varied thrush, bluebirds, Townsend's solitaire, and the typical thrushes. Members of this family are on the whole friendly birds that do not hesitate to come into our yards and gardens.

Several members of the family are westerners that only rarely appear east of the Great Plains. The varied thrush and Townsend's solitaire now and then appear as strays at feeding stations in the East.

AMERICAN ROBIN

This is a bird we see most often when it is hopping about the lawn looking for worms. Its appearances close to the habitations of man often lead to the false assumption that the robin is one of the most domesticated of birds and needs only a little encouragement to partake of whatever bounty we have to offer. The truth of the matter is that the robin is less interested in our food than anything else we have to offer. It comes to our yards during the warmer months to build a nest and raise young. Often thirsty, it makes frequent use of bird baths for drinking. After quenching its thirst, it may abandon itself to lengthy communal bathing. Finally, our closely cut lawns make ideal feeding grounds where in damp weather the robin can find the earthworms that are such a favorite food.

When the robins that nest with us leave for the South, their places may be taken by robins from farther north. Not all robins by any means withdraw to a sunnier climate for the winter; some stay as far north as the Great Lakes, New England, and Nova Scotia. Robins that winter in the north are for the most part hardy, independent birds with little use for feeding stations. It is a different story with robins that have gone south for the winter. Many do visit feeding stations, and now and then a particularly domineering robin will attempt to chase every other bird away from the feeder in much the same way that many mockingbirds do.

It is on the way north in spring that robins may temporarily become dependent upon feeding stations. When caught by spring snowstorms hundreds of migrating robins may come flocking to our yards. Frantically hungry, such birds may strip the last remaining apples from trees and seek refuse in garbage pits. Ravenous robins ate every bit of the contents from a full crate of honey that had been inadvertently left outside during a late snowstorm in Nova Scotia. When hard-pressed by weather conditions, robins will eat almost anything they happen to find.

The versatile robin has mastered many kinds of feeders including bird tables, trays on posts, window trays, suet holders, and hummingbird feeders.

By fluttering before food-filled holes, they even at times make use of hanging log feeders. Window feeders are popular with robins, and in Nebraska robins came to a feeding station on a second-story porch. In the same yard robins were in the habit of coming to halved apples impaled on twigs. In a North Dakota yard robins came to a box on a post where raisins were always available. Among the foods that are tempting to robins are suet, suet mixtures, peanut butter, peanut hearts, raisins, currants, pecan meats, cottage cheese, American cheese, cooked spaghetti, doughnuts, cornbread, white bread, sliced apple and pear, strawberries, and cherries.

WOOD THRUSH

This is one of the few birds that has to be tamed before it will accept our bounty. Although the wood thrush, like the robin, has become domesticated to the extent that it will frequent well-planted yards, it is essentially a shy bird that for the most part remains hidden by the densest foliage in our yards. All summer we hear the wood thrush's superb song but only rarely do we see it venture out onto the lawn.

216

*Birds
That
Visit
Feeding
Stations*

One place where we do see this bird is at the bird bath. The wood thrush has the same liking for water that is seen in the robin.

Noting the frequent appearances of wood thrushes at a bird bath in their yard, observers at Belmont, Massachusetts,* tried leaving raisins near the bath. This proved to be successful the several summers that the experiment was tried. A pair that nested in the yard accepted the raisins eagerly. One fall the birds became tame enough to pick up raisins that were tossed in their direction. Before the birds left that fall, they would come running toward anyone who had raisins to offer.

Others have had similar success in taming the wood thrush. Occasionally a bird will stay on through the fall and into winter. Such individuals become tame and completely dependent upon offerings at feeding stations. A wood thrush that had lost its tail feathers was present as late as Christmas Day at a feeder in Bay City, Michigan. This bird subsisted upon raisins, prunes, and cracked sunflower seeds. Other foods that meet with the wood thrush's approval are suet, peanut butter, and white bread. Occasionally the wood thrush accepts a little of the seed or grain mixture offered at a feeder. Although not apt to take food at feeders, the wood thrush will at times visit bird tables, trays on posts, suet holders, and sometimes hummingbird feeders. Its preference is for food on the ground.

HERMIT THRUSH

This is one of the hardiest members of the family and also the thrush that is most likely to appear at feeding stations. The hermit thrush has the same wide distribution as the robin in winter, and many stay behind to brave the cold of our northern states and southern Canada. In summer we must look for this bird in wilder parts of this country, especially the more northern states, and in the north woods of Canada. The hermit thrush is easily recognized by its habit of slowly raising and lowering the tail.

"Hermit" is a good name to apply to this thrush, for it is usually seen by itself and in wilder regions. However, thanks to the taming process that has brought so many birds to our yards and feeding stations, this small thrush is not unexpected

*George A. Drew, Jr., "Tameness of Wood Thrushes," *Bulletin of Massachusetts Audubon Society*, 34, No. 7, October 1950.

about habitations in winter. One that was present at a Florida feeding station became so tame that it remained on the feeder when a dog was romping about or someone was close-by. Sometimes more than one of these thrushes appear together at the feeder. There have been reports of five or more feeding together peacefully.

If there is a choice between using elevated feeders and taking food on the ground, the hermit thrush is apt to divide its time about equally between both places. It comes quite readily to bird tables, trays on posts, and window trays. Sometimes this thrush will flutter briefly before a hanging feeder. Almost anything on the menu is acceptable including small seeds and finely cracked grain. Among the foods that are most readily taken are suet, suet mixtures, peanut butter, peanut hearts, pecan meats, raisins, sliced apple, doughnuts, and white bread.

SWAINSON'S THRUSH

Briefly in late spring and again in the fall we may observe brown-backed thrushes in our yard that seem somewhat different in appearance from the ones we are used to. If the thrushes you see are uniformly gray-brown and have buffy eye-rings and cheeks, they are Swainson's thrushes, birds of the northern spruce belt. Of the hundreds that may pass our way en route to the tropics in the fall, a few may find our bird baths and fewer still our feeding stations.

Next to water, the best enticement for these birds is fruits and berries. Try placing such food near the bird bath where the thrushes are coming to drink and bathe. Eventually you may get a few of the birds coming to the feeders. Those that do come will adapt readily to different feeding devices.

Natural fruits and berries that can be used to attract this bird include wild grapes, pokeberries, Virginia creeper, elderberries, and wild cherries. In lieu of such fare, try chopped apple, raisins, currants, and store grapes. A Swainson's thrush at a Maine feeder in late November fed solely upon suet in spite of the presence of other foods. Other more conventional foods taken by this thrush include suet mixtures, white bread, and occasional items from seed and grain mixtures. The Swainson's thrush prefers food on the ground but may occasionally appear at bird tables, trays, and suet holders.

This is one of our most difficult visitors when it comes to identification. However, this thrush is well named, and if you can distinguish gray cheeks and note the absence of an eye-ring on a bird that looks like a Swainson's thrush there is little doubt but that you have spotted one of these little-known thrushes.

Nesting in northern Canada and with us only briefly while on migration, the gray-cheek is not a familiar bird by any means. Our only acquaintanceship is likely to come in late spring and again in the fall, when this thrush puts in an appearance at bird baths and sometimes at feeding stations. A bird bander in Illinois has reported that the gray-cheek was seen in her yard most commonly in the spring. This bander normally captured between twenty and thirty gray-cheeks a year.

The food tastes of this thrush seem to be almost identical to those of the Swainson's. It readily accepts suet, suet mixtures, raisins, white bread, and fruits and berries. Like the Swainson's, the gray-cheeked thrush is partial to food on the ground.

EASTERN BLUEBIRD

Twenty-five to forty years ago this species was seen more often at feeders than it is today. Even so, the bluebird was never well adapted to living close to man. It was, and still is, primarily a bird of open woodlands and farming country. The appearance of this bird near human habitations is usually associated with cold weather in winter.

Not many bluebirds remain in the North as this species is poorly adapted to cold; even in the South where most bluebirds pass the winter there are times, such as the winter of 1958, when bluebirds perish by the thousands because of inclement weather. The few that do remain in the North for the most part stay close to the coast. From the coast of the Carolinas to Cape Cod there are always a few hardy bluebirds that attempt to pass the winter not far from the sound of crashing waves. Only a scattered few brave the colder temperatures that occur inland.

During the winter of 1953, three bluebirds appeared at the feeder of Arthur H. Fast of Arlington, Virginia. These three birds survived the winter nicely on a diet of peanut hearts. The next winter six birds appeared, and these, too, fared very well.

The following winter Mr. Fast was host to no less than fifteen bluebirds. One of the highest winter feeding station counts I know of was eighteen at a Chappaqua, New York, feeder on January 27, 1961. Even farther north on Cape Cod in Massachusetts bluebirds are sometimes fairly common in winter and some of them appear at feeding stations.

The reason there are fewer bluebirds at feeders today lies in an overall decline in numbers that has been particularly noticeable since the winter of 1958. As mentioned in Chapter 8, the present plight of the bluebird is closely associated with scarcity of nesting sites, and a prime factor in this is competition by other hole-nesting birds, especially the starling.

Bluebirds are quite versatile and will accept food at bird tables, trays on posts, window trays, suet holders, and some hanging feeders. While peanut hearts seem to be one of the best foods to try with this species, there are a number of others that are also well received. Bluebirds have been recorded taking peanut hearts, pecan meats, suet, raisins, currants, white bread, cornbread, doughnuts, pie crust, cottage cheese, and baked apple.

KINGLETS

The large family of Old World warblers is represented at feeding stations by two of the smallest of our customers—golden-crowned and ruby-crowned kinglets. When we see one of these birds we may at first decide that we have a vireo or one of the New World warblers in view. The kinglets, if anything, are even more animated than warblers, which always seem to be moving quickly from place to place. The kinglets are also far better adapted to our northern winters. The golden-crowned is found from the Great Lakes and New England southward in winter, while the somewhat less hardy ruby-crowned ranges from Maryland and Virginia southward. Although both occasionally appear at feeding stations in winter, neither species shows any sign of being dependent upon our bounty. In spite of the smallness of their size, the kinglets are independent birds that somehow manage to eke out a living even in winter at the northern limits of their ranges.

GOLDEN-CROWNED KINGLET

If you should see any of these kinglets outside your windows, you will be impressed by the tireless way they search twigs and especially the needles of conifers. Every part of a twig or needle is carefully searched for insect eggs or other minute fare. Sometimes a kinglet will hover before a clump of pine needles as it attempts to procure something that otherwise would be out of reach. This kinglet even outperforms the chickadees when it comes to getting food from awkward places.

Rarely do golden-crowneds become regular visitors to feeding stations. If they come at all, it is usually a brief visit that may have been inspired by the presence of other feeding birds. This kinglet does not need any lessons in how to obtain food from small hanging feeders, suet holders, and food logs. It hovers expertly before such devices and sometimes joins other birds at a feeding shelf. The only foods that seem to have any appeal to this kinglet are suet, suet mixtures, and peanut butter.

RUBY-CROWNED KINGLET

Although generally considered to be less hardy than the golden-crowned, this kinglet sometimes surprises us by appearing in winter well north of its normal winter range. Several were present one winter at a Nova Scotia feeder and occurrences in winter as far north as Quebec and Ontario are not uncommon. Birds that spend the winter this far north, or in more northern states, almost always seem to require the extra food advantages of feeding stations. In this respect, the ruby-crowned is a less hardy bird than the golden-crowned. Of the two species, the ruby-crowned is much more likely to take advantage of feeding stations and this holds true in more southern parts of the winter range as well.

There is little difference in the habits of the two species at feeders. The ruby-crowned is a more commonly expected guest and much more likely to stay longer. A little more versatile than the golden-crowned, the ruby-crowned kinglet will visit bird tables, trays, suet holders, small hanging feeders, logs, and occasionally hummingbird feeders. Foods accepted by this bird include suet, suet mixtures, peanut butter, peanut hearts, finely cracked pecans and other cracked nuts, cornbread, and doughnuts.

WAXWINGS

The bohemian waxwing of western North America and the smaller cedar waxwing, which ranges from coast to coast, are generally regarded as fruit and berry eaters that rarely, if ever, touch other foods. The waxwings have gained this reputation because of the way whole flocks descend upon fruiting trees and shrubs and each member then gorges itself until it can hold no more. Sometimes we can divert these fruit-eaters from their natural fare with generous supplies of raisins. Although justly described as greedy birds and sometimes called gluttons, the waxwings are well mannered in their feeding habits and few other birds have such a handsome, gentle-manly appearance. The cedar waxwing is the species to look for in eastern states.

CEDAR WAXWING

Ordinarily this waxwing will not come to a feeding station on its own. It has to be lured. The time to do this is when a flock is in your yard feasting upon pyracantha or some other fruiting tree or shrub. Place some of the foods the waxwings are eating on a feeding tray in full view of the flock. Also supply one or two of the feeding station foods that are especially well favored. Raisins, currants, or chopped or halved apples are well suited for this purpose. Even after being offered such fare, waxwings may not take notice. They are one of our more difficult birds to attract. If this waxwing accepts food at all, it will be in fairly open situations. At times it visits bird tables, trays, and places on the ground where suitable foods have been scattered.

When they do respond, waxwings come with a rush that will remind us of the
eagerness with which a flock of starlings descends upon food. In a few minutes a flock
will consume a pint or so of raisins. When Arthur H. Fast of Arlington, Virginia,
played host to a large flock of cedar waxwings that first appeared in early March, he
wisely substituted halved apples for the raisins he had been offering. For two and a
half months his feeders were inundated by one flock after another of hungry cedar
waxwings. Ten to twelve apples were supplied the birds daily as well as some raisins
and currants.

In spite of their appetites, the waxwings show more decorum toward one another
than most feeding station birds. Even when a flock is feeding at close quarters, there
is no shoving or pecking. A bond of fellowship prevails which dictates that each bird
is fully entitled to its share of the feast. The cedar waxwing at times seems to exceed
even this extraordinary politeness. Birds have sometimes been seen lined up on a
branch passing a berry back and forth from one bill to another and not a bird willing
to eat it. Such performances are believed to be part of their courtship ritual.

Although we may not be able to lure this bird with food, we do have a good
chance of doing so with water. Like the robin and other fruit and berry eaters, the
cedar waxwing has an unquenchable thirst. After filling up on water at our bird
baths, waxwings usually go in for a session of bathing. Little else besides raisins,
currants, and halved apple appeal to this bird at feeding stations.

STARLINGS

It is too bad that we should have received one of the most quarrelsome and aggressive members of this Old World family. From stock that was introduced in New York City in 1890 and 1891, the starling has spread to most sections of this continent and can now be regarded as one of our most numerous bird species. Thanks to its intelligence and adaptability, the starling has conquered other sizable sections of the globe as well. After man has given it small footholds, the starling has become well established in Australia, Tasmania, New Zealand, South Africa, and such lands to the south as Mexico, Jamaica, and Chile.

The only other member of the starling family to reach North America is the crested myna, which was introduced in Vancouver in British Columbia. Unlike the starling, this member has not spread much beyond the place of introduction. In spite of many bad points, the starling does have some redeeming features. It is helpful in controlling many insect pests including the Japanese beetle. Even at the feeding station it is not a serious nuisance except when too many come at one time.

It usually takes a snowstorm or prolonged cold weather before starlings descend upon feeding stations in large numbers. When hordes of starlings do appear, it is time to take action as through sheer weight of numbers as well as quarrelsomeness, the starling imposes a serious hardship upon other feeding station visitors.

Although a cantankerous bully, the starling is surprisingly docile when handled. Birds that are caught in banding traps remain quiet until removed. When we pick them up there is no struggling or attempts to peck us. For all its bluster, the starling is basically mild mannered, if not timid. Banding also reveals the cleverness of the bird. This is the only species, to my knowledge, that has the ingenuity to lift the door of a "Potter-type" drop-door banding trap with its bill and in this way escape. A bird will insert its bill under the bottom rung of the door and lift upward. Birds have been known to escape within two minutes after capture by using this method.

The starling arrives late at feeding stations and departs well before dusk. This is fortunate timing for birds that can take advantage of early and late feedings. However, in bad weather starlings settle down in the vicinity of a feeding station and make a day of it. While some are eating, others are waiting in nearby trees or on rooftops. There is a constant coming and going so that normal visitors to the feeders have little time to themselves.

Starlings are not particular about where they obtain their food. In keeping with its adaptive nature, the starling will come to almost any feeder containing food that is well favored. Therefore, this hearty eater may be expected at bird tables, trays on posts, window trays, suet holders, hanging feeders, logs, and ground feeding areas. If anything, the ground is the most favored eating place. Although they quickly master most feeders, they tend to be wary about coming close to the house. With some shooing and banging upon windowpanes, we can usually keep nearby feeders reserved for birds we would rather have. Other details on how to keep starlings from overrunning feeders and lists of what they will and will not eat are provided on pages 274–5.

WARBLERS

No less than thirty-eight out of the fifty-three warbler species known within our borders have been recorded at feeding stations. Many times visits consist of nothing more than a bird coming briefly to a sugar-water feeder for hummingbirds or picking up something in the way of food at a feeding station. Nonetheless, this is enough interest to indicate that warblers are reasonably well aware of our food offerings. The myrtle, or yellow-rumped, warbler is more than a chance visitor. This warbler is commonly attracted to feeding stations in winter and in some localities will be one of the most numerous guests.

The other warblers are not as accommodating. We see most of them only briefly, if at all, when they pass through twice annually on their migrations between our continent and the tropics. There is a better enticement than food, however, if we wish to gain their attention. The magical lure that will bring them to a spot where we can see them is water. The slow drip of water into a shallow pan or bird bath brings them timidly at first, then with greater courage so that the warblers that have congregated may soon abandon themselves to an orgy of drinking and bathing. Food is usually an afterthought. The sight of other birds at the feeder may bring an inquisitive visit or two. This is as true in the spring as it is in late summer or fall. On the other hand, there are always a number of warblers that for unknown reasons do not continue on the long fall trek to the tropics but drop out somewhere along the way. We call such stay-behinds "stragglers." We have already met such individuals among the thrushes and we will meet more tardy birds of this description in the families that follow. With careful attention to food, we can sometimes coax such birds to our feeders. Given enough care and attention, the warbler that has stayed behind will sometimes make it through even the coldest of winters.

ORANGE-CROWNED WARBLER

The most difficult thing about this bird is its identification. Any warbler at the feeding station that cannot readily be recognized is likely to be a member of this species. Look for a plain greenish warbler that has no well-defined markings. Another clue to this warbler's identification is its enormous winter range. There are a few winter records as far north as British Columbia and Nova Scotia. In the East this warbler winters along the coast and may be found sparingly from Maine southward along the Atlantic and Gulf coasts.

The orange-crowned is a solitary bird, and almost always no more than one appears at a feeding station. Those that do take up feeding station habits often become persistent visitors that we see off and on all day. One that appeared at a Florida feeder in December was described as precise as an old grandfather clock, appearing about every twenty-five minutes until late afternoon. This bird continued to come through early spring. Others have had similar experiences with this plain but not unexciting warbler. It is a bird that is always missed when it finally does leave.

If favorite foods are present, this warbler will come to bird tables and window shelf feeders. Small hanging feeders are very much to its liking. Fairly versatile when it comes to feeders, the orange-crowned will also accept food at trays on posts, suet holders, and hummingbird feeders. We cater to its tastes with suet, suet mixtures, peanut butter, finely chopped nutmeats, raisins, doughnuts, cake, and sliced apple.

CAPE MAY WARBLER

This is another one of the confusing fall warblers, but not as difficult to identify, as a rule, as the orange-crowned. Although this warbler is sometimes a straggler, like the orange-crowned, the main reason it visits us is not necessity but a taste for sweets. Those who have hummingbird feeders up in late summer and early fall are sometimes visited by migrating Cape May warblers that have discovered the delights of the

228

*Birds
That
Visit
Feeding
Stations*

sweetened solutions. Now and then a Cape May stays for the winter. One spent the winter successfully at a Morgantown, West Virginia, feeder and another was at a feeder in Pennsylvania as late as January. These late stayers no longer come to sweets but take more substantial fare in the form of suet or peanut butter.

YELLOW-RUMPED WARBLER

This warbler, formerly known as the myrtle warbler, is the only member of the family that is hardy enough consistently to brave our northern winters. By making use of berries of red cedar, poison ivy, bayberry, and little else, the yellow-rumped warbler ekes out a living where other warblers would fail. There are some winters when this warbler is common in coastal thickets from the Carolinas north to Massachusetts. In the Deep South this warbler is an abundant winter resident wherever good supplies of natural food exist.

Not only is this *the* warbler to look for in winter over much of the East, but it is the most common warbler at feeding stations. In fact, this warbler is sometimes so plentiful that it overruns food supplies. There is a constant coming and going of these warblers when bad weather or shortage of natural foods causes them to take extra advantage of our feeders. When the bayberry supply around Thomasville, Georgia, failed one winter, yellow-rumped warblers came swarming to feeders in such numbers that it was difficult to keep them stocked with enough food. Even as far north as Connecticut and Massachusetts feeders in winter are sometimes crowded with these birds.

The yellow-rumped is also a bird to look for during migration. It is one of the latest warblers to pass through in the fall and one of the first to appear in the spring. As with the family in general, water is the best attractant. This warbler, however, needs far less invitation than the others to come to food. The sight of other birds draws it to the feeders, and once on to our offerings, it becomes a scrappy, if not domineering, guest. Some individuals try vainly to keep other birds away. Usually after a day or two of futile chasing about, a bird will lose its aggressiveness and become more reasonable.

One of the best ways to lure yellow-rumped warblers to feeders is to supply

*Yellow-rumped
warbler.*

natural foods birds are coming to in the wild. Some of us do this by gathering branches of bayberry whenever we visit the coast. Later, a few at a time, we place the berry-laden branches at our feeders. If warblers do not take the waxy berries, other birds soon will.

Yellow-rumped warblers respond well to almost any feeder that contains favorite foods. The preference seems to be for small hanging feeders, but this warbler makes itself at home at bird tables, trays on posts, window trays, suet holders, and hummingbird feeders. In addition to such standard fare as suet, suet mixtures, peanut butter, peanut hearts, finely cracked corn, and finely crushed nutmeats, yellow-rumped warblers take a surprising variety of kitchen leftovers. These include bakery products, halved orange, cooked sweet potato, and cooked squash. Grape jelly is an excellent cold-weather food for this and other late warblers.

PINE WARBLER

This yellowish warbler with white wing bars is somewhat more often expected than the orange-crowned but usually is less common at feeding stations than the yellow-rumped. The pine warbler is a gregarious bird that joins the mixed flocks that are a feature of southern woodlands in winter. Small flocks of pine warblers sometimes appear at feeding stations in the South after cold weather sets in. I observed as many as ten feeding at one time at a feeding station near Thomasville, Georgia. Judging from the appetite of these birds, natural sources of food may not have been any too plentiful. Although pine warblers may eat ravenously, they get along well among themselves and with other visitors to feeding stations.

In common with several other of the warblers, occasional pine warblers may remain behind in the North where they are obliged to face the perils of northern winters. As a rule, we are not aware of such stragglers until cold weather brings them to our feeding stations. Pine warblers have been recorded at winter feeding stations as far north as the Great Lakes and New England. Usually such stragglers are found near the coast.

We will have little difficulty in catering to the food needs of this warbler. Not only do pine warblers accept the customary warbler diet of suet, peanut butter, and

230

*Birds
That
Visit
Feeding
Stations*

finely crushed nutmeats, but they take finely ground scratch feed, bits of sunflower kernels, and cooked or uncooked cornmeal. This bird mainly chooses small hanging feeders and hanging logs. The pine warbler also comes to bird tables, trays on posts, window trays, and suet holders.

YELLOW-BREASTED CHAT

During the summer this warbler of dense thickets and tangles is rarely seen and is usually known only through its weird repertoire of calls and whistles. During the fall there appears to be much moving about before the bulk of the population leaves for the tropics. Numbers of chats even move northward in late summer and early fall. These travelers appear in New England and as far north as the maritime provinces of Canada. That this typically southern bird should embark on these ventures is one of the riddles of bird migration.

In recent years more and more chats are staying behind to attempt our winters rather than make the long flight to the tropics. These birds appear at feeding stations all the way from our southern states to New England. Although a welcome visitor, the chat is not an easy bird to coax through the winter. This is seen in the experiences of a host at Rye, New Hampshire, who was obliged to go to great lengths to keep a bedraggled chat from starving or freezing to death.* The bird had appeared in mid-November, and at first rejected every food offered except doughnuts and peanut butter. In order that the bird receive some protection from the weather, food was placed in a breezeway. For a while the bird seemed to thrive. But by mid-January the once-jaunty chat began to look more and more dejected. Banana was tried in this emergency. The bird responded by eating half a banana a day, and soon the bird's appearance and actions had improved so much that the host began to feel there was a good chance of getting this bird through the winter after all. By the time the winter was over, the bird had gone through two severe snowstorms and much near-zero weather. During the worst of the winter, an infrared heat lamp had been giving warming rays over the food tray where the bird ate. Such extra attentions as these had seen this delicate tropical warbler safely through a northern winter.

*John Fernald, "A Chat Winters in New Hampshire," *Bulletin of Massachusetts Audubon Society*, 36, No. 9, December 1952.

Besides doughnuts, peanut butter, and banana, chats are known to take other feeding station foods including suet, suet mixtures, chopped apple, soaked raisins, grapes, white bread, and cornbread. Grape jelly is a food well worth trying. Appearances of this bird in late fall and winter are usually at protected feeders near the house. Therefore, the chat can be expected at bird tables and feeding trays close to windows.

WEAVER FINCHES

Two members of this family have become established in North America. One is the European tree sparrow, which has long maintained itself in the vicinity of St. Louis, Missouri, and the other is the ubiquitous house sparrow.

HOUSE SPARROW

In his *Life Histories*, A. C. Bent states that during the peak of its abundance, the house sparrow, except in heavily forested, alpine, and desert regions, was undoubtedly the most abundant bird in the United States. Within its favorite haunts one could easily see twice as many sparrows as all other birds combined. This was years ago. At the present time, what with losses due to disease and other checks and balances, the house sparrow is no longer an overwhelmingly abundant bird. In fact, in many areas the house sparrow has all but disappeared and the decline in its numbers continues. Part of this decline has been due to a fatal bacterial infection known as salmonella to which the house sparrow seems particularly subject.

Much of the house sparrow's aggression and notorious bullying has disappeared during this period of decline. We can be thankful for this because during its heyday the house sparrow was so bothersome to other birds that few could nest in our yards, and in many areas feeding stations were all but impossible. The much more restrained house sparrow we see today is neither much of an asset nor a detriment to a feeding station operation. The main complaint is that this sparrow takes a fair share of our food offerings and provides little in return. A small flock that frequented my feeders in Virginia probably consumed around fifteen dollars' worth of grain a year.

One advantage in having this sparrow is that it seems to draw other birds to the feeder. Whenever dickcissels have been found at feeding stations in the East, they have almost always been with house sparrows. There is also an element of protection in having a flock of house sparrows at the feeders. None of our guests is so jittery and given to flying off with such little provocation as is the house sparrow. Some of the sparrow's nervousness is communicated to other birds, and they too get in the habit of making sudden departures. The overall effect seems to be to keep the entire feeding station company a little more alerted to cats, bird-hawks, and other dangers.

The house sparrow's ability to find its way to most feeders should not conceal the fact that it has some decided preferences. House sparrows tend to avoid wobbly or free-swinging feeders or any device that upsets their equilibrium. On the other hand, they will flock to all securely anchored feeders and freely take food from the ground. First preference is for the ground and second is for large tables and trays. The house sparrow comes to hanging feeders only when it has to and tends to avoid any that do not provide firm footing. It sometimes visits hummingbird feeders. The biggest attractions to these birds are wheat, cracked corn, bakery products, and kitchen scraps. Other popular foods include millet, canary seed, rape, buckwheat, suet (rarely), and cantaloupe seed. Occasional birds accept sunflower.

House sparrows.

BLACKBIRDS AND ORIOLES

A distinctive New World family, the blackbirds, including orioles, cowbirds, grackles, meadowlark, and bobolink, are enterprising, successful birds that have filled every habitat and are making themselves more and more at home in our yards. The orioles were the first to discover the advantages of yards with shade trees and supplies of food and water. As early as the 1890s, the northern oriole was a feeding station visitor. Not until somewhat later did the blackbirds begin to take notice. The appearance of a male red-winged blackbird at a northern Michigan feeder in late 1921 was cause for comment. By 1950 blackbirds of several species had become common visitors to feeding stations. Today our feeders are sometimes so inundated by dark-plumaged birds that we have to take steps to discourage them (see Chapter 6). The blackbirds, including cowbirds and grackles, may come flocking to our yards in

*A red-winged blackbird helps itself to seed from
a hanging coconut feeder.*

immense numbers one day and be absent the next. The two orioles we meet in the East, the northern and orchard orioles, on the other hand, are normally daily visitors that appear in pairs or sometimes family groups. One of the more interesting ornithological events of this century has been the increased appearance of northern orioles in winter throughout the East. Feeding stations seem to have had a major influence in changing the migratory patterns of this species and, to some degree, those of other members of this family.

EASTERN MEADOWLARK

Rarely does this open-country bird appear in quarters as cramped as our lawns and gardens. The eastern meadowlark is most at home on wide open plains, fields, and pastures. As a rule, only during severe winter weather does this hardy bird take refuge in barnyards or join the company of birds at feeding stations. Yet the lure of boundless plenty is beginning to compromise even the meadowlark. One example is seen in a flock of a dozen or so birds that came regularly all winter to a feeder located on motel grounds along a busy highway in South Carolina. The birds came, good weather or bad, and the location was not particularly open. Though primarily a ground-feeder, the meadowlark will now and then feed briefly at a tray on a post or a window tray.

When the meadowlark does visit a feeder, it is always grain on the ground that attracts it at first. Once acclimated to a location, birds may become bold enough to try an elevated feeder or even a windowsill feeder. The meadowlark has a decided preference for seeds and grain and will take corn, scratch feed, wheat, oats, barley, sorghum, millet, and canary seed.

RED-WINGED BLACKBIRD

Although this common blackbird has only recently discovered our feeders, it has learned quickly, and now we sometimes feel obliged to take steps to discourage this guest. The problem with redwings is not hostility toward other birds but the weight of numbers when a large flock settles down to feed. Luckily for us, redwings are impatient birds. A flock that has been feeding busily at every feeder may suddenly

236

*Birds
That
Visit
Feeding
Stations*

depart before the meal seems half-finished. As likely as not, this flock will be seen no more that day. Redwings forage widely through both the suburbs and the countryside. Our feeders will be only one of their many stopping places.

Redwings are often regarded as harbingers of spring. The males, resplendent in their red epaulets, arrive in flocks several weeks ahead of the females. Although those of us living in more northern states always take pleasure in the arrival of these flocks, we need to remind ourselves that many redwings do not fly south in the fall. We become aware of this fact when redwings sometimes appear at our feeders in midwinter. For the most part, redwings are spring, summer, and fall visitors in the North; in southern states redwings are almost exclusively winter visitors. The tendency, however, is for more and more redwings to stay behind in northern states in spite of the cold and snow. A secure food supply at feeding stations may be the main reason behind this trend.

Flocks of redwings that appear at feeders are frequently composed entirely of one sex or another. Flocks composed entirely of males are seen more commonly than all-female flocks. When there are representatives of both sexes in a flock, usually one sex will greatly outnumber the other. Still another tendency is for each sex to feed at different times of the day. In late June at a feeder on Cape Cod, for example, females came early in the morning while males appeared later in the day, usually well along in the afternoon. Separation of sexes is not a usual phenomenon among feeding station birds. It is seen most often in the redwing and also in grackles and cowbirds.

Not only do redwings tend to eat separately according to sex, but they have an aversion to eating with other closely related species. Rarely, for example, do redwings eat along with grackles or cowbirds. When forced to eat in close proximity, one species, if it is possible, will go to an elevated feeder while the other will eat on the ground. This kind of segregation is not accomplished without a certain amount of scrapping. The dominant species always takes the elevated feeder while the subordinate one eats on the ground. Redwings at a South Carolina feeder ate at an elevated tray. Cowbirds fed below upon whatever tidbits sifted down to them. Much the same arrangement was seen at a Florida feeding station, only this time the redwings were in the humble position of feeding on the ground while grackles ate above.

Redwings are up to mastering almost any type of feeder and even feed successfully from hanging log feeders. The redwing will accept food at bird tables, trays on posts, window trays, small hanging feeders, logs, and on the ground. Where large numbers of redwings are in the habit of coming for food, it is easiest simply to scatter food on the ground. Use walks and driveways for this purpose. Redwings are open-country birds and do not need nearby cover in the form of trees and shrubs.

When it comes to kinds of food to use, redwings are not discriminating. They happily eat any kind of seeds and grain tossed their way. Foods that have the most appeal are sunflower, scratch feed, cracked corn, wheat, sorghum, millet, canary seed, buckwheat, rice (cooked or uncooked), peanut hearts, pecan meats, cornbread, and white bread.

ORCHARD ORIOLE

This demure-looking bird of orchards and shade trees does not properly seem to belong among the blackbirds. However, the orioles are close relatives of the blackbirds and the orchard oriole reveals this in several ways. Males arrive ahead of the females in the spring and immediately set about establishing breeding territories. Like the blackbirds, orchard orioles are inclined to be gregarious, and this is seen in the sizable numbers that sometimes appear at feeders.

There is only one reasonably successful way to attract this oriole. This is with sugar-water. While with us during a brief nesting season that lasts no later than July, orchard orioles can readily be attracted to the same feeders that draw hummingbirds. Usually some modification of the typical hummingbird feeder is needed if orioles are to utilize it. A perch is essential and also a larger supply of sugar-water than is offered in most hummingbird feeders. Ruth Thomas* solved the problems of orchard oriole feeders very nicely in her Arkansas yard by fastening empty cold cream jars to fence posts and similar places where birds would readily come to feed. The jars were dressed with red ribbon frills in order to make them look like flowers. They were filled with the same sugar-water solutions used in feeding hummingbirds. By the end of several seasons the orioles had responded so well to these overtures that as many as eight pairs along with their offspring were coming to the feeders. Although several other species, including ruby-throated hummingbirds, used these feeders, they were primarily drinking places for the nectar-loving orchard orioles.

*"Orioles Like Sugar Water," *Audubon Magazine*, July–August 1958.

238

*Birds
That
Visit
Feeding
Stations*

Orchard orioles have not followed the example of the northern oriole and rarely stay behind during the fall. There are only occasional records of stragglers in fall and winter, and these have appeared anywhere from the Great Lakes and New England to the Gulf states. Should such a guest appear at feeders, substitute fruit, suet, suet mixtures, and white bread for sugar-water. Halved apples and oranges are foods that are always well liked by orchard orioles. So long as favorite foods are present, the orchard oriole will come to a variety of feeders. It may visit bird tables, trays, suet holders, hanging feeders, logs, hummingbird feeders, and jars holding sweetish solutions.

NORTHERN ORIOLE

The colorful birdlife of the tropics is ours when this bird, formerly called the Baltimore oriole, visits our feeders. The orange and black male is particularly well garbed for a sunny climate, and the natural foods of orioles are found in greatest profusion in the tropics. Therefore, it would seem to be to the advantage of orioles to visit our continent only long enough to complete the vital function of raising families and then to return to the tropics for nine months of sunshine.

This was the time-honored tradition of the northern oriole until very recently. In recent years, as described in Chapter 9, northern orioles have succumbed to the temptations of feeding stations and a somewhat warmer climate and many no longer make the long trek to the tropics.

A bright-colored adult male that arrived at my feeders on a blustery January 3, when I was living near the coast in Massachusetts, seemed so bedraggled and woebegone that I wondered how I could pull him through the winter. The food that brought him to my feeders and that he subsisted upon the first few days was halved orange. Several of his first feeding sessions lasted as long as fifteen minutes. As he became better adjusted, he ate for shorter periods of time and less frequently. By the third day of his stay, he was eating almost nothing but grape jelly at my feeders. This was the preferred food by far.

After the oriole had successfully weathered both a snowstorm and a rainy spell, I began to hold out more hope for him. Not only did I attribute this change for the better to the grape jelly but also to a thorough bath and grooming on January 7. On this date, with the temperature at 37 degrees and sunny, the oriole had soaked himself completely in water from melted snow; then he had spent half an hour preening and grooming his feathers while perched on a tree limb near the feeder.

Feathers that have been thoroughly cleaned and groomed provide much better insulation against the cold than dirty, bedraggled feathers. The oriole had taken one of the best possible precautions against the cold weather that was to come. Except for showing obvious discomfort so far as its feet were concerned, this bird seemed undaunted by the coldest days and fully equal to a northern winter. To be sure, the feeding station was a vital necessity to get him safely through.

So much has been said of the northern oriole in winter that it should not be forgotten that this oriole is a common summer resident over much of the East. Like the orchard oriole, it can be attracted in summer with sugar-water feeders such as those used for hummingbirds but with adequate perches. Many other foods will also lure the northern oriole, and it adapts well to almost any kind of feeder. So long as there is not strenuous competition from other birds, it comes readily to bird tables, trays, hanging feeders, logs, hanging coconuts, suet holders, and sometimes the ground. It is especially partial to hummingbird feeders and jars holding sweetish solutions.

One never knows which foods will appeal to this temperamental guest. Some northern orioles like one thing, some another; also birds suddenly change to a new

*Fruit is one of the best lures
when it comes to inviting
the northern oriole.*

240

*Birds
That
Visit
Feeding
Stations*

food and reject foods that they had been coming to. The only plan is to keep experimenting with different foods when you are host to this bird. There is a long list to choose from. Northern orioles are known to take suet, suet mixtures, peanut butter, doughnuts, pie crust, white bread soaked in milk, halved apple and orange, cooked raisins, grapes, banana, grape and strawberry jelly, cooked rice, small pieces of cracked corn, millet, and pecan meats.

RUSTY BLACKBIRD

Although much like a small grackle in appearance, the rusty does not conform closely to the behavior patterns seen in other members of the blackbird family. It is a bird of wilder regions, nesting in the northern wilderness of Canada, and, for the most part, spending the winter in swamps and wet woodlands of our South. Only in recent years has this blackbird begun to show much interest in feeding stations. It stops by during fall migration while en route to its winter quarters or when, as sometimes happens, it has remained in the North for the winter. The rusty, one of the hardiest of the blackbirds, occasionally winters as far north as Alaska.

In striking contrast to other blackbirds, rusty blackbirds do not arrive in the yard in large flocks but appear two or three at a time, as a rule, or as a solitary visitor. A bird at my feeding station in Massachusetts one fall went out of its way to avoid feeding with other birds. Its favorite feeding place was the bare ground just outside the kitchen door. It would come here many times during the day to eat the scratch feed that I made available especially for its use. Coming so often, as it did, and eating lengthy meals, the bird had a surprising capacity to hold food. Only small pieces of grain were eaten. Larger pieces were picked up but soon discarded. Any item of food as large as a pea seems too bulky for the rusty blackbird. As the bird fed near my doorstep, it walked about constantly and seemed to give vent to a certain nervousness by frequent flicks of the tail.

The rusty blackbird is probably a more common visitor to feeding stations than is generally realized. The difficulty with this bird is that many people mistake it for some other member of the blackbird family. Look for a blackbird that superficially resembles a grackle and always consult a bird guide to make sure of your identification.

Rusty blackbirds are fond of scratch feed, especially cracked corn, and they also take sunflower, sorghum, and millet. Most feeding by this blackbird is on the ground, but occasionally it visits bird tables and trays on posts.

COMMON GRACKLE

Keeping an eye out for leftovers and dropping down into trash barrels, this grackle makes itself at home at every wayside and picnic area. It has also discovered our yards, and comes flocking to our feeders in such numbers that we must make drastic changes in the menu if we would rather see less of this hulking bird that always seems to have a crafty gleam in its eye (page 64). The common grackle has increased greatly in numbers in recent years; thus there is concern about the way it is presently invading residential areas. Along with the increase in numbers, there has been a tendency on the part of the grackle, as well as other blackbirds, to stay farther north in winter. Common grackles are now not unexpected in winter as far north as Minnesota, southern Ontario, and Maine. Many of us, whether we like it or not, now have the common grackle with us the year round.

In spite of our reservations, grackles make themselves thoroughly at home and go about their business as though we had no say in their affairs. We see them strutting about the lawn, prying into everything with their heavy beaks, and sometimes even walking on tops of newly clipped hedges. Every once in a while, one will cease whatever it is doing and gaze skyward as though nervous about something overhead. "Sky-gazing," as it is called, may be followed by other displays, such as bowing and fluffing of body feathers. These antics on the part of the male seem directed sometimes at females, other times at males. It all seems related in some way to courtship.

Common grackles very often continue with their displays when they are at the feeders. Here they seem to feign haughty aloofness from other birds. Grackles may often be seen eating peacefully with other blackbirds at feeders and other birds as well. Smaller birds in time gain confidence and join the throng. However, there is a lack of dependability in the grackle. One never knows when this large guest may turn upon smaller ones and wreak havoc. Numerous observers have told of grackles killing house sparrows at feeders and then dismembering the victims and eating

242

Birds
That
Visit
Feeding
Stations

portions of them. The brains seem to be a special delicacy. During a single spring, an observer in Rhode Island counted no fewer than thirteen house sparrows killed by a single grackle. This grackle would pounce upon an unsuspecting house sparrow, decapitate it, and then fly off with the head.

Grackle predation seems to take place mainly during the nesting season, and the victims are almost invariably house sparrows. Why the house sparrow is singled out over other species is something of a mystery. It has been suggested that the house sparrow, through its importuning ways, antagonizes the larger bird. Lacking any refinement, the house sparrow pushes in among other feeding birds and sometimes boldly snatches food from their beaks. Whether the grackle feels obliged to retaliate or is simply seeking a change in diet is not known. In any event, the house sparrow never seems to learn. It continues to feed confidently alongside its large partner.

One of the best foods to give grackles is white bread. Not only do the grackles have a special liking for bread but they often go through an elaborate dunking ceremony before eating it. Bread may be taken to a bird bath or other watering place and there dropped in to soak or held under by the bill. The wet bread is then consumed. Sometimes other foods, including sunflower and kernels of corn, are dunked before they are eaten. In early summer grackles may be seen flying off with food they have dunked at the bird bath or other source of water. This food is being taken to young that are either in the nest or have already fledged. Wetting helps the food go down more easily.

Stale bakery products are a good food for these birds. Expert dunkers that they are, the food is soon softened. Grackles are as accomplished at dunking pieces of doughnut as we are! The list of other foods that are to the liking of this omnivorous bird is long indeed. Among the foods that have special appeal to grackles are sunflower, white bread, bread and milk, peanuts (shucked) and whole or cracked corn. A wide range of other foods are taken by this bird, including wheat, oats, barley, buckwheat, sorghum, popcorn, rice, millet, suet, suet mixtures, peanut hearts, peanut butter, buttermilk, cottage cheese, and boiled white potato.

The common grackle is surprisingly versatile in its reaction to feeders. Equally at home on the ground or at raised feeders, the grackle readily finds its way to bird tables, feeding trays, and many hanging feeders. If food is scarce on bird tables, trays, and the ground, this grackle will cling to sides of small hanging feeders. For

a bird of its size, it manages to balance quite handily on perches of hanging feeders.
Ordinarily it is too wary to come to window feeders.

BROWN-HEADED COWBIRD

This least respectable member of the blackbird family is very much at home at bird feeders. Most of us do not object to its presence but we are likely to withhold our approval of this bird if we are aware of its parasitic habits. Every cowbird we see has been reared by a foster parent. The female cowbird simply deposits her eggs in the nests of other birds. Her timing is so perfect that her eggs hatch about the same time as those of the rightful owners. The young cowbirds outgrow their nest mates and are soon receiving the greatest share of the food. Many times it is the offspring of usurping cowbirds that win out at the expense of the legitimate brood.

If we can forgive cowbirds for their waywardness, we may find ourselves enjoying these odd, interesting birds. Flocks arrive at our feeders almost any time of the year. If we live in more northern states, we can expect cowbirds in some numbers through spring, summer, and fall. In the South the cowbird is chiefly a winter visitor. The well-disciplined cowbird flocks that appear at our feeders eat quietly and do not intentionally disturb other guests. A problem arises only if too many arrive at one time. Large flocks, that sometimes invade feeders and then move on, do disrupt the feeding routine of other birds.

As with redwings, there is often a preponderance of one sex or another. In spring and early summer males go through a ludicrous courtship performance. A bird will puff out its feathers, especially those around the neck, and with wings stiffly curved, take a hop forward. This movement is followed by a low bow, so low sometimes that the head may actually strike the ground. These actions are accompanied by strange gurgling noises that sound like water being poured from a bottle.

During the mating season the courtship ritual of the male seems to take up more time than eating. Frequently performances take place at feeding trays. The females, seemingly unimpressed, go about their feeding activities and soon fly off to leave the still bowing males in full possession.

Cowbirds seem to prefer feeding in compact flocks. Therefore they need plenty

244

Birds
That
Visit
Feeding
Stations

of space. If we are going to cater to their needs, we should scatter food on the ground well out in the open or place it on large bird table feeders. However, cowbirds will, if necessary, adapt to window trays, trays on posts, and small hanging feeders. There is little incentive to provide this none-too-welcome visitor with expensive fare. In fact, the cowbird is content with nothing more than cracked corn or scratch feed. If other foods are available, the cowbird will not hesitate to use them. Its tastes run to sunflower, wheat, sorghum, canary seed, rape, buckwheat, rice, peanut hearts, pecan meats, cornbread, and white bread.

TANAGERS

Like the orioles, the tanagers are vividly colored birds whose ties are with the American tropics. Of four that fly north to nest within our borders, only the scarlet and summer tanagers occur in the East. The recently introduced blue-gray tanager has a precarious foothold in the Miami, Florida, region. Tanagers, as a rule, do not come readily to feeding stations. People living north of Virginia and Kentucky are more likely to receive visits from the scarlet tanager; those living in these states or to the south are more likely to see the summer tanager.

SCARLET TANAGER

There is no mistaking the handsome red and black male scarlet tanager. No other feeding station visitor, with the possible exception of the male painted bunting, is more brilliantly colored. Would that we had more of both sexes of this tanager at our feeders!

When they do come, scarlet tanagers are retiring birds that eat quietly in one place for a long time. We are highly privileged if we succeed in luring a pair. If there is a nest nearby, the parents may carry off food to the young; later the young may appear along with parents at the feeders.

A male was seen feeding for half an hour at a northern Michigan feeder in late May. This bird made frequent visits to a window feeder and also took food from the ground. Although the bird soon disappeared, there was a return visit by this bird or

246

*Birds
That
Visit
Feeding
Stations*

another one in late October—later than normal for the scarlet tanager to be in North America. When feeding birds in Massachusetts, I had a scarlet tanager at a second-story feeder in late September.

There is no sure way to lure the scarlet tanager. If one or two start coming to your feeding station, try fruit and place it where there will be little competition from other birds. Preference seems to be for first- and second-story window trays; the scarlet tanager also comes to bird tables, trays on posts, suet holders, and food on the ground. Besides fruit, including sliced apple, bananas, cherries, and raisins, try a few birdseeds, suet, suet mixtures, cornbread, white bread, and pie crust. Probably this species and other tanagers would eat granulated white sugar or brown sugar, foods that are used to attract many tanagers in the tropics.

SUMMER TANAGER

Male summer tanagers and male cardinals share the distinction of being the only virtually all-red birds to visit feeding stations in the East. The male summer tanager can be distinguished by absence of a crest and a more slender bill. Summer tanagers are far less common than cardinals, and those who live in the South are lucky to have

There's nothing like a banana, raisins, and an orange section to bring out the elusive scarlet tanager.

a pair in their yard or coming to their feeders. A summer resident in our southern states, the summer tanager sometimes appears as a stray in northern states in late summer or early fall. A tendency by this species to stay behind in winter was first widely noted during the winter of 1972–1973.

Once on to our fare, summer tanagers come boldly without fear of people who may be watching. Intolerant of other birds, this tanager, like the scarlet, loses interest if there is too much competition for food. A pair that was coming to my Florida feeder deserted when a mockingbird began to employ aggressive tactics. Alexander Sprunt writes that this tanager will exhibit remarkable tameness when coming for food. Birds will visit a porch where people are sitting and carry away crumbs and other food to their young.

Food tastes are much the same as those of the scarlet tanager. The same fruits, including sliced apple and orange, banana, and raisins, are taken and such other foods as suet, sunflower, pecan meats, peanut hearts, pound cake, white bread, and butter. The summer tanager has about the same feeder preferences as the scarlet. It visits bird tables, trays on posts, window trays, and sometimes hummingbird feeders.

GLOSSARY OF FOODS AND PRECAUTIONS

ALFALFA MEAL AND PELLETS   poultry or livestock mixtures that contain alfalfa meal are well liked by starlings.

ALMOND   a soft-shelled nut whose chopped kernels are readily taken by woodpeckers, titmice, chickadees, jays, nuthatches, Carolina wrens, mockingbirds, and red crossbills.

AMERICAN CHEESE   one of the best cheeses for bird feeding. Users include downy woodpecker, Carolina wren, robin.

ANIMAL FATS   fats used in bird feeding, including suet, lard, and grease, promote growth and efficient use of feed in domestic poultry. The same doubtless applies to wild birds. The fats we offer at our feeders are high-energy foods, rich in calories, that are particularly well suited to winter feeding. They are well received by nearly all visitors including many sparrows and finches, birds that are regarded as dominantly seed-eating. See also *grease, suet,* and *suet mixtures.*

APPLE   has advantages in its relatively low cost and the ease with which it can be served. Most popular with birds during the spring and also has many users through the summer. Impale halved apples on twigs or nails.

APPLE, BAKED   many birds, particularly the bluebird, respond to apple if it is baked.

APPLE, RAW, SLICED   chief users are robin, hermit thrush, cedar waxwing, starling, yellow-breasted chat, and orioles.

APPLE JELLY   a good winter food that birds take because of its sweetness.

APPLE SEEDS   many birds, including evening grosbeak, begin taking apple seeds after the pulp has been consumed.

APRICOT   taken by the house finch.

ASHES   see *mineral matter*.

BACON DRIPPINGS   see *suet mixtures* and *kitchen wastes*.

BAKERY PRODUCTS   the bread, toast, rolls, muffins, cornbread, cake, crackers, and doughnuts that come under this heading are high in carbohydrates and, as a whole, have a food value about three-fourths that of grain. Do not rely too heavily upon these foods. They supply bulk but are lacking in many important nutritional ingredients.

BANANA   there is much variation in the way birds react to this food. Sometimes well received by mockingbird, catbird, Carolina wren, yellow-breasted chat, and northern oriole.

BARLEY   this grain has little attraction for most birds. Taken to some extent by meadowlark, grackle, cardinal, and towhee.

BAYBERRY   the waxy fruits of this largely seacoast shrub are well suited for winter feeding. Especially attractive to yellow-rumped warbler.

BEEF BONE   see *meat bone*.

BEEF FAT   see *suet*.

BIRD SEED MIXTURE   most mixtures sold commercially contain liberal portions of millet, sorghum, and sometimes canary seed. Lesser portions of rape and sunflower are sometimes included. Little objection can be made to the ingredients that go into these mixtures. The main question is whether the proportions will be right for the birds that visit our feeders. By buying the ingredients separately and then mixing our own we can hope to arrive at a mixture well suited to the needs of our clientele. Changes may be necessary with the seasons as our guest list will also be undergoing frequent change.

BLACK WALNUT   a native nut whose tasty meats are excellent for bird feeding. Crack the hard shell with a hammer and let birds pick out the meats. Chief users are woodpeckers, chickadees, titmice, and nuthatches. See also *nutmeats* and *pecan*.

BLUEBERRY   together with the closely similar huckleberry, this soft berry is an excellent food for young birds and will attract shyer species, like thrushes, to the feeder.

BREAD   see *white bread*.

BROWNTOP MILLET   see *millet*.

BUCKWHEAT   although rejected by many birds, buckwheat seeds are well received by doves, cardinal, and purple finch.

BUTTER   leftover scraps are well liked by catbird and summer tanager.

BUTTERMILK   appeals to the common grackle.

BUTTERNUT   a close relative of the black walnut, with a somewhat more northerly range. The meats are especially favored by black-capped chickadee, titmice, nuthatches, and pine siskin.

CAKE, COOKIE, AND BREAD CRUMBS   see *crumbs*.

CANADA, OR FIELD, PEA   appeals to the domestic pigeon.

CANARY SEED   (*Phalaris canariensis*) ranks with millet as the grass seed most favored by birds at feeding stations. Since the mineral and protein content of this common ingredient in birdseed mixtures is not high, this seed should be used with other more nutritious foods. Users include doves, bobwhite, red-bellied woodpecker, titmice, house sparrow, blackbirds, and most sparrows and finches.

CANTALOUPE SEED   see *melon seeds*.

CEREALS   see *chick feed, cornmeal, dry cereal, grain, hot cereal*.

CHARCOAL   see *mineral matter*.

CHEESE   a popular food for feeding birds in England. The three kinds that are occasionally used in this country are American cheese, cottage cheese, and cream cheese. The first one is the most used and perhaps the most favored by birds. See also *American cheese*.

CHERRIES   the cherries sold in grocery stores are too expensive for regular use, yet there is nothing like a bright red maraschino or other cherry to get the attention of an otherwise indifferent robin, thrush, or tanager.

CHICK FEED   this food, composed of corn, wheat, sorghum, and oat groats ground to almost powder fineness, is one of the best for attracting sparrows. Good for all species treated in Part II of this book and also vesper and Lincoln's sparrows.

CLAY   see *mineral matter*.

COCONUT   somehow the coconut has not caught on as well in this country as in England. The meat makes a good winter food for woodpeckers, chickadees, and titmice, and the shell a handsome bird feeder suitable for hanging from a tree limb. Shredded coconut meats are risky in that the meat swells after being swallowed. Another disadvantage is that the meat in any form is overly popular with gray squirrels.

CORN, CANNED   appeals to the starling.

CORN, CRACKED   many wonder why they should continue to buy more expensive foods when cracked corn is so universally well liked by birds. This popular cereal grain does have a few disadvantages. When cracked, corn spoils quickly in bad weather, and it attracts many guests we are dubious about, including squirrels, starlings, house sparrows, and blackbirds. Corn is a good heat- and energy-producing food, being largely carbohydrates and oil, but like other grains, it is low in crude protein and especially deficient in mineral matter. An advantage is the Vitamin A present in yellow corn.

CORN, WHOLE KERNELS   some of the disadvantages of cracked corn are overcome with the use of whole kernels. As whole kernels or corn on the cob, the grains are much more resistant to spoilage and they attract fewer unwanted guests (see *selective foods*). Users include bobwhite, ring-necked pheasant, mourning dove, domestic pigeon, red-bellied woodpecker, blue jay, blackbirds, cardinal, and blue grosbeak.

CORNBREAD   good keeping qualities and fair nutrition make this a better food than white bread for bird feeding. Use crumbled or in broken pieces. See page 272 for special recipe for birds.

CORNMEAL   used chiefly with other ingredients as an additive to suet mixtures. Yellow cornmeal is preferred for bird feeding because of the presence of Vitamin A. Dry cornmeal is taken by red crossbills. See also *suet mixtures*.

CORNMEAL MUSH   a soft, easily downed food that is made by cooking cornmeal. Well suited to warblers and as a food for young birds. Not well adapted for use in winter because it freezes hard in cold weather.

COTTAGE CHEESE   a good food to try with young birds when they appear at feeders. Also can be used with robin, bluebird, and grackle.

CRACKER CRUMBS   one of the kitchen odds and ends that is apt to be overlooked. Well received by blue jay, house wren, and chipping sparrow.

CRANBERRIES   appeals to the pine grosbeak.

CREAM CHEESE   appeals to the white-breasted nuthatch.

CRUMBS   stale crumbs of bakery products, especially those of cake, cookies, and bread, are suitable for use at the feeder and can be mixed, along with other ingredients, into rendered suet in the preparation of suet mixtures.

CURRANTS, COOKED   well liked by catbird and robin.

CURRANTS, RAW   taken by the same birds that accept raisins, if anything, they have a somewhat wider appeal because of the smaller size. See also *raisins*.

DATES   appeal to the house finch.

DISEASE AT BIRD FEEDERS   if disease breaks out among birds eating at bird feeders, it is usually a sign that insufficient care has been taken to maintain cleanliness at feeders and bird baths. Disease is most often encountered in wet weather. Moldy food contaminated by droppings is to blame in many instances. See also *sanitation at feeders*.

DOG BISCUITS, SOAKED popular with birds as seen by the number that come to dog dishes to get leftovers. Users include blue jay, starling, and grackle.

DOUGHNUTS when first exposed at feeders, doughnuts are sometimes left untouched. Crumble them and birds will quickly catch on to this highly popular food. Suspended on wire holders, doughnuts make unique feeders in that birds eat their way through the food they are clinging to. There is little wastage as fallen pieces are consumed by birds that are waiting on the ground. Users include blue jay, bluebird, ruby-crowned kinglet, yellow-rumped warbler, yellow-breasted chat, northern oriole, and house finch.

DRIED PRUNES, SLICED appeal to the wood thrush.

DRY CEREAL cornflakes, puffed wheat, and other dry cereals appeal more to birds when moistened with milk. Favored by the catbird. Dry farina was taken by red crossbills.

ECONOMICAL PURCHASING one of the biggest savings that can be made in bird food is to buy seeds and grain in 50- or 100-pound sacks and store the contents in safe, tight containers. Twenty-gallon trash cans with tight lids are recommended as storage bins. See page 24.

EGGS, BOILED, FRIED, OR SCRAMBLED users include blue jay, catbird, mockingbird, starling, and grackle.

EGGSHELL, BROKEN OR GROUND an excellent source of calcium. Deficiency of this mineral in the diet is said to lead to nest robbing by blue jays. Broken pieces of eggshell can be offered near feeders or in suet mixtures. If placed on the ground near nesting colonies, eggshell is eagerly consumed by purple martins. See also *kitchen wastes* and *suet mixtures*.

ENGLISH WALNUT well liked by birds but expensive. Users include jays, chickadees, titmice, house sparrow, goldfinch, and white-crowned sparrow.

FATS AND FAT MIXTURES see *animal fats*, *suet*, and *suet mixtures*.

FIELD PEA see *Canada pea*.

FIG   liked by the mockingbird and house finch.

FISH, FRIED   appeals to the catbird.

FLAXSEED   appeals to the purple finch, pine grosbeak, redpoll.

FLOUR   can be used with cornmeal or alone as a binder in suet mixtures. See also *suet mixtures*.

FOODS FOR YOUNG BIRDS   much of the food supplied in early summer is taken by parents to feed young that are in the nest. Later many of these same young will follow parents to the feeders and here will clamor incessantly for more and more food. There will be a period when only soft, moist foods are suitable for these youngsters. We can choose from a long list. Among those to offer are cottage cheese, bread soaked in milk, pablum with milk, cornmeal mush, cooked oatmeal with raisins, raisins and currants (cooked or soaked), grapes, cherries, mashed banana, blueberries, raspberries, and strawberries. Mealworms, though troublesome, are something else to consider. Suet that has been properly rendered is another good food for young birds, but it is usually too difficult to handle for birds just out of the nest. Parents will do the feeding. Peanut butter and other ingredients can be added to the suet. See also *suet mixtures; suet, how to use in summer*; and *mealworm*.

FOODS, FREEZING   because they become hard and unpalatable after freezing, a number of foods are not well adapted for use during northern winters. This applies to fruits of all kinds, cornmeal mush, hot cereals, and many kitchen scraps. Melted suet or grease protects some foods from freezing, and for this reason it is desirable to use suet recipes including currants and raisins when the weather is cold. See *suet mixtures*.

FOODS, HARMFUL   see *harmful foods*.

FOODS, LONG-LASTING   see *long-lasting foods*.

FOODS TO ATTRACT ATTENTION   when starting a new feeding station, there is nothing like white bread to advertise our intentions (see page 12). Other foods, especially suet and sunflower, thistle, and scratch feed, should quickly follow. The main thing is to get birds in the habit of coming to a certain place for food. See also *white bread*.

FOXTAIL MILLET   see *millet*.

FRUIT BOWL   when properly cut and served, fresh fruit makes an excellent bird food. Serve by placing in a shallow bowl along with the juice. Almost any kind of fruit, including chopped pieces of apple, orange, banana, pear, and grape, is suitable for this purpose. While fruit has its greatest appeal in summer, we should not overlook the needs of occasional over-wintering fruit-eaters, such as the northern oriole and yellow-breasted chat. Birds that respond in summer include catbird, mockingbird, thrushes, orioles, tanagers, and rose-breasted grosbeak.

GRAIN OR CEREAL GRAIN   cereal grains are members of the grass family that are cultivated for the production of food for man and his domestic animals. Some cereal grains, including corn, wheat, millet, sorghum, and canary seed, are out-standing bird foods. The cereal grains are rather low in protein and completely lacking in vitamins C and D. They do contain vitamins of the B group and are rich in carbohydrates. The latter makes them good energy foods. In view of the several deficiencies of cereal grains, we should not build our feeding program entirely around them. A balanced menu, using not only cereal grains but other seeds, nutmeats, fruits, kitchen scraps, and suet mixtures, is greatly to be pre-ferred. Nevertheless, the cereal grains are the backbone of any bird feeding program and one of the main attractions that keep birds coming.

GRAPEFRUIT   usually scorned, but halved fruits are sometimes taken eagerly by crows and starlings.

GRAPE JELLY   may be used at any season, but especially useful in winter as it doesn't freeze and attracts such over-wintering birds as yellow-rumped warbler and northern oriole.

GRAPES, CULTIVATED OR WILD   wintering northern orioles in North Carolina refused fresh grapes placed on a feeding shelf; on the other hand, partly rotten, crushed grapes lying on the ground were accepted eagerly. Reaction by birds to grapes, as well as to other fruits, varies greatly. Sometimes grapes are the most popular fruit we can supply. Users include mockingbird, yellow-breasted chat, northern oriole, house finch, and towhee.

GRAPES, WHITE SEEDLESS   this grocery store variety is one of the best grapes to use in order to get a prompt response.

GREASE   leftover kitchen grease in the form of melted lard, cooking oils, and bacon drippings should be saved for the many recipes (pages 272–5) that make use of these products. See also *animal fats, kitchen wastes,* and *suet mixtures.*

GRIT   an essential ingredient in the diets of most birds and especially important in winter when it is hard for birds to find because of snow cover. A large variety of small, hard objects come under the heading of grit. Some are more important as suppliers of mineral matter, others are essentially grinding agents. Grit can be supplied in such forms as ashes, charcoal, clay, coarse sand, cuttlefish bone, eggshell, ground limestone, ground oyster and clam shell, fine gravel, and dry mortar such as may be found clinging to old bricks. Grit can be obtained from poultry suppliers and pet stores. See also *mineral matter.*

HARMFUL FOODS   luckily there are very few foods that need to be avoided because they are harmful to birds. See *peanut butter* for precautions to take with this extremely popular bird food. It is less well known that millet is sometimes fatal to cowbirds, red-winged blackbirds, and perhaps other birds as well. The small, round seeds are sometimes exactly the right size to enter the windpipe and cause asphyxiation. Foods that swell with the absorption of moisture are also hazardous. Too much dry rolled oats or desiccated coconut meat can lead to internal injuries. Many foods spoil in wet weather, hence the inadvisability of overstocking feeders. See *moldy foods, hazards of.*

HAY CHAFF   a rich source of seeds of alfalfa, clover, timothy, and other grasses, hay is a storehouse of food for birds. Birds can be supplied by simply sprinkling hay chaff from a barn loft onto the snow or bare ground. The seeds from timothy hay are particularly welcomed by birds. Coming to chaff from timothy hay in Michigan one winter were horned lark, redpoll, savannah sparrow, vesper sparrow, and snow bunting.

HEMPSEED   formerly much used in bird feeding and relished by many of the same species that take sunflower seeds. Presently this seed is not readily available commercially and only parched seeds can be sold legally, because this plant is the producer of marijuana. The parched seeds seem less acceptable to birds.

HICKORY NUT   the sweet flavored nutmeats of mockernut are well liked by birds. This hickory and several others have users that include woodpeckers, chickadees, titmice, warblers, cardinal, goldfinch, and pine siskin.

HONEY   Although once recommended as a hummingbird food, honey has since been found to be harmful to hummingbirds and should not be used at all in feeding.

HOT CEREAL   cooked oatmeal and other hot cereals provide something slightly different to use on the menu. Cooked oatmeal with raisins is one of the foods to offer young birds that visit feeders during the nesting season.

JAPANESE MILLET   see *millet*.

KITCHEN WASTES   a wide variety of wastes and leftovers can be saved for bird feeding. But care must be taken not to overdo this kind of economy. Some wastes, such as melon rinds and soft fruit, can lead to unsightliness, and others are risky from a health standpoint. Avoid using moldy bread and other spoiled foods. Also avoid using food that is highly seasoned. Wastes best suited for use in bird feeding include fats and grease, eggshell, melon seeds, pieces of cheese, and stale bakery products. See also page 12 and *moldy foods, hazards of*.

LONG-LASTING FOODS   it is sometimes necessary to make provision for our bird guests during absences from home. Besides stocking hopper-type feeders with sufficient amounts of seed and grain, we should offer foods that will last and not be quickly consumed. Unless discovered by hordes of hungry starlings, suet is excellent for this purpose. See page 274 for a hard suet mixture that will withstand the inroads of starlings. Corn on the cob is so unwieldy that birds cannot consume it quickly. Tie ears securely so that squirrels or other mammals will not make off with them. See *Osage orange* for another food that is long lasting. Birds have to wait for this one to rot before they can get at the seeds. See also *suet*.

LOQUAT   appeals to the house finch.

MEALWORM   the time and effort required to establish mealworm cultures make this form of live bird food impracticable for most of us. However, it is an excellent food for rearing young birds and for finicky adults that we may be holding as convalescents. Mealworms are a real treat for parents and young at the height of the nesting season. Offer in a dish or the bird bath so the more active worms won't crawl away. Mealworm cultures may be started in a box or tray containing fine meal or flour plus coarse material such as scraps of paper. Some moisture should be supplied in the form of apple, carrot, or raw potato. Mealworms are the larval stage of a common beetle, *Tenebrio molitor*.

MEAT SCRAPS   these can be offered to birds in the form of beef bones, lamb bones, ham scraps, bacon rind, hamburger, hot dogs, or as small scraps from our dinner plates. Offer meat that has been cooked. That many birds have a craving for meat is seen in the avid way it is taken by several hawks, gulls, certain woodpeckers, crows, jays, chickadees, titmice, starling, and white-winged crossbill. As with other leftovers, meat scraps may cause unsightliness. One solution is to hang a meat bone where it is not readily visible and let birds pick off the edible meat.

MELON SEEDS   those of cantaloupe, watermelon, pumpkin, and squash are readily taken by birds and sometimes with the same enthusiasm that greets sunflower seeds. So that the edible kernels are readily available, we should put such seeds through a meat or coffee grinder. Make a practice of saving all the melon seeds you can; otherwise you won't have nearly enough for winter bird feeding. Users include mourning dove, blue jay, chickadees, titmice, nuthatches, starling, house sparrow, cardinal, rose-breasted grosbeak, purple finch, and towhee.

MILK   appeals to the catbird.

MILLET   the small, nearly round seeds of millet make up one of the most important groups of foods used in bird feeding. In fact, millet constitutes the largest portion of most commercial birdseed mixtures. Although millet is well liked by birds generally and has many users, especially among doves, blackbirds, sparrows, and finches, there are fairly wide differences in how the several kinds are received. This is seen in the considerable amount of wastage sometimes noted when commercial birdseed mixtures are offered at feeding stations. It pays to find the right millet for the birds that come to your feeders. The following are kinds that are frequently used in bird feeding:

1. Browntop millet (*Panicum ramosum*) was well received when tested at feeding stations in Georgia.

2. Better known is foxtail millet (*Setaria italica*) and its several varieties—golden, German, and Hungarian. All are good for bird feeding, especially golden.

3. Japanese millet (*Echinochloa frumentacea*) is frequently planted as a waterfowl food but it is not too well received by birds at feeding stations.

4. Better results are obtained from pearl millet (*Pennisetum glaucum*), also known as cattail millet. This millet is planted as a dove food and also attracts many sparrows and finches.

5. Proso millet (*Panicum miliaceum*), also known as common millet, has three varieties named after their color—white, yellow, and red. It is one of the best millets for bird feeding. White proso millet ranks first in acceptance, then red, and slightly less favored is yellow proso. Contrary to some opinion, red proso is not an inferior millet for bird feeding. Most birds accept it readily enough.

MINERAL MATTER   the craving that birds sometimes show for ashes, charcoal, clay, salt, and other such substances reveals possible mineral deficiencies in the diet. Regular feeding station visitors, in contrast to birds living in the northern wilderness, rarely seem in need of this extra mineral matter. This may partly reflect the well-balanced diets we provide. In any event, we probably need to do nothing more than continue to offer a variety of wholesome foods and from time to time supply some form of grit. See also *grit* and *salt*.

MOLDY FOODS, HAZARDS OF   one of the questions that frequently arises in bird feeding is whether or not to offer birds slightly moldy foods. Also many people wonder whether they should take pains to remove any food at feeders that has become moldy. Dampness causes mold and this is why leftover food on trays or food in hoppers or storage containers tends to become moldy in wet weather. Is there a health hazard to birds when foods become moldy?

Little is known on this subject so far as wild birds are concerned. It seems probable that some species can tolerate fairly high levels of mold in their foods while other species cannot. The late Herbert L. Stoddard, authority on the bobwhite quail, has warned that this species sickens after eating cracked corn that has become moldy on exposure to wet weather. Moldy foods, according to Philip J. Schaible,* are not necessarily harmful to the poultry eating them and sometimes the mold may have a beneficial effect. Schaible states that mold causes food to have less nutritional value, and he also points to examples of mortality in poultry caused by eating moldy foods. In 1960 over 10,000 turkeys died in Great Britain from eating peanuts containing a mycotoxin mold. Losses have also resulted from a mold in wheat known as ergot and another mold found in barley. Several avian diseases, including aspergillosis, thrush, and favus, are caused by toxic fungi.

In view of the many hazards present in moldy foods, it seems best to take extra pains with the foods we offer. Avoid using foods that are already moldy, keep feeders clean, and remove foods that have become moldy. See also *sanitation at feeders*.

MUSHROOMS, COOKED   appeal to the catbird.

NIGER   see *thistle*.

NUTMEATS   one of the best extra nutrition foods for use at the feeder. They are such a rich source of heat and energy, however, that we should curtail their use during warmer parts of the year. Birds seem as eager for exotic nutmeats as for those they know in the wild. One difficulty with some nuts is that the shells clutter up the feeders and the ground below. The only recourse is periodically to sweep up this debris and take it to the compost heap. Nutmeats are sometimes not recognized by birds in the North; in the South, where nutmeats are better known to birds in the wild, they are generally eagerly received at feeders. See also *almond, black walnut, coconut, English walnut, hickory nut, peanut* (and peanut products), and *pecan*.

OATMEAL   see *hot cereal*.

OATS AND OAT GROATS   for the most part, oats are less attractive to birds than corn or wheat. One obstacle to birds is the tight hull. When this is removed, oats are more easily handled by birds and therefore more palatable. Hulled oats are called

Poultry: Feeds and Nutrition, Westport, Conn., Avi Publishing Co., 1970.

oat groats. They go into chick feed, scratch feed, and other mixtures used in bird feeding. Among the many users of oat groats are mourning dove, domestic pigeon, flicker, house sparrow, meadowlark, blackbirds, cardinal, dickcissel, purple finch, towhee, junco, and snow bunting.

ORANGES   as with many other fruits, oranges may be totally ignored or taken with enthusiasm. Freezing temperatures limit the use of oranges during northern winters. Nevertheless, it is a good policy to keep a halved orange, frozen or not, on the feeder. This is one of the best ways to lure the northern oriole. Users are most numerous in summer and include red-bellied woodpecker, catbird, northern oriole, summer tanager, scarlet tanager, and rose-breasted grosbeak. Oranges can be used in several ways—halves impaled on twigs or nails, halves left on feeder shelves, or pieces cut up and used in fruit bowls. See also *fruit bowl*.

OSAGE ORANGES   although the sprawling Osage orange hedges that once separated fields in farming country are fast disappearing, there are still enough plants left in some areas to supply needs at bird feeders. The fruits contain seeds that are well liked by many visitors. Simply place the fruits on the ground, and as they slowly decay the seeds will become available to the many birds that like them. See also *long-lasting foods*.

OYSTER SHELL   useful both as grit and as a supplier of mineral matter. Should be finely ground. See also *grit*.

PEACHES   appeal to the house finch.

PEANUT   although an underground tuber, the peanut has much the same appeal and usefulness in bird feeding as nuts from trees. Peanuts are rich in calories and equally attractive to birds whether raw, cooked, or salted. But it is best not to offer birds a diet rich in peanuts or peanut products in summer: it is difficult for young birds to digest, and peanuts can become rancid in hot weather.

PEANUT BUTTER   this taste treat is safer and more economical when it is used as an ingredient in suet mixtures. It takes only a little peanut butter to impart the flavor and some of the nutritional value. See also *harmful foods* and *suet mixtures*.

PEANUT, CHOPPED   providing chopped peanuts is one way to insure smaller birds their share of this popular food. The smaller bits are taken by warblers and sparrows.

PEANUT HEARTS   these are the embryos of the peanut, which are removed in making peanut butter. Up until recently this was an economical food that was commonly sold as a bird food. Now it is less readily available. Has much the same appeal to birds as other nutmeats and comes in small pieces that can easily be taken by smaller birds. Sometimes a popular food but more often hardly touched at all. Avoid offering it in wet weather as these meats quickly spoil.

PEANUTS IN THE SHELL   thanks to a brittle shell, the kernels are available to strong-billed birds, including woodpeckers, blue jay, titmice, nuthatches, and grackle. You can enjoy the antics of birds trying to get at the tasty kernels by stringing together a row of peanuts and hanging this food chain somewhere near the feeder.

PEARS, HALVED   appeal to the mockingbird and robin.

PEARL MILLET   see *millet*.

PECAN   culls and leftovers from packing plants in the South have for many years been used in the manufacture of a highly popular bird food. The cracked nutmeats can be protected from the weather by mixing into suet mixtures. When tested with other nutmeats at a feeder in Athens, Georgia, this nut was found by Verne E. Davison to rank with black walnut as the nut food most preferred by bird visitors.

PIE CRUST   liked by the chickadee, bluebird, northern oriole, and scarlet tanager.

PLUMS   appeal to the house finch.

POPCORN   when popped, taken by crow, blue jay, chickadees, and grackle. Around Christmas time, the popped kernels, along with cranberries and other highly colored objects, can be strung on living evergreens to make showy "birds' Christmas trees."

POTATO   see *white potato*.

POTATO PEELINGS, COOKED   appeal to the blue jay.

PROSO MILLET   see *millet*.

PUMPKIN   see *melon seeds*.

RAISINS   many times this food goes untouched at the feeder. Nevertheless, raisins have a special use in inviting less easily persuaded birds to our feeders or window-sills. Users include blue jay, catbird, mockingbird, brown thrasher, robin, blue-bird, cedar waxwing, northern oriole, scarlet tanager, summer tanager, cardinal, and rose-breasted grosbeak. Soaked or steamed raisins are a good food for young birds in summer. See also *currants* and *foods for young birds*.

RANCID SUET   see *suet, how to use in summer*.

RAPE   should be given a try if for no other reason than its unusually high protein and fat content and the presence of many minerals. The small black seeds may at first be ignored. Always a good food to try with the house finch and sometimes taken by mourning dove, chickadee, cowbird, evening grosbeak, and junco.

RICE, COOKED OR UNCOOKED   however offered, rice has few takers and this is probably just as well. The mineral content of processed rice is lower than that of corn and the nutritional value is generally poor. Cooked rice seems to be more appreciated than is uncooked. Rice in its several forms is taken by bobwhite, doves, starling, meadowlark, blackbirds, northern oriole (relishes cooked rice), and many sparrows and finches.

ROLLED OATS   appeal to pine siskin, towhee, and several other sparrows and finches. See also *harmful foods*.

RYE   the least popular with birds of the cereal grains used in bird feeding. Users include bobwhite, ring-necked pheasant, mourning dove, house sparrow, and cardinal.

SAFFLOWER   a relative newcomer to the market, safflower is increasingly popular in bird feeding for much the same reason as thistle. It is eaten by birds most of us want and not eaten, or rarely eaten, by a long list of others. Even though the white seeds look like sunflower, birds are slow to catch on to them. If offering safflower for the first time, use in hanging feeders with sunflower. Cardinals are usually the first to eat them. Other takers include doves, chickadees, titmice, jays, nuthatches, purple finches, evening grosbeaks, and goldfinches.

SALT   birds, such as northern finches, that have predominantly vegetable diets often exhibit a strong craving for salt. When we are hosts to such birds, we may want to supply extra salt. This can best be done by pouring a saline water solution over a stump or piece of wood until crystals form. A craving for salt has been noted in doves, downy and hairy woodpecker, crows, jays, titmice, nuthatches, house sparrow, evening grosbeak, purple finch, house finch, pine grosbeak, redpoll, pine siskin, goldfinch, and crossbills.

Birds can probably obtain most of their salt requirements from the bakery products, bacon grease, peanut butter, and salted nuts we offer. To be on the safe side, do not offer too much bacon grease or other salty foods and do not purposely add salt to foods. See also *mineral matter*.

SANITATION AT BIRD BATHS   the dangers of spreading disease are probably greatest at improperly maintained bird baths. Dirty water produces not only molds but harmful bacteria that may lead to coccidiosis and salmonella infection. Prevention is simple enough if we will take the trouble. When baths are heavily used, empty and refill several times a day. This is the only way to insure that fecal matter and other dirt doesn't accumulate in the baths. Baths should be scrubbed and cleaned several times a week. These precautions are less necessary in wet weather when baths are receiving little or no use.

SANITATION AT FEEDERS   when moldy food is allowed to collect along with droppings and other debris, there is a real danger that birds will become infected with aspergillosis or other bird diseases. The remedy is to put out small amounts of food at frequent intervals and to keep feeders and immediate surroundings as clean as possible. Feeders should be cleaned with a stiff brush every few days and at the same time the ground below should be swept clean in order to get rid of any litter. As a precaution against disease, feeder trays and tubular feeders should be scrubbed at frequent intervals using a detergent/warm water solution and thoroughly rinsed and dried. This is wise if there is evidence of any sickness in the feeding station flock. But generally, cleanliness and a little care about the proper amounts of food to put out seem to be all the precautions that are needed.

SAUERKRAUT   try with starling.

SCRATCH FEED   this commercial and popular food is a mainstay at many feeding stations. Scratch feed is basically a mixture of wheat and cracked corn. Other grains, particularly barley or oat groats, may be substituted for the wheat. Additional ingredients sometimes include sorghum, buckwheat, and Canada peas. Scratch comes in coarse, medium, and fine. The grade to ask for depends upon your users. Finer grades are more acceptable to small birds, especially sparrows. For birds that would take larger pieces, see *corn, whole kernels*. An advantage in fine or medium scratch is that the pieces cannot be removed so quickly by blue jays and blackbirds. The problem of spoilage that occurs with cracked corn applies to scratch feed. See also *corn, cracked*.

SELECTIVE FOODS   so long as you have no serious problems, you can go on using plentiful amounts of such popular foods as cracked corn, scratch feed, sunflower, millet, canary seed, suet, doughnuts, and cornbread. But if you need to dampen certain appetites and still keep most of the birds you want, you will need to pay special attention to selective foods. Few foods will be completely ignored by unwanted guests, but those listed below are seldom taken by the four species in question except possibly under stress of extreme hunger.

	STARLING	HOUSE SPARROW	RED-WINGED BLACKBIRD	COMMON GRACKLE
Apple, sliced		x	x	x
Buckwheat	x			
Coconut	x	x	x	x
Corn, whole kernels	x	x		
Currants		x	x	x
Orange, halved	x	x	x	x

	STARLING	HOUSE SPARROW	RED-WINGED BLACKBIRD	COMMON GRACKLE
Peanut, chopped		x		
Raisins		x	x	x
Rape		x	x	x
Safflower	x	x	x	x
Suet		x	x	
Suet, hardened mix	x	x	x	x
Sunflower	x			
Thistle	x	x	x	x

x = taken sparingly or not at all

SORGHUM   several varieties of *Sorghum vulgare*, including milo and kafir, are common ingredients in birdseed mixtures. Sorghum also occasionally appears in scratch feed. The brownish, or sometimes whitish, globular seeds are several times the size of millet. Sorghum has somewhat less fat than corn but slightly more protein. Unlike yellow corn, sorghum has no Vitamin A. Relative cheapness and fair acceptability with birds make sorghum, including milo, a common substitute for corn. Overuse of this grain, however, leads to wastage. Main users of milo are gallinaceous birds, mourning dove, house sparrow, blackbirds, and sparrows and finches. See also *scratch feed*.

SPAGHETTI, COOKED   the worm-like appearance may make this food inviting to its one occasional user, the robin.

SQUASH   see *melon seeds*.

SQUASH, COOKED   appeals to yellow-rumped warbler.

STRAWBERRIES   appeal to catbird, robin.

SUDAN GRASS   (*Sorghum sudanense*) a cultivated grass not to be confused with grain sorghum. The seeds are taken by bobwhite, mourning dove, and many sparrows and finches.

SUET   a standard food that has been offered since the earliest days of bird feeding. Beef suet is preferred by birds to any other. Suet, for best results, should be fresh, firm, white in color, and not stringy. Cut pieces to fit suet holders. Suet is easier to cut and will not shatter when it has been warmed to room temperature or above. If not well secured, suet will be carried away by larger birds or mammals. See also *animal fats*.

SUET HOLDERS, HAZARDS   the simple wire hardware-cloth suet holders are excellent for holding suet. However, there is the danger of birds' feet, tongues, or even eyes sticking to the metal in freezing weather. This hazard can be avoided by making suet holders out of plastic-coated hardware cloth. Also suet can be placed in woven mesh bags such as those used by grocery stores to hold citrus fruits. These can be hung at suitable places outside the window.

SUET, HOW TO USE IN SUMMER   a valuable food in summer, but steps should be taken in warm weather to prevent suet from becoming rancid. Rancid suet is much less palatable and has a lower nutritional value. Suet that has been rendered in such a way as to remove impurities and moisture will stay fresh in spite of warm weather. The first step is to place suet that has been ground or cut into small pieces in a saucepan partially filled with water. Render over slow heat. After the suet has melted, turn off the heat and let stand. After some cooling, remove the solidified fat that has risen to the surface. Place this purified fat where it will drain and then put into containers and store in the refrigerator until needed. Offer only at feeders that are in partial or complete shade.

SUET MIXTURES   since the early days of bird feeding, it has been known that suet goes further and has greater appeal to birds when it is melted and other ingredients are mixed in. The basic step in preparing any one of several recipes using suet (pages 272–4) is to cut the suet into pieces, pass these through a meat grinder, and then render over slow heat. While the suet is melting, begin stirring in cornmeal, peanut butter, and such other ingredients as bacon grease, lard, honey, syrup, sugar, flour, rolled oats, chick feed, fine scratch feed, eggshell, raisins, currants, peanut hearts, nutmeats, and stale bread crumbs. Save seeds for use elsewhere. They are superfluous in mixtures and tend to block birds' access to the other ingredients. Pour into containers or holes in hanging log feeders and offer as needed. The mixtures made in this manner are wholesome and nutritious and are welcomed by nearly all the birds that come to feeding stations.

SUGAR   a basic ingredient in solutions for hummingbirds (pages 167–9) and sometimes taken by birds in a dry, granulated form. In the American tropics, especially the West Indies, granulated sugar is commonly offered in bowls to woodpeckers, honeycreepers, tanagers, and other birds.

SUMMER FEEDING   when warm weather comes, it is important to use fewer high-calorie or heating foods. One way to do this is to eliminate or greatly reduce offerings of oil-rich seeds and nuts. Some of the ones to eliminate are rape, hemp, peanuts, walnuts, pecans, and coconut. Other energy foods, like sunflower, suet, and suet mixtures containing peanut butter, are so useful that they may be continued. Birds are pretty good judges of their needs. During the summer most species turn largely to insects and other natural fare. As a rule, only the few that nest near us find it convenient to supplement their natural diet with some of our foods. We can supply these birds with much the same menu we have used all winter but with reduced amounts of high-energy foods. In addition, try supplying cut-up fruits in fruit bowls, sugar-water in feeders for hummingbirds, and soft, moist foods for young birds. See *foods for young birds* and *fruit bowls*.

SUNFLOWER   in many respects this is *the* food that is most popular with birds and which keeps them coming when nothing else will. Birds spoiled on sunflower may leave feeders temporarily after the supply has become exhausted. This has been noted in the black-capped chickadee, evening grosbeak, and American goldfinch. Black oil sunflower, which is smaller and entirely black, has largely superseded gray- and black-striped sunflower in bird feeding. The oil seed contains proportionately more edible kernel and less hull than the larger seed. It is also easier for birds to open. Although mainly a winter food, sunflower can be continued in summer for the value it has in attracting such colorful birds as cardinal, rose-breasted grosbeak, and blue grosbeak. In winter we often find it hard to supply enough sunflower to keep up with the demands of chickadees, titmice, nuthatches, and sparrows and finches. We are likely to be particularly hard-pressed when large flocks of northern finches descend upon us from the north. For those who would rather not have empty hulls to contend with, sunflower kernels or pieces of kernel are the answer. They are available at bird-food outlets but are more expensive than seeds in the shell.

SWEET POTATO, COOKED   appeals to the starling and yellow-rumped warbler.

THISTLE   the seed that is commonly sold as "thistle" is in reality niger (*Guizotia abyssinica*), a member of the thistle family imported from Africa and India. Ethiopia is the main source of supply. This seed, long popular as a food for cage birds, is a fairly recent discovery at bird feeders and is valued for the special appeal it has for a rather select group, including the purple finch, house finch, redpoll, pine siskin, and goldfinch. Although the price of thistle may make it seem a luxury item, it is actually an economical food if you consider the limited number of species that eat it and the fact that the small, black seeds cannot be rapidly consumed.

    Thistle is used most successfully in tubular hanging feeders designed for its use. On bird tables or on the ground, it is not quite such a selective food and may sometimes attract the attention of mourning doves, house sparrows, and members of the blackbird family.

WALNUT   see *black walnut* and *English walnut*.

WATER   this necessity is all too often overlooked when we establish a feeding program. Water should be provided the year round and is especially important in winter (see pages 58–9). See also *sanitation at bird baths*.

WATERMELON   the pulp is taken by the house finch. See also *melon seeds*.

WAX MYRTLE   see *bayberry*.

WEED SEED   many so-called weeds, including barnyard and foxtail grass, are relatives of cultivated millet, which is such an important supplier of birdseed. We can use seeds of these wild grasses just as well, and also those of more noxious weeds. However, it is a chore to gather enough of this food to make a difference. Some may hesitate to use this food because of the chance that unwanted weeds will take root. In any event, weed seed should be used in the same way as hay chaff. Scatter seed heads on the snow or bare ground and let birds take whatever they wish.

WHEAT   Seldom is wheat offered by itself; it is most often fed to birds in the form of scratch or chick feed. Except in coarser grades, the wheat comes in broken or cracked pieces. Birds seem to find wheat a little less attractive than corn. While wheat has a somewhat higher protein content than corn, the food values of the two grains are about the same. Wheat is taken by bobwhite, ring-necked pheasant, mourning dove, blue jay, chickadee, brown thrasher, house sparrow, blackbirds, cardinal, blue grosbeak, evening grosbeak, purple finch, pine siskin, goldfinch, towhee, and several sparrows, including song sparrow.

WHITE BREAD   Now that enriched white bread is more readily available, we need not be quite so concerned about giving birds and ourselves a nutritionally poor food. White bread has a place in attracting birds to new feeders and is an occasional treat to give birds at any time of the year. What it is about white bread that makes it so popular, we do not know. Whether fresh or stale, it is a food that birds come to as readily as any. The best way to offer it is in small broken pieces. Other breads, including brown bread, are not nearly so well received. Users of white bread include not only virtually every species that comes to feeding stations but the waterfowl that take handouts in city parks. We should take pity on these park birds and offer them something more nutritious. Corn and other grains are far better suited for their needs than white bread. See also *foods to attract attention*.

WHITE POTATO   one never knows what the birds' response will be to kitchen scraps. Potato is a food we seldom think of offering. Yet the white potato in its several forms (fried, mashed, boiled, or as potato chips) has a number of users. The brown creeper is known to take small bits of boiled potato. Look for some use among omnivorous feeders such as crow, blue jay, catbird, starling, and grackle.

YOUNG BIRDS AT FEEDERS   see *foods for young birds*.

RECIPES AND MENUS

A SWEET-TASTING MIXTURE WITH WIDE APPEAL

Heat to boiling:

6 cups water
1 cup shortening or melted suet

Add:

2 cups cornmeal
½ cup flour
1 cup white or brown sugar or syrup

Mix and bring to boil. Cover and turn off heat. Finally, add whatever extras in the way of seeds, raisins, nutmeats, peanut butter, or other tidbits may seem appropriate. Pour into pans and chill before placing at feeders.

CORNBREAD FOR THE BIRDS

3 pints yellow cornmeal
3 teaspoons baking powder
⅔ cup shortening
3 pints water

Bake in a deep pan slowly (425° F for 25 minutes) so as not to form a hard crust. The amounts given above can be reduced proportionately.

3 cups melted suet

1 cup cornmeal

1 cup peanut butter

1 cup birdseed or nutmeats

1 cup coarse brown sugar

1 cup raisins or currants

Combine ingredients and add enough water to achieve the consistency of porridge. Cook over hot water until blended. For use at coconut shell feeders or other, more exclusive hanging feeders. A rich mixture that is well liked by birds in winter.

A STANDARD MIXTURE OF WASTE FATS

*2 cups melted fat (suet, lard, bacon drippings, or any fat that does not contain rich
seasoning)*

2 cups cornmeal (yellow preferred)

1 cup peanut butter

Stir cornmeal, peanut butter, and any other suitable ingredients into melted fat and cook for several minutes. Pour into shallow cups or dishes appropriate for use at feeders. Handy dishes can be made by cutting down cardboard milk cartons to a desirable size. After mixture has solidified, wedge filled containers into holders. This is necessary if they are to be kept in place.

INGREDIENTS FOR A SUCCESSFUL BIRD FEEDING PROGRAM

1. Bakery products: white bread (use sparingly), cornbread, doughnuts, cake and cracker crumbs.

2. Birdseed mixtures composed of such seeds as millet, canary seed, rape, and flax. White proso millet is one of the best of the millets.

3. Buckwheat for quail and doves.

4. Fruit: grapes, cherries, bananas, and halved apples and oranges, and pears.

5. Grit: coarse sand, finely crushed oyster shell, and eggshell.

6. Nutmeats: especially chopped peanut (or peanut hearts), pecan, and almond. Also most native nuts that can be harvested in the wild.

7. Suet (preferably beef suet).

8. Suet mixtures (including cornmeal and peanut butter).

9. Scratch feed composed of cracked corn, wheat, and sometimes other ingredients.

10. Sunflower seed (black oil most popular).

11. Thistle seed for mourning doves, titmice, sparrows and finches (especially gold-finches).

12. Water: keep ice-free in winter and always maintain cleanliness of bird baths.

ANTI-STARLING MEASURES

1. When starlings are troublesome, substitute a hard mixture for suet or softer mixtures. The following hard suet mixtures are particularly effective in cold weather:

> *2 parts rendered beef suet*
> *3 parts white or yellow cornmeal*
>   or
> *1 part peanut butter*
> *2 parts rendered beef suet*
> *4 parts finely cracked corn*
> *4 parts white or yellow cornmeal*

Prepare in the same way as other suet mixtures and, for still greater hardness, melt a second time and then pour back into containers.

2. Foods that starlings won't take:

Buckwheat	*Peanuts in the shell*	*Sunflower (unhulled)*
Coconut in the shell	*Rape*	*Thistle*
Corn (whole kernels)	*Safflower*	

3. Foods that appeal to starlings:

Alfalfa meal and pellets	*Currants*	*Meat bone*
American cheese	*Dogfood (canned)*	*Peanut butter*
Apples (halved)	*Dogfood, biscuits (soaked)*	*Peanut hearts*
Bacon grease	*Doughnuts*	*Potato chips*
Birdseed	*Eggs, cooked in various*	*Raisins*
Bread (white)	*ways*	*Rice (cooked)*
Corn (canned)	*Grapefruit (halved)*	*Sauerkraut*
Corn (cracked)	*Laying mash for chickens*	*Suet*
Cornbread	*Mashed potato*	*Table scraps*

Use at feeders designated especially for starlings or eliminate these foods altogether if you would temporarily ban starlings (a brief ban may cause them to go elsewhere).

BIRDS THAT VISIT EASTERN FEEDERS

Vultures, hawks, owls, and shrikes on this list were observed taking suet or other feeding station foods.

BLACKBIRDS AND ORIOLES

Blackbird, red-winged*	Grackle, boat-tailed	Oriole, northern*
Blackbird, rusty	Grackle, common	Oriole, orchard
Cowbird, brown-headed	Meadowlark, eastern	

CHICKADEES AND TITMICE

Chickadee, black-capped*	Chickadee, boreal*	Titmouse, tufted*
	Chickadee, Carolina*	

CREEPERS

Creeper, brown*

DOVES

Dove, ground	Dove, mourning	Pigeon, domestic*

FLYCATCHERS

Phoebe, eastern

FOWL-LIKE BIRDS

Bobwhite*	Pheasant, ring-necked*	Turkey
Grouse, ruffed*		

*Included in Gilbert H. Trafton's list of birds coming to feeders in *Methods of Attracting Birds*, Boston, Houghton Mifflin, 1910.

277

Birds
That
Visit
Eastern
Feeders

GNATCATCHERS AND KINGLETS

Gnatcatcher, blue-gray   Kinglet, golden-crowned*   Kinglet, ruby-crowned

HUMMINGBIRDS

Hummingbird, ruby-throated*

JAYS AND CROWS

Crow, common*   Jay, blue*   Jay, gray*

LARKS

Lark, horned*

MIMIC THRUSHES

Catbird, gray*   Mockingbird*   Thrasher, brown

NUTHATCHES

Nuthatch, brown-headed   Nuthatch, red-breasted*   Nuthatch, white-
                                                        breasted*

OWLS

Boreal   Saw-whet   Screech*

ROBINS AND THRUSHES

Bluebird, eastern*   Thrush, hermit*   Veery
Robin, American*   Thrush, Swainson's
Thrush, gray-cheeked   Thrush, wood

SHRIKES

Shrike, loggerhead   Shrike, northern

SPARROWS AND FINCHES

Bunting, indigo   Finch, purple*   Redpoll, common*
Bunting, painted   Goldfinch, American*   Redpoll, hoary
Bunting, snow*   Grosbeak, blue   Siskin, pine*
Cardinal*   Grosbeak, evening*   Sparrow, chipping*
Crossbill, red*   Grosbeak, pine*   Sparrow, field
Crossbill, white-winged*   Grosbeak, rose-breasted*   Sparrow, fox*
Dickcissel   Junco, dark-eyed*   Sparrow, grasshopper
Finch, house   Longspur, Lapland*   Sparrow, Lincoln's

*Included in Gilbert H. Trafton's list of birds coming to feeders in *Methods of Attracting Birds*, Boston, Houghton Mifflin, 1910.

Sparrow, savannah
Sparrow, song*
Sparrow, swamp*

Sparrow, tree*
Sparrow, vesper*
Sparrow, white-crowned*

Sparrow, white-throated*
Towhee, rufous-sided

STARLINGS
Starling*

TANAGERS
Tanager, scarlet*   Tanager, summer

VULTURES, HAWKS, AND FALCONS
Hawk, Cooper's   Hawk, red-tailed   Vulture, black
Hawk, red-shouldered   Kestrel, American   Vulture, turkey

WARBLERS
Chat, yellow-breasted   Warbler, Cape May   Warbler, yellow-throated
Ovenbird   Warbler, orange-crowned Warbler, Wilson's
Redstart, American   Warbler, palm   Waterthrush, northern
Warbler, black-and-white Warbler, pine*   Yellowthroat, common
Warbler, blackpoll   Warbler, Tennessee
Warbler, black-throated Warbler, yellow
blue   Warbler, yellow-rumped*

WAXWINGS
Waxwing, cedar

WEAVER FINCHES
Sparrow, house*

WOODPECKERS
Flicker, northern*   Woodpecker, downy*   Woodpecker, pileated
Sapsucker, yellow-bellied Woodpecker, hairy*   Woodpecker, red-bellied*
Woodpecker, black-backed Woodpecker, northern   Woodpecker, red-headed

WRENS
Wren, Bewick's   Wren, house
Wren, Carolina   Wren, winter*

*Included in Gilbert H. Trafton's list of birds coming to feeders in *Methods of Attracting Birds*, Boston, Houghton Mifflin, 1910.

WESTERN STRAYS SOMETIMES SEEN AT EASTERN FEEDERS

BLACKBIRDS AND ORIOLES
Blackbird, Brewer's
Blackbird, yellow-headed
Oriole, northern (western race known as Bullock's)

DOVES
Dove, white-winged

HUMMINGBIRDS
Hummingbird, rufous

JAYS, CROWS, AND MAGPIES
Magpie, black-billed
Nutcracker, Clark's

MIMIC THRUSHES
Thrasher, curve-billed

ROBINS AND THRUSHES
Solitaire, Townsend's
Thrush, varied

SPARROWS AND FINCHES
Bunting, lark
Finch, gray-crowned rosy
Grosbeak, black-headed
Junco, dark-eyed (western races)
Sparrow, black-throated
Sparrow, clay-colored
Sparrow, golden-crowned
Sparrow, Harris'
Sparrow, lark
Towhee, green-tailed

TANAGERS
Tanager, western

WARBLERS
Warbler, yellow-rumped (western race known as Audubon's)

WAXWINGS
Waxwing, bohemian

WOODPECKERS
Woodpecker, Lewis'

ESCAPED CAGE BIRDS AND OTHER EXOTICS

Especially in cities and adjoining suburbs there is always the possibility of a parrot-like bird, a foreign finch, or some other exotic appearing at feeding stations. Some may have escaped from zoos and others been lost by private owners. Also owners sometimes tire of their pets and deliberately release them. The exotic seen at feeders is usually a bewildered, hungry bird that would be better off back in captivity. However, a number have become adapted to our cities and do quite nicely with the aid of feeding stations. Some that are breeding in the wild are maintaining their numbers or actually increasing.

The outstanding example of a potentially successful acclimatization is afforded by the quaker, or monk, parakeet. This hardy parakeet from southern South America is presently found individually or in small flocks in many of our northern cities and as far south as southern Florida. It builds a bulky stick nest both for communal roosting and nesting purposes. Our cold northern winters seem to impose no hardship on this bird. Almost unknown in the wild in this country in 1968, the quaker parakeet has appeared in dozens of towns and cities in the eastern portion of the United States. Regarded with suspicion because of depredations to crops in its native home, the quaker parakeet has been blacklisted by some state game departments, and its numbers in these states are being rigidly controlled. This parakeet has a good appetite for food offerings and sometimes dominates feeders. Foods taken by quaker parakeets at feeders include suet, meat scraps, sunflower, millet, corn (especially fresh corn on the cob), bread, cake, raisins, currants, apple, and other fruits.

A second member of the parrot family is sometimes also seen in northern cities—the canary-winged parakeet of tropical South America. Its stronghold in this country is the region of southern Florida around Miami. Here noisy, fast-flying flocks of these birds are a common sight. Probably about 2,000 of these parakeets are presently established in the wild in the Miami region.

Southern Florida is also the home of a number of other exotics. The jaunty red-whiskered bulbul thrives in Kendall, a residential suburb south of Miami; the hill myna is found in small numbers from Homestead to Palm Beach; the spotted-breasted oriole adorns tropical yards from Homestead to Jensen Beach, which lies north of Palm Beach; the blue-gray tanager exists in small numbers in the Miami region; the Java sparrow is fairly widespread but has its main headquarters in Coral Gables; since the early 1980s the collared dove, from Asia and Europe, has become established in Southern Florida and is spreading northward; and at least ten members of the parrot family not yet mentioned share this "great outdoor zoo" with the other exotics. St. Petersburg, on the west coast of Florida, is the focal point for the ringed turtle dove and budgerigar. Hundreds of the latter birds live in a wild or semi-wild condition in communities to the north and south as well as in St. Petersburg itself.

In addition to the exotics mentioned above, game birds are sometimes deliberately released by state game departments. Besides the familiar ring-necked pheasant, some other less well-known game birds such as the gray partridge, chukar, and black francolin are sometimes released into the wild. Chances of the appearance of any of these birds, except the ring-necked pheasant, at feeders in the East are slight.

An altogether different bird is the European goldfinch that is sometimes seen at feeders in more northern states. Since this colorful goldfinch once bred for a time on Long Island, there is still a suspicion that it breeds in the wild in this country. It seems more likely, however, that the occasional bird seen at feeding stations is an escapee from captivity.

The following are exotics that may be expected at Florida feeding stations and in several instances have appeared at more northern feeders:

BLACKBIRDS AND ORIOLES
Oriole, spotted-breasted
Troupial

BULBULS
Bulbul, red-whiskered

Escaped
Cage
Birds
and
Other
Exotics

DOVES
Dove, collared
Dove, ringed turtle

PARROTS AND PARAKEETS
Amazon, green-cheeked
Budgerigar
Cockatiel

Conure, halfmoon
(or Petz)
Parakeet, bee bee
(or tovi)

Parakeet, canary-winged
Parakeet, quaker
(or monk)
Parakeet, ringneck

SPARROWS AND FINCHES
Cardinal, red-crested

STARLINGS AND MYNAHS
Mynah, hill

TANAGERS
Tanager, blue-gray

WAXBILLS
Sparrow, Java (or ricebird)

appendix f
CHANGES IN COMMON NAMES

Although the scientific name of each bird species is the safest name to go by, common names have become relatively standardized, with the result that many popular works, including this one, rely entirely upon them. However, common names do change and the reader may not readily recognize some of the latest names that are listed below.

APPROVED NAME	NO LONGER ACCEPTED
BLACKBIRDS AND ORIOLES	
Grackle, common	*Grackle, purple*
Oriole, northern	*Oriole, Baltimore*
CHICKADEES AND TITMICE	
Chickadee, boreal	*Chickadee, brown-headed*
	Chickadee, Hudsonian
JAYS AND CROWS	
Crow, common	*Crow*
Jay, gray	*Jay, Canada*
FOWL-LIKE BIRDS	
Turkey	*Turkey, wild*
MIMIC THRUSHES	
Catbird, gray	*Catbird*

OWLS
Owl, boreal   *Owl, Richardson's*

ROBINS AND THRUSHES
Robin, American   *Robin*
Thrush, Swainson's   *Thrush, olive-backed*

SPARROWS AND FINCHES
Goldfinch, American   *Goldfinch, common*
Junco, dark-eyed   *Junco, slate-colored*
Towhee, rufous-sided   *Towhee, eastern*
                                         Towhee, red-eyed

VULTURES, HAWKS, AND FALCONS
Kestrel, American   *Hawk, sparrow*

WARBLERS
Warbler, yellow-rumped   *Warbler, myrtle*
Yellowthroat, common   *Yellowthroat*

WEAVER FINCHES
Sparrow, house   *Sparrow, English*

WOODPECKERS
Flicker, northern   *Flicker, yellow-shafted*
Woodpecker, black-backed   *Woodpecker, Arctic three-toed*
Woodpecker, northern   *Woodpecker, American three-toed*

Note: Several of the recent name changes reflect "lumping," or combining into one species what had been two or more species. Northern flicker, yellow-rumped warbler, northern oriole, and dark-eyed junco are names that have come into being after dominantly eastern or western species have been combined into one single species. The northern flicker, for example, is the single species that has evolved after the more easterly ranging yellow-shafted flicker and more western red-shafted flicker were no longer regarded as separate species. The two flickers are now regarded as races of a single species. The same thing has happened with myrtle warbler and Audubon's warbler, Baltimore oriole and Bullock's oriole, slate-colored junco and several western juncos.

SOME NATIONAL PUBLICATIONS ABOUT BIRDS, NATURE, AND THE ENVIRONMENT

American Birds
700 Broadway
New York, N.Y. 10003

Audubon
700 Broadway
New York, N.Y. 10003

Birder's World
720 E. 8th Street
Holland, Mich. 49423

Birding
American Birding Association
P. O. Box 6599
Colorado Springs, Colo. 80934

The Bird's Eye reView
National Bird-Feeding Society
P. O. Box 23
Northbrook, Ill. 60065

Bird Watcher's Digest
P. O. Box 110
Marietta, Ohio 45750

FeederWatch News
Cornell Laboratory of Ornithology
159 Sapsucker Woods Road
Ithaca, N.Y. 14850

Living Bird Quarterly
Cornell Laboratory of Ornithology
159 Sapsucker Woods Road
Ithaca, N.Y. 14850

Nature Society News
Griggsville, Ill. 62340

WildBird
P. O. Box 6050
Mission Viejo, Calif. 92690

INDEX

A Note on the Type

The text of this book was set in Garamond, a modern rendering
of the type first cut by Claude Garamond (1510–1561). Garamond was a pupil of Geoffroy Tory and is believed to have based
his letters on the Venetian models, although he introduced a
number of important differences, and it is to him we owe the
letter which we know as old style. He gave to his letters a
certain elegance and a feeling of movement that won for their
creator an immediate reputation and the patronage of
Francis I of France.

Composed by Crane Typesetting Service, Inc.,
West Barnstable, Massachusetts
Printed and bound by The Haddon Craftsmen,
Scranton, Pennsylvania
Based on a design by Susan Mitchell